Contents

Language Implementation Patterns

Create Your Own Domain-Specific and General Programming Languages

Language Implementation Patterns

Create Your Own Domain-Specific and General Programming Languages

Terence Parr

The Pragmatic Bookshelf
Raleigh, North Carolina   Dallas, Texas

Many of the designations used by manufacturers and sellers to distinguish their products are claimed as trademarks. Where those designations appear in this book, and The Pragmatic Programmers, LLC was aware of a trademark claim, the designations have been printed in initial capital letters or in all capitals. The Pragmatic Starter Kit, The Pragmatic Programmer, Pragmatic Programming, Pragmatic Bookshelf and the linking *g* device are trademarks of The Pragmatic Programmers, LLC.

With permission of the creator we hereby publish the chess images in Chapter 11 under the following licenses:

Permission is granted to copy, distribute and/or modify this document under the terms of the GNU Free Documentation License, Version 1.2 or any later version published by the Free Software Foundation; with no Invariant Sections, no Front-Cover Texts, and no Back-Cover Texts. A copy of the license is included in the section entitled "GNU Free Documentation License"
(http://commons.wikimedia.org/wiki/Commons:GNU_Free_Documentation_License).

Every precaution was taken in the preparation of this book. However, the publisher assumes no responsibility for errors or omissions, or for damages that may result from the use of information (including program listings) contained herein.

Our Pragmatic courses, workshops, and other products can help you and your team create better software and have more fun. For more information, as well as the latest Pragmatic titles, please visit us at

http://www.pragprog.com

ISBN-10: 1-934356-45-X

ISBN-13: 978-1-934356-45-6

Printed on acid-free paper.

P1.0 printing, December 2009

Version: 2009-12-7

Acknowledgments

I'd like to start out by recognizing my development editor, the talented Susannah Pfalzer. She and I brainstormed and experimented for eight months until we found the right formula for this book. She was invaluable throughout the construction of this book.

Next, I'd like to thank the cadre of book reviewers (in no particular order): Kyle Ferrio, Dragos Manolescu, Gerald Rosenberg, Johannes Luber, Karl Pfalzer, Stuart Halloway, Tom Nurkkala, Adam Keys, Martijn Reuvers, William Gallagher, Graham Wideman, and Dan Bornstein. Although not an official reviewer, Wayne Stewart provided a huge amount of feedback on the errata website. Martijn Reuvers also created the ANT build files for the code directories.

Gerald Rosenberg and Graham Wideman deserve special attention for their ridiculously thorough reviews of the manuscript as well as provocative conversations by phone.

Preface

The more language applications you build, the more patterns you'll see. The truth is that the architecture of most language applications is freakishly similar. A broken record plays in my head every time I start a new language application: "First build a syntax recognizer that creates a data structure in memory. Then sniff the data structure, collecting information or altering the structure. Finally, build a report or code generator that feeds off the data structure." You even start seeing patterns within the tasks themselves. Tasks share lots of common algorithms and data structures.

Once you get these language implementation design patterns and the general architecture into your head, you can build pretty much whatever you want. If you need to learn how to build languages pronto, this book is for you. It's a pragmatic book that identifies and distills the common design patterns to their essence. You'll learn why you need the patterns, how to implement them, and how they fit together. You'll be a competent language developer in no time!

Building a new language doesn't require a great deal of theoretical computer science. You might be skeptical because every book you've picked up on language development has focused on compilers. Yes, building a compiler for a general-purpose programming language requires a strong computer science background. But, most of us don't build compilers. So, this book focuses on the things that we build all the time: configuration file readers, data readers, model-driven code generators, source-to-source translators, source analyzers, and interpreters. We'll also code in Java rather than a primarily academic language like Scheme so that you can directly apply what you learn in this book to real-world projects.

What to Expect from This Book

This book gives you just the tools you'll need to develop day-to-day language applications. You'll be able to handle all but the really advanced or esoteric situations. For example, we won't have space to cover topics such as machine code generation, register allocation, automatic garbage collection, thread models, and extremely efficient interpreters. You'll get good all-around expertise implementing modest languages, and you'll get respectable expertise in processing or translating complex languages.

This book explains how existing language applications work so you can build your own. To do so, we're going to break them down into a series of well-understood and commonly used patterns. But, keep in mind that this book is a learning tool, not a library of language implementations. You'll see many sample implementations throughout the book, though. Samples make the discussions more concrete and provide excellent foundations from which to build new applications.

It's also important to point out that we're going to focus on building applications for languages that already exist (or languages you design that are very close to existing languages). Language design, on the other hand, focuses on coming up with a syntax (a set of valid sentences) and describing the complete semantics (what every possible input means). Although we won't specifically study how to design languages, you'll actually absorb a lot as we go through the book. A good way to learn about language design is to look at lots of different languages. It'll help if you research the history of programming languages to see how languages change over time.

When we talk about language applications, we're not just talking about *implementing* languages with a compiler or interpreter. We're talking about any program that processes, analyzes, or translates an input file. Implementing a language means building an application that executes or performs tasks according to sentences in that language. That's just one of the things we can do for a given language definition. For example, from the definition of C, we can build a C compiler, a translator from C to Java, or a tool that instruments C code to isolate memory leaks. Similarly, think about all the tools built into the Eclipse development environment for Java. Beyond the compiler, Eclipse can refactor, reformat, search, syntax highlight, and so on.

You can use the patterns in this book to build language applications for any computer language, which of course includes domain-specific languages (DSLs). A domain-specific language is just that: a computer language designed to make users particularly productive in a specific domain. Examples include Mathematica, shell scripts, wikis, UML, XSLT, makefiles, PostScript, formal grammars, and even data file formats like comma-separated values and XML. The opposite of a DSL is a general-purpose programming language like C, Java, or Python. In the common usage, DSLs also typically have the connotation of being smaller because of their focus. This isn't always the case, though. SQL, for example, is a lot bigger than most general-purpose programming languages.

How This Book Is Organized

This book is divided into four parts:

- *Getting Started with Parsing*: We'll start out by looking at the overall architecture of language applications and then jump into the key language recognition (parsing) patterns.

- *Analyzing Languages*: To analyze DSLs and programming languages, we'll use parsers to build trees that represent language constructs in memory. By walking those trees, we can track and identify the various symbols (such as variables and functions) in the input. We can also compute expression result-type information (such as **int** and **float**). The patterns in this part of the book explain how to check whether an input stream makes sense.

- *Building Interpreters*: This part has four different interpreter patterns. The interpreters vary in terms of implementation difficulty and run-time efficiency.

- *Translating and Generating Languages*: In the final part, we will learn how to translate one language to another and how to generate text using the StringTemplate template engine. In the final chapter, we'll lay out the architecture of some interesting language applications to get you started building languages on your own.

The chapters within the different parts proceed in the order you'd follow to implement a language. Section 1.2, *A Tour of the Patterns*, on page 5 describes how all the patterns fit together.

What You'll Find in the Patterns

There are 31 patterns in this book. Each one describes a common data structure, algorithm, or strategy you're likely to find in language applications. Each pattern has four parts:

- *Purpose*: This section briefly describes what the pattern is for. For example, the purpose of Pattern 21, *Automatic Type Promotion*, on page 193 says "...how to automatically and safely promote arithmetic operand types." It's a good idea to scan the Purpose section before jumping into a pattern to discover exactly what it's trying to solve.

- *Discussion*: This section describes the problem in more detail, explains when to use the pattern, and describes how the pattern works.

- *Implementation*: Each pattern has a sample implementation in Java (possibly using language tools such as ANTLR). The sample implementations are not intended to be libraries that you can immediately apply to your problem. They demonstrate, in code, what we talk about in the Discussion sections.

- *Related Patterns*. This section lists alternative patterns that solve the same problem or patterns we depend on to implement this pattern.

The chapter introductory materials and the patterns themselves often provide comparisons between patterns to keep everything in proper perspective.

Who Should Read This Book

If you're a practicing software developer or computer science student and you want to learn how to implement computer languages, this book is for you. By computer language, I mean everything from data formats, network protocols, configuration files, specialized math languages, and hardware description languages to general-purpose programming languages.

You don't need a background in formal language theory, but the code and discussions in this book assume a solid programming background.

To get the most out of this book, you should be fairly comfortable with recursion. Many algorithms and processes are inherently recursive. We'll use recursion to do everything from recognizing input, walking trees, and building interpreters to generating output.

How to Read This Book

If you're new to language implementation, start with Chapter 1, *Language Applications Cracked Open*, on page 3 because it provides an architectural overview of how we build languages. You can then move on to Chapter 2, *Basic Parsing Patterns*, on page 21 and Chapter 3, *Enhanced Parsing Patterns*, on page 49 to get some background on grammars (formal language descriptions) and language recognition.

If you've taken a fair number of computer science courses, you can skip ahead to either Chapter 4, *Building Intermediate Form Trees*, on page 73 or Chapter 5, *Walking and Rewriting Trees*, on page 101. Even if you've built a lot of trees and tree walkers in your career, it's still worth looking at Pattern 14, *Tree Grammar*, on page 119 and Pattern 15, *Tree Pattern Matcher*, on page 123.

If you've done some basic language application work before, you already know how to read input into a handy tree data structure and walk it. You can skip ahead to Chapter 6, *Tracking and Identifying Program Symbols*, on page 131 and Chapter 7, *Managing Symbol Tables for Data Aggregates*, on page 155, which describe how to build symbol tables. Symbol tables answer the question "What is *x*?" for some input symbol *x*. They are necessary data structures for the patterns in Chapter 8, *Enforcing Static Typing Rules*, on page 181, for example.

More advanced readers might want to jump directly to Chapter 9, *Building High-Level Interpreters*, on page 219 and Chapter 12, *Generating DSLs with Templates*, on page 313. If you really know what you're doing, you can skip around the book looking for patterns of interest. The truly impatient can grab a sample implementation from a pattern and use it as a kernel for a new language (relying on the book for explanations).

If you bought the e-book version of this book, you can click the gray boxes above the code samples to download code snippets directly. If you'd like to participate in conversations with me and other readers, you can do so at the web page for this book[1] or on the ANTLR user's

---

1. http://www.pragprog.com/titles/tpdsl

list.[2] You can also post book errata and download all the source code on the book's web page.

Languages and Tools Used in This Book

The code snippets and implementations in this book are written in Java, but their substance applies equally well to any other general programming language. I had to pick a single programming language for consistency. Java is a good choice because it's widely used in industry.[3,4] Remember, this book is about design patterns, not "language recipes." You can't just download a pattern's sample implementation and apply it to your problem without modification.

We'll use state-of-the-art language tools wherever possible in this book. For example, to recognize (parse) input phrases, we'll use a parser generator (well, that is, after we learn how to build parsers manually in Chapter 2, *Basic Parsing Patterns*, on page 21). It's no fair using a parser generator until you know how parsers work. That'd be like using a calculator before learning to do arithmetic. Similarly, once we know how to build tree walkers by hand, we can let a tool build them for us.

In this book, we'll use ANTLR extensively. ANTLR is a parser generator and tree walker generator that I've honed over the past two decades while building language applications. I could have used any similar language tool, but I might as well use my own. My point is that this book is not about ANTLR itself—it's about the design patterns common to most language applications. The code samples merely help you to understand the patterns.

We'll also use a template engine called StringTemplate a lot in Chapter 12, *Generating DSLs with Templates*, on page 313 to generate output. StringTemplate is like an "unparser generator," and templates are like output grammar rules. The alternative to a template engine would be to use an unstructured blob of generation logic interspersed with print statements.

You'll be able to follow the patterns in this book even if you're not familiar with ANTLR and StringTemplate. Only the sample implementations use them. To get the most out of the patterns, though, you should walk

---

2. http://www.antlr.org/support.html
3. http://langpop.com
4. http://www.tiobe.com/index.php/content/paperinfo/tpci/index.html

through the sample implementations. To really understand them, it's a good idea to learn more about the ANTLR project tools. You'll get a taste in Section 4.3, *Quick Introduction to ANTLR*, on page 84. You can also visit the website to get documentation and examples or purchase *The Definitive ANTLR Reference* [Par07] (shameless plug).

One way or another, you're going to need language tools to implement languages. You'll have no problem transferring your knowledge to other tools after you finish this book. It's like learning to fly—you have no choice but to pick a first airplane. Later, you can move easily to another airplane. Gaining piloting skills is the key, not learning the details of a particular aircraft cockpit.

I hope this book inspires you to learn about languages and motivates you to build domain-specific languages (DSLs) and other language tools to help fellow programmers.

Terence Parr
December 2009
parrt@cs.usfca.edu

Part I

Getting Started with Parsing

## Chapter 1

Language Applications Cracked Open

In this first part of the book, we're going to learn how to recognize computer languages. (A *language* is just a set of valid sentences.) Every language application we look at will have a parser (recognizer) component, unless it's a pure code generator.

We can't just jump straight into the patterns, though. We need to see how everything fits together first. In this chapter, we'll get an architectural overview and then tour the patterns at our disposal. Finally, we'll look at the guts of some sample language applications to see how they work and how they use patterns.

1.1 The Big Picture

Language applications can be very complicated beasts, so we need to break them down into bite-sized components. The components fit together into a multistage pipeline that analyzes or manipulates an input stream. The pipeline gradually converts an input sentence (valid input sequence) to a handy internal data structure or translates it to a sentence in another language.

We can see the overall data flow within the pipeline in Figure 1.1, on the next page. The basic idea is that a reader recognizes input and builds an *intermediate representation* (IR) that feeds the rest of the application. At the opposite end, a generator emits output based upon the IR and what the application learned in the intermediate stages. The intermediate stages form the *semantic analyzer* component. Loosely speaking,

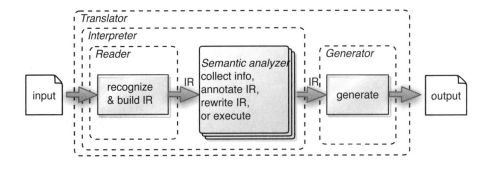

Figure 1.1: The multistage pipeline of a language application

semantic analysis figures out what the input means (anything beyond syntax is called the *semantics*).

The kind of application we're building dictates the stages of the pipeline and how we hook them together. There are four broad application categories:

- *Reader*: A reader builds a data structure from one or more input streams. The input streams are usually text but can be binary data as well. Examples include configuration file readers, program analysis tools such as a method cross-reference tool, and class file loaders.

- *Generator*: A generator walks an internal data structure and emits output. Examples include object-to-relational database mapping tools, object serializers, source code generators, and web page generators.

- *Translator* or *Rewriter*: A translator reads text or binary input and emits output conforming to the same or a different language. It is essentially a combined reader and generator. Examples include translators from extinct programming languages to modern languages, wiki to HTML translators, refactorers, profilers that instrument code, log file report generators, pretty printers, and macro preprocessors. Some translators, such as assemblers and compilers, are so common that they warrant their own subcategories.

- *Interpreter*: An interpreter reads, decodes, and executes instructions. Interpreters range from simple calculators and POP protocol servers all the way up to programming language implementations such as those for Java, Ruby, and Python.

1.2 A Tour of the Patterns

This section is a road map of this book's 31 language implementation patterns. Don't worry if this quick tour is hard to digest at first. The fog will clear as we go through the book and get acquainted with the patterns.

Parsing Input Sentences

Reader components use the patterns discussed in Chapter 2, *Basic Parsing Patterns*, on page 21 and Chapter 3, *Enhanced Parsing Patterns*, on page 49 to *parse* (recognize) input structures. There are five alternative parsing patterns between the two chapters. Some languages are tougher to parse than others, and so we need parsers of varying strength. The trade-off is that the stronger parsing patterns are more complicated and sometimes a bit slower.

We'll also explore a little about grammars (formal language specifications) and figure out exactly how parsers recognize languages. Pattern 1, *Mapping Grammars to Recursive-Descent Recognizers*, on page 29 shows us how to convert grammars to hand-built parsers. ANTLR[1] (or any similar parser generator) can do this conversion automatically for us, but it's a good idea to familiarize ourselves with the underlying patterns.

The most basic reader component combines Pattern 2, *LL(1) Recursive-Descent Lexer*, on page 33 together with Pattern 3, *LL(1) Recursive-Descent Parser*, on page 38 to recognize sentences. More complicated languages will need a stronger parser, though. We can increase the recognition strength of a parser by allowing it to look at more of the input at once (Pattern 4, *LL(k) Recursive-Descent Parser*, on page 43).

When things get really hairy, we can only distinguish sentences by looking at an entire sentence or phrase (subsentence) using Pattern 5, *Backtracking Parser*, on page 55.

Backtracking's strength comes at the cost of slow execution speed. With some tinkering, however, we can dramatically improve its efficiency. We just need to save and reuse some partial parsing results with Pattern 6, *Memoizing Parser*, on page 62.

For the ultimate parsing power, we can resort to Pattern 7, *Predicated Parser*, on page 68. A predicated parser can alter the normal parsing flow based upon run-time information. For example, input T(i) can mean

---

1. http://www.antlr.org

different things depending on how we defined T previously. A predicate parser can look up T in a dictionary to see what it is.

Besides tracking input symbols like T, a parser can execute actions to perform a transformation or do some analysis. This approach is usually too simplistic for most applications, though. We'll need to make multiple passes over the input. These passes are the stages of the pipeline beyond the reader component.

Constructing Trees

Rather than repeatedly parsing the input text in every stage, we'll construct an IR. The IR is a highly processed version of the input text that's easy to traverse. The nodes or elements of the IR are also ideal places to squirrel away information for use by later stages. In Chapter 4, *Building Intermediate Form Trees*, on page 73, we'll discuss why we build trees and how they encode essential information from the input.

The nature of an application dictates what kind of data structure we use for the IR. Compilers require a highly specialized IR that is very low level (elements of the IR correspond very closely with machine instructions). Because we're not focusing on compilers in this book, though, we'll generally use a higher-level tree structure.

The first tree pattern we'll look at is Pattern 8, *Parse Tree*, on page 90. Parse trees are pretty "noisy," though. They include a record of the rules used to recognize the input, not just the input itself. Parse trees are useful primarily for building syntax-highlighting editors. For implementing source code analyzers, translators, and the like, we'll build *abstract syntax trees* (ASTs) because they are easier to work with.

An AST has a node for every important token and uses operators as subtree roots. For example, the AST for assignment statement this.x=y; is as follows:

The AST implementation pattern you pick depends on how you plan on traversing the AST (Chapter 4, *Building Intermediate Form Trees*, on page 73 discusses AST construction in detail).

Pattern 9, *Homogeneous AST*, on page 94 is as simple as you can get. It uses a single object type to represent every node in the tree. Homogeneous nodes also have to represent specific children by position within a list rather than with named node fields. We call that a *normalized child list*.

If we need to store different data depending on the kind of tree node, we need to introduce multiple node types with Pattern 10, *Normalized Heterogeneous AST*, on page 96. For example, we might want different node types for addition operator nodes and variable reference nodes. When building heterogeneous node types, it's common practice to track children with fields rather than lists (Pattern 11, *Irregular Heterogeneous AST*, on page 99).

Walking Trees

Once we've got an appropriate representation of our input in memory, we can start extracting information or performing transformations.

To do that, we need to traverse the IR (AST, in our case). There are two basic approaches to tree walking. Either we embed methods within each node class (Pattern 12, *Embedded Heterogeneous Tree Walker*, on page 113) or we encapsulate those methods in an external visitor (Pattern 13, *External Tree Visitor*, on page 116). The external visitor is nice because it allows us to alter tree-walking behavior without modifying node classes.

Rather than build external visitors manually, though, we can automate visitor construction just like we can automate parser construction. To recognize tree structures, we'll use Pattern 14, *Tree Grammar*, on page 119 or Pattern 15, *Tree Pattern Matcher*, on page 123. A tree grammar describes the entire structure of all valid trees, whereas a tree pattern matcher lets us focus on just those subtrees we care about. You'll use one or more of these tree walkers to implement the next stages in the pipeline.

Figuring Out What the Input Means

Before we can generate output, we need to analyze the input to extract bits of information relevant to generation (semantic analysis). Language analysis is rooted in a fundamental question: for a given symbol reference x, what is it? Depending on the application, we might need to know whether it's a variable or method, what type it is, or where it's defined. To answer these questions, we need to track all input symbols using one of the *symbol tables* in Chapter 6, *Tracking and Identifying Program Symbols*, on page 131 or Chapter 7, *Managing Symbol Tables for Data Aggregates*, on page 155. A symbol table is just a dictionary that maps symbols to their definitions.

The semantic rules of your language dictate which symbol table pattern to use. There are four common kinds of scoping rules: languages with a single scope, nested scopes, C-style **struct** scopes, and class scopes. You'll find the associated implementations in Pattern 16, *Symbol Table for Monolithic Scope*, on page 141, Pattern 17, *Symbol Table for Nested Scopes*, on page 146, Pattern 18, *Symbol Table for Data Aggregates*, on page 161, andPattern 19, *Symbol Table for Classes*, on page 167.

Languages such as Java, C#, and C++ have a ton of semantic compile-time rules. Most of these rules deal with type compatibility between operators or assignment statements. For example, we can't multiply a string by a class name. Chapter 8, *Enforcing Static Typing Rules*, on page 181 describes how to compute the types of all expressions and then check operations and assignments for type compatibility. For non-object-oriented languages like C, we'd apply Pattern 22, *Enforcing Static Type Safety*, on page 201. For object-oriented languages like C++ or Java, we'd apply Pattern 23, *Enforcing Polymorphic Type Safety*, on page 208. To make these patterns easier to absorb, we'll break out some of the necessary infrastructure in Pattern 20, *Computing Static Expression Types*, on page 184 and Pattern 21, *Automatic Type Promotion*, on page 193.

If you're building a reader like a configuration file reader or Java .class file reader, your application pipeline would be complete at this point. To build an interpreter or translator, though, we have to add more stages.

Interpreting Input Sentences

Interpreters execute instructions stored in the IR but usually need other data structures too, like a symbol table. Chapter 9, *Building High-Level Interpreters*, on page 219 describes the most common interpreter implementation patterns, including Pattern 24, *Syntax-Directed Interpreter*, on page 225, Pattern 25, *Tree-Based Interpreter*, on page 230, Pattern 27, *Stack-Based Bytecode Interpreter*, on page 259, and Pattern 28, *Register-Based Bytecode Interpreter*, on page 267. From a capability standpoint, the interpreter patterns are equivalent (or could be made equally powerful). The differences between them lie in the instruction set, execution efficiency, interactivity, ease-of-use, and ease of implementation.

Translating One Language to Another

Rather than interpreting a computer language, we can translate programs to another language (at the extreme, compilers translate high-level programs down to machine code). The final component of any translator is a generator that emits structured text or binary. The output is a function of the input and the results of semantic analysis. For simple translations, we can combine the reader and generator into a single pass using Pattern 29, *Syntax-Directed Translator*, on page 296. Generally, though, we need to decouple the order in which we compute output phrases from the order in which we emit output phrases. For example, imagine reversing the statements of a program. We can't generate the first output statement until we've read the final input statement. To decouple input and output order, we'll use a model-driven approach. (See Chapter 11, *Translating Computer Languages*, on page 279.)

Because generator output always conforms to a language, it makes sense to use a formal language tool to emit structured text. What we need is an "unparser" called a *template engine*. There are many excellent template engines out there but, for our sample implementations, we'll use StringTemplate.[2] (See Chapter 12, *Generating DSLs with Templates*, on page 313.)

So, that's how patterns fit into the overall language implementation pipeline. Before getting into them, though, it's worth investigating the architecture of some common language applications. It'll help keep everything in perspective as you read the patterns chapters.

1.3 Dissecting a Few Applications

Language applications are a bit like fractals. As you zoom in on their architecture diagrams, you see that their pipeline stages are themselves multistage pipelines. For example, though we see compilers as black boxes, they are actually deeply nested pipelines. They are so complicated that we have to break them down into lots of simpler components. Even the individual top-level components are pipelines. Digging deeper,

---

2. http://www.stringtemplate.org

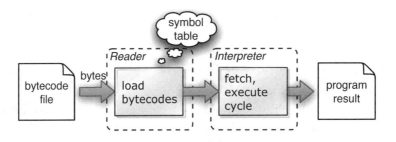

Figure 1.2: BYTECODE INTERPRETER PIPELINE

the same data structures and algorithms pop up across applications and stages.

This section dissects a few language applications to expose their architectures. We'll look at a bytecode interpreter, a bug finder (source code analyzer), and a C/C++ compiler. The goal is to emphasize the architectural similarity between applications and even between the stages in a single application. The more you know about existing language applications, the easier it'll be to design your own. Let's start with the simplest architecture.

Bytecode Interpreter

An *interpreter* is a program that executes other programs. In effect, an interpreter simulates a hardware processor in software, which is why we call them *virtual machines*. An interpreter's instruction set is typically pretty low level but higher level than raw machine code. We call the instructions*bytecodes* because we can represent each instruction with a unique integer code from 0..255 (a byte's range).

We can see the basic architecture of a bytecode interpreter in Figure 1.2. A reader loads the bytecodes from a file before the interpreter can start execution. To execute a program, the interpreter uses a *fetch-decode-execute cycle*. Like a real processor, the interpreter has an instruction pointer that tracks which instruction to execute next. Some instructions move data around, some move the instruction pointer (branches and calls), and some emit output (which is how we get the program result). There are a lot of implementation details, but this gives you the basic idea.

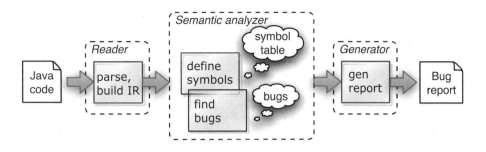

Figure 1.3: SOURCE-LEVEL BUG FINDER PIPELINE

Languages with bytecode interpreter implementations include Java, Lua,[3] Python, Ruby, C#, and Smalltalk.[4] Lua uses Pattern 28, *Register-Based Bytecode Interpreter*, on page 267, but the others use Pattern 27, *Stack-Based Bytecode Interpreter*, on page 259. Prior to version 1.9, Ruby used something akin to Pattern 25, *Tree-Based Interpreter*, on page 230.

Java Bug Finder

Let's move all the way up to the source code level now and crack open a Java bug finder application. To keep things simple, we'll look for just one kind of bug called *self-assignment*. Self-assignment is when we assign a variable to itself. For example, the setX() method in the following Point class has a useless self-assignment because this.x and x refer to the same field x:

```
class Point {
    int x,y;
    void setX(int y) { this.x = x; } // oops! Meant setX(int x)
    void setY(int y) { this.y = y; }
}
```

The best way to design a language application is to start with the end in mind. First, figure out what information you need in order to generate the output. That tells you what the final stage before the generator computes. Then figure out what that stage needs and so on all the way back to the reader.

3. http://www.lua.org
4. http://en.wikipedia.org/wiki/Smalltalk_programming_language

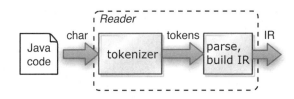

Figure 1.4: PIPELINE THAT RECOGNIZES JAVA CODE AND BUILDS AN IR

For our bug finder, we need to generate a report showing all self-assignments. To do that, we need to find all assignments of the form this.x = x and flag those that assign to themselves. To do that, we need to figure out (*resolve*) to which entity this.x and x refer. That means we need to track all symbol definitions using a symbol table like Pattern 19, *Symbol Table for Classes*, on page 167. We can see the pipeline for our bug finder in Figure 1.3, on the previous page.

Now that we've identified the stages, let's walk the information flow forward. The parser reads the Java code and builds an intermediate representation that feeds the semantic analysis phases. To parse Java, we can use Pattern 2, *LL(1) Recursive-Descent Lexer*, on page 33, Pattern 4, *LL(k) Recursive-Descent Parser*, on page 43, Pattern 5, *Backtracking Parser*, on page 55, and Pattern 6, *Memoizing Parser*, on page 62. We can get away with building a simple IR: Pattern 9, *Homogeneous AST*, on page 94.

The semantic analyzer in our case needs to make two passes over the IR. The first pass defines all the symbols encountered during the walk. The second pass looks for assignment patterns whose left-side and right-side resolve to the same field. To find symbol definitions and assignment tree patterns, we can use Pattern 15, *Tree Pattern Matcher*, on page 123. Once we have a list of self-assignments, we can generate a report.

Let's zoom in a little on the reader (see Figure 1.4). Most text readers use a two-stage process. The first stage breaks up the character stream into vocabulary symbols called*tokens*. The parser feeds off these tokens to check syntax. In our case, the tokenizer (or*lexer*) yields a stream of vocabulary symbols like this:

... void setX (int y) { ...

As the parser checks the syntax, it builds the IR. We have to build an IR in this case because we make multiple passes over the input. Retokenizing and reparsing the text input for every pass is inefficient and makes it harder to pass information between stages. Multiple passes also support forward references. For example, we want to be able to see field x even if it's defined after method setX(). By defining all symbols first, before trying to resolve them, our bug-finding stage sees x easily.

Now let's jump to the final stage and zoom in on the generator. Since we have a list of bugs (presumably a list of Bug objects), our generator can use a simple **for** loop to print out the bugs. For more complicated reports, though, we'll want to use a template. For example, if we assume that Bug has fields file, line, and fieldname, then we can use the following two StringTemplate template definitions to generate a report (we'll explore template syntax in Chapter 12, *Generating DSLs with Templates*, on page 313).

```
report(bugs) ::= "<bugs:bug()>" // apply template bug to each bug object
bug(b) ::= "bug: <b.file>:<b.line> self assignment to <b.fieldname>"
```

All we have to do is pass the list of Bug objects to the **report** template as attribute bugs, and StringTemplate does the rest.

There's another way to implement this bug finder. Instead of doing all the work to read Java source code and populate a symbol table, we can leverage the functionality of the javac Java compiler, as we'll see next.

Java Bug Finder Part Deux

The Java compiler generates .class files that contain serialized versions of a symbol table and AST. We can use Byte Code Engineering Library (BCEL)[5] or another class file reader to load .class files instead of building a source code reader (the fine tool FindBugs[6] uses this approach). We can see the pipeline for this approach in Figure 1.5, on the following page.

The overall architecture is roughly the same as before. We have just short-circuited the pipeline a little bit. We don't need a source code parser, and we don't need to build a symbol table. The Java compiler has already resolved all symbols and generated bytecode that refers to unique program entities. To find self-assignment bugs, all we have to

---

5. http://jakarta.apache.org/bcel/
6. http://findbugs.sourceforge.net/

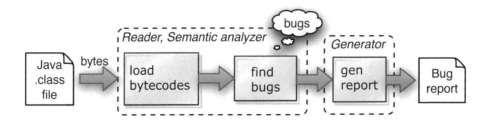

Figure 1.5: JAVA BUG FINDER PIPELINE FEEDING OFF .CLASS FILES

do is look for a particular bytecode sequence. Here is the bytecode for method setX():

```
0:    aload_0      // push 'this' onto the stack
1:    aload_0      // push 'this' onto the stack
2:    getfield #2; // push field this.x onto the stack
5:    putfield #2; // store top of stack (this.x) into field this.x
8:    return
```

The #2 operand is an offset into a symbol table and uniquely identifies the x (field) symbol. In this case, the bytecode clearly gets and puts the same field. If this.x referred to a different field than x, we'd see different symbol numbers as operands of getfield and putfield.

Now, let's look at the compilation process that feeds this bug finder. javac is a compiler just like a traditional C compiler. The only difference is that a C compiler translates programs down to instructions that run natively on a particular CPU.

C Compiler

A C compiler looks like one big program because we use a single command to launch it (via **cc** or **gcc** on UNIX machines). Although the actual C compiler is the most complicated component, the C compilation process has lots of players.

Before we can get to actual compilation, we have to preprocess C files to handle includes and macros. The preprocessor spits out pure C code with some line number directives understood by the compiler. The compiler munches on that for a while and then spits out assembly code (text-based human-readable machine code). A separate assembler translates the assembly code to binary machine code. With a few command-line options, we can expose this pipeline.

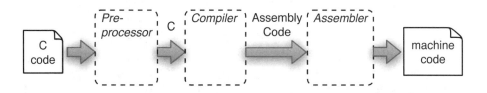

Figure 1.6: C COMPILATION PROCESS PIPELINE

Let's follow the pipeline (shown in Figure 1.6) for the C function in file t.c:

```
void f() { ; }
```

First we preprocess t.c:

```
$ cpp t.c tmp.c          # preprocess t.c, put output into tmp.c
$
```

That gives us the following C code:

```
# 1 "t.c"                // line information generated by preprocessor
# 1 "<built-in>"         // it's not C code per se
# 1 "<command line>"
# 1 "t.c"
void f() { ; }
```

If we had included stdio.h, we'd see a huge pile of stuff in front of f(). To compile tmp.c down to assembly code instead of all the way to machine code, we use option -S. The following session compiles and prints out the generated assembly code:

```
$ gcc -S tmp.c           # compile tmp.c to tmp.s
$ cat tmp.s              # print assembly code to standard output
        .text
.globl _f
_f:                             ; define function f
        pushl   %ebp            ; do method bookkeeping
        movl    %esp, %ebp      ; you can ignore this stuff
        subl    $8, %esp
        leave                   ; clean up stack
        ret                     ; return to invoking function
        .subsections_via_symbols
$
```

To assemble tmp.s, we run as to get the object file tmp.o:

```
$ as -o tmp.o tmp.s          # assemble tmp.s to tmp.o
$ ls tmp.*
tmp.c   tmp.o   tmp.s
$
```

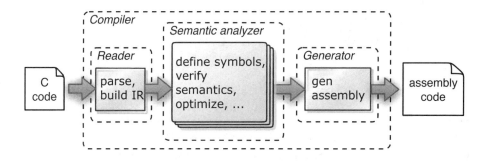

Figure 1.7: ISOLATED C COMPILER APPLICATION PIPELINE

Now that we know about the overall compilation process, let's zoom in on the pipeline inside the C compiler itself.

The main components are highlighted in Figure 1.7. Like other language applications, the C compiler has a reader that parses the input and builds an IR. On the other end, the generator traverses the IR, emitting assembly instructions for each subtree. These components (the *front end* and *back end*) are not the hard part of a compiler.

All the scary voodoo within a compiler happens inside the semantic analyzer and optimizer. From the IR, it has to build all sorts of extra data structures in order to produce an efficient version of the input C program in assembly code. Lots of set and graph theory algorithms are at work. Implementing these complicated algorithms is challenging. If you'd like to dig into compilers, I recommend the famous "Dragon" book: *Compilers: Principles, Techniques, and Tools* [ALSU06] (Second Edition).

Rather than build a complete compiler, we can also leverage an existing compiler. In the next section, we'll see how to implement a language by translating it to an existing language.

Leveraging a C Compiler to Implement C++

Imagine you are Bjarne Stroustrup, the designer and original implementer of C++. You have a cool idea for extending C to have classes, but you're faced with a mammoth programming project to implement it from scratch.

To get C++ up and running in fairly short order, Stroustrup simply reduced C++ compilation to a known problem: C compilation. In other

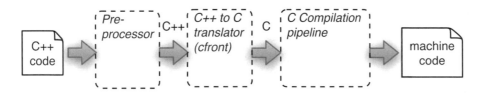

Figure 1.8: C++ (CFRONT) COMPILATION PROCESS PIPELINE

words, he built a C++ to C translator calledcfront. He didn't have to build a compiler at all. By generating C, his nascent language was instantly available on any machine with a C compiler. We can see the overall C++ application pipeline in Figure 1.8. If we zoomed in on cfront, we'd see yet another reader, semantic analyzer, and generator pipeline.

As you can see, language applications are all pretty similar. Well, at least they all use the same basic architecture and share many of the same components. To implement the components, they use a lot of the same patterns. Before moving on to the patterns in the subsequent chapters, let's get a general sense of how to hook them together into our own applications.

1.4 Choosing Patterns and Assembling Applications

I chose the patterns in this book because of their importance and how often you'll find yourself using them. From my own experience and from listening to the chatter on the ANTLR interest list, we programmers typically do one of two things. Either we implement DSLs or we process and translate general-purpose programming languages. In other words, we tend to implement graphics and mathematics languages, but very few of us build compilers and interpreters for full programming languages. Most of the time, we're building tools to refactor, format, compute software metrics, find bugs, instrument, or translate them to another high-level language.

If we're not building implementations for general-purpose programming languages, you might wonder why I've included some of the patterns I have. For example, all compiler textbooks talk about symbol table management and computing the types of expressions. This book also spends roughly 20 percent of the page count on those subjects. The reason is that some of the patterns we'd need to build a compiler are also critical to implementing DSLs and even just processing general-purpose languages. Symbol table management, for example, is the bedrock of most language applications you'll build. Just as a parser is the key to analyzing the syntax, a symbol table is the key to understanding the semantics (meaning) of the input. In a nutshell, syntax tells us what to do, and semantics tells us what to do it to.

As a language application developer, you'll be faced with a number of important decisions. You'll need to decide which patterns to use and how to assemble them to build an application. Fortunately, it's not as hard as it seems at first glance. The nature of an application tells us a lot about which patterns to use, and, amazingly, only two basic architectures cover the majority of language applications.

Organizing the patterns into groups helps us pick the ones we need. This book organizes them more or less according to Figure 1.1, on page 4. We have patterns for reading input (part I), analyzing input (part II), interpreting input (part III), and generating output (part IV). The simplest applications use patterns from part I, and the most complicated applications need patterns from I, II, and III or from I, II, and IV. So, if all we need to do is load some data into memory, we pick patterns from part I. To build an interpreter, we need patterns to read the input and at least a pattern from part III to execute commands. To build a translator, we again need patterns to parse the input, and then we need patterns from part IV to generate output. For all but the simplest languages, we'll also need patterns from part II to build internal data structures and analyze the input.

The most basic architecture combines lexer and parser patterns. It's the heart of Pattern 24, *Syntax-Directed Interpreter*, on page 225 and Pattern 29, *Syntax-Directed Translator*, on page 296. Once we recognize input sentences, all we have to do is call a method that executes or translates them. For an interpreter, this usually means calling some implementation function like assign() or drawLine(). For a translator, it means printing an output statement based upon symbols from the input sentence.

The other common architecture creates an AST from the input (via tree construction actions in the parser) instead of trying to process the input on the fly. Having an AST lets us sniff the input multiple times without having to reparse it, which would be pretty inefficient. For example, Pattern 25, *Tree-Based Interpreter*, on page 230 revisits AST nodes all the time as it executes **while** loops, and so on.

The AST also gives us a convenient place to store information that we compute in the various stages of the application pipeline. For example, it's a good idea to annotate the AST with pointers into the symbol table. The pointers tell us what kind of symbol the AST node represents and, if it's an expression, what its result type is. We'll explore such annotations in Chapter 6, *Tracking and Identifying Program Symbols*, on page 131 and Chapter 8, *Enforcing Static Typing Rules*, on page 181.

Once we've got a suitable AST with all the necessary information in it, we can tack on a final stage to get the output we want. If we're generating a report, for example, we'd do a final pass over the AST to collect and print whatever information we need. If we're building a translator, we'd tack on a generator from Chapter 11, *Translating Computer Languages*, on page 279 or Chapter 12, *Generating DSLs with Templates*, on page 313. The simplest generator walks the AST and directly prints output statements, but it works only when the input and output statement orders are the same. A more flexible strategy is to construct an output model composed of strings, templates, or specialized output objects.

Once you have built a few language applications, you will get a feel for whether you need an AST. If I'm positive I can just bang out an application with a parser and a few actions, I'll do so for simplicity reasons. When in doubt, though, I build an AST so I don't code myself into a corner.

Now that we've gotten some perspective, we can begin our adventure into language implementation.

## Chapter 2

Basic Parsing Patterns

Language recognition is a critical step in just about any language application. To interpret or translate a phrase, we first have to recognize what kind of phrase it is (sentences are made up of phrases). Once we know that a phrase is an assignment or function call, for example, we can act on it. To recognize a phrase means two things. First, it means we can distinguish it from the other constructs in that language. And, second, it means we can identify the elements and any substructures of the phrase. For example, if we recognize a phrase as an assignment, we can identify the variable on the left of the = and the expression substructure on the right. The act of recognizing a phrase by computer is called *parsing*.

This chapter introduces the most common parser design patterns that you will need to build recognizers by hand. There are multiple parser design patterns because certain languages are harder to parse than others. As usual, there is a trade-off between parser simplicity and parser strength. Extremely complex languages like C++ typically require less efficient but more powerful parsing strategies. We'll talk about the more powerful parsing patterns in the next chapter. For now, we'll focus on the following basic patterns to get up to speed:

- Pattern 1, *Mapping Grammars to Recursive-Descent Recognizers*, on page 29. This pattern tells us how to convert a grammar (formal language specification) to a hand-built parser. It's used by the next three patterns.

- Pattern 2, *LL(1) Recursive-Descent Lexer*, on page 33. This pattern breaks up character streams into tokens for use by the parsers defined in the subsequent patterns.

- Pattern 3, *LL(1) Recursive-Descent Parser*, on page 38. This is the most well-known recursive-descent parsing pattern. It only needs to look at the current input symbol to make parsing decisions. For each rule in a grammar, there is a parsing method in the parser.

- Pattern 4, *LL(k) Recursive-Descent Parser*, on page 43. This pattern augments an *LL(1)* recursive-descent parser so that it can look multiple symbols ahead (up to some fixed number *k*) in order to make decisions.

Before jumping into the parsing patterns, this chapter provides some background material on language recognition. Along the way, we will define some important terms and learn about grammars. You can think of grammars as functional specifications or design documents for parsers. To build a parser, we need a guiding specification that precisely defines the language we want to parse.

Grammars are more than designs, though. They are actually executable "programs" written in a domain-specific language (DSL) specifically designed for expressing language structures. Parser generators such as ANTLR can automatically convert grammars to parsers for us. In fact, ANTLR mimics what we'd build by hand using the design patterns in this chapter and the next.

After we get a good handle on building parsers by hand, we'll rely on grammars throughout the examples in the rest of the book. Grammars are often 10 percent the size of hand-built recognizers and provide more robust solutions. The key to understanding ANTLR's behavior, though, lies in these parser design patterns. If you have a solid background in computer science or already have a good handle on parsing, you can probably skip this chapter and the next.

Let's get started by figuring out how to identify the various substructures in a phrase.

2.1 Identifying Phrase Structure

In elementary school, we all learned (and probably forgot) how to identify the parts of speech in a sentence like *verb* and *noun*. We can do the same thing with computer languages (we call it *syntax analysis*). Vocabulary symbols (*tokens*) play different roles like *variable* and *operator*. We can even identify the role of token subsequences like *expression*.

Take return x+1;, for example. Sequence x+1 plays the role of an expression and the entire phrase is a return statement, which is also a kind of statement. If we represent that visually, we get a sentence diagram of sorts:

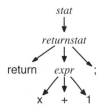

Flip that over, and you get what we call a *parse tree*:

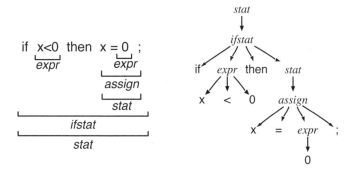

Tokens hang from the parse tree as leaf nodes, while the interior nodes identify the phrase substructures. The actual names of the substructures aren't important as long as we know what they mean. For a more complicated example, take a look at the substructures and parse tree for an if statement:

Parse trees are important because they tell us everything we need to know about the syntax (*structure*) of a phrase. To parse, then, is to conjure up a two-dimensional parse tree from a flat token sequence.

2.2 Building Recursive-Descent Parsers

A parser checks whether a sentence conforms to the syntax of a *language*. (A language is just a set of valid sentences.) To verify language membership, a parser has to identify a sentence's parse tree. The cool thing is that the parser doesn't actually have to construct a tree data structure in memory. It's enough to just recognize the various substructures and the associated tokens. Most of the time, we only need to execute some code on the tokens in a substructure. In practice, we want parsers to "do this when they see that."

To avoid building parse trees, we trace them out implicitly via a function call sequence (a call tree). All we have to do is make a function for each named substructure (interior node) of the parse tree. Each function, say, *f*, executes code to match its children. To match a substructure (subtree), *f* calls the function associated with that subtree. To match token children, *f* can call a match() support function. Following this simple formula, we arrive at the following functions from the parse tree for return x+1;:

```
/** To parse a statement, call stat(); */
void stat()       { returnstat(); }
void returnstat() { match("return"); expr(); match(";"); }
void expr()       { match("x"); match("+"); match("1"); }
```

Function match() advances an input cursor after comparing the current input token to its argument. For example, before calling match("return"), the input token sequence looks like this:

```
return  x + 1 ;
  ↑
```

match("return") makes sure that current (first) token is return and advances to the next (second) token. When we advance the cursor, we *consume* that token since the parser never has to look at it again. We can represent consumed tokens with a dark gray box:

```
return  x + 1 ;
        ↑
```

To make things more interesting, let's figure out how to parse the three kinds of statements found in our parse trees: **if**, **return**, and assignment statements. To distinguish what kind of statement is coming down the road, stat() needs to branch according to the token under the input cursor (the light gray box). We call that token the *lookahead token*. Here's one way to implement stat():

```
void stat() {
    if ( «lookahead token is return» )            returnstat();
    else if ( «lookahead token is identifier» ) assign();
    else if ( «lookahead token is if» )          ifstat();
    else «parse error»
}
```

We call this kind of parser a *top-down parser* because it starts at the top of the parse tree and works its way down to the token leaf nodes.

More specifically, we're using Pattern 3, *LL(1) Recursive-Descent Parser*, on page 38. *Descent* refers to its top-down nature, and *recursive* refers to the fact that its functions potentially call themselves. For example, in Section 2.1, *Identifying Phrase Structure*, on page 22, the *stat* substructure for the assignment statement appears within (under) the *stat* for the if statement. Nesting in a parse tree begets recursion in a recursive-descent parser. The formal designation for a top-down parser that uses a single lookahead token is *LL(1)*. The first *L* means "read the input from left to right." The second *L* means "descend into parse tree children from left to right." For complicated languages, we can use more lookahead yielding Pattern 4, *LL(k) Recursive-Descent Parser*, on page 43.

At this point, we've got a parser that can recognize the various substructures using different functions. But, that's all it does. To execute application-specific code upon seeing a particular substructure, we have to add code to the appropriate function. For example, if we want to print "found return" every time we see a return statement, we can add the following anywhere in returnstat():

```
System.out.println("found return");
```

The patterns that follow this introductory material fill in some details, but that's really all there is to building parsers: predicting which kind of phrase approaches, invoking functions to match substructures, matching tokens, and executing application-specific actions (code).

The first few recursive-descent parsers you build are pretty fun. After a while, though, building them is monotonous. The parsing functions are so similar and consistent that we can easily generate them automatically. The only problem is describing the structure of our language to the computer. Since most languages have an infinite number of sentences, we can't just delineate them. For the same reason, we can't delineate all possible parse trees. What we need is a DSL for specifying languages.

2.3 Parser Construction Using a Grammar DSL

Building recursive-descent parsers in a general-purpose programming language is tedious and error-prone. We have to type the same code templates over and over again. It's much more productive to use a DSL specifically designed for describing languages. "Programs" in this DSL are called *grammars*. Tools that translate grammars to parsers are called *parser generators*. Grammars are concise and act like functional specifications for languages. They are much easier to read than the equivalent recursive-descent parser implementations.

Substructures in the parse tree and functions in the parser correspond to *rules* in a grammar. The children of a substructure become references to rules and tokens on the right side of a rule definition. The if-then-else code template in the parser becomes a | separated list of alternative substructures. Here is one way to encode the recursive-descent parser from the previous section as an ANTLR grammar:

```
stat        : returnstat            // "return x+0;" or
            | assign                // "x=0;" or
            | ifstat                // "if x<0 then x=0;"
            ;
returnstat : 'return' expr ';' ; // single-quoted strings are tokens
assign      : 'x' '=' expr ;
ifstat      : 'if' expr 'then' stat ;
expr        : 'x' '+' '0'           // used by returnstat
            | 'x' '<' '0'           // used by if conditional
            | '0'                   // used in assign
            ;
```

This example foreshadows much of Pattern 1, *Mapping Grammars to Recursive-Descent Recognizers*, on page 29.

Read rule **stat** as "A **stat** can be either a **returnstat**, an **assign**, or an **ifstat**." We can use a *syntax diagram* to visualize the control flow within that rule (using ANTLRWorks):

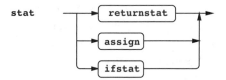

If there is only one alternative, such as in rule **returnstat**, the syntax diagram shows just a sequence of elements:

When rules get more complicated, syntax diagrams come in handy. For example, here is the syntax diagram for rule **expr**:

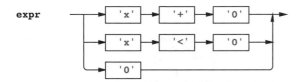

Rule **expr** might look a little funny to you, and it should. It says that expressions can only be one of three alternative token sequences. Further, variables can only be x, and integers can only be 0. This brings us to the last piece of the language recognition puzzle: combining input characters into vocabulary symbols (tokens).

2.4 Tokenizing Sentences

Humans unconsciously combine letters into words before recognizing grammatical structure while reading. As adults, we are so good at it that we don't notice it. Beginning readers, on the other hand, move along with their fingers trying to sound out the words.

Reading Morse code exposes this hidden process nicely by forcing us to move character by character. Before interpreting a sentence as English, we have to convert the dots and dashes to letters and then combine the letters into words. Once we have words, we can apply English grammatical structure. For example, here is print 34 in Morse code:

```
.--. .-. .. -. - ...-- ....-
p   r   i  n  t 3    4
```

Recognizers that feed off character streams are called *tokenizers* or *lexers* (see Pattern 2, *LL(1) Recursive-Descent Lexer*, on page 33). Just as an overall sentence has structure, the individual tokens have structure. At the character level, we refer to syntax as the *lexical structure*.

Grammars describe language structures, and so we can also use them for lexical specifications.

For example, here are suitable definitions for numbers and identifiers:

```
Number : '0'..'9'+ ;           // 1-or-more digits (0..9)
ID     : ('a'..'z'|'A'..'Z')+ ; // 1-or-more upper or lower case letters
```

Now we can make a better version of rule **expr** using generic variable names and numbers instead of specific ones:

```
expr      : ID '+' Number  // used by returnstat
          | ID '<' Number  // used by if conditional
          | Number         // used in assign
          ;
```

This rule still isn't general enough, but it demonstrates how lexical and syntactic rules can interact.

To make things more concrete, let's look at a real grammar for a simple language. Say we want to recognize lists of names such as [a,b,c] and nested lists such as [a,[b,c],d]. We could use the following ANTLR grammar with three syntactic rules and one lexical rule (lexical rules start with an uppercase letter):

parsing/topdown/NestedNameList.g

```
grammar NestedNameList;
list      : '[' elements ']' ;          // match bracketed list
elements : element (',' element)* ;    // match comma-separated list
element  : NAME | list ;               // element is name or nested list
NAME     : ('a'..'z'|'A'..'Z')+ ;       // NAME is sequence of >=1 letter
```

We can see the parse trees for those two sentences in Figure 2.1, on the next page. The leaves of the parse tree (highlighted nodes) are the tokens from the input stream. The interior nodes are rule names from the grammar. Pattern 2, *LL(1) Recursive-Descent Lexer*, on page 33 and Pattern 3, *LL(1) Recursive-Descent Parser*, on page 38 show how to build a lexer and parser for this grammar.

When reading the lexer and parser design patterns, you'll notice that they are nearly identical. This makes sense given that both patterns look for structure in input sequences. The only difference lies in the type of their input symbols, characters or tokens. We can even take this one step further. Pattern 14, *Tree Grammar*, on page 119 recognizes structure in tree node sequences.

With this preparatory grammar and parsing discussion out of the way, we can define four classic parsing patterns. After looking at them, we'll be able to build parsers for lots of languages. Ultimately we'll use ANTLR grammars rather than hand-built recursive-descent parsers because it's a lot easier. Knowledge of these parsing design patterns still

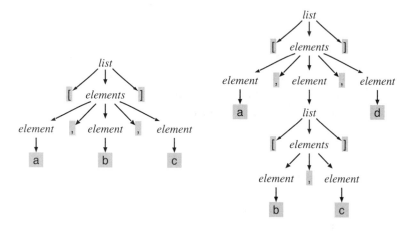

Figure 2.1: PARSE TREES FOR [A,B,C] AND [A,[B,C],D] WITH HIGHLIGHTED
TOKEN LEAVES

matters, though, because grammars are what drive our parser generators. We still need a good understanding of the underlying mechanism
to build grammars effectively.

1 Mapping Grammars to Recursive-Descent Recognizers

Purpose

*This translates a grammar to a recursive-descent recognizer that matches
phrases and sentences in the language specified by the grammar.*

This pattern identifies the core control-flow framework for any recursive-descent lexer, parser, or tree parser.

Discussion

Even when building lexers and parsers by hand, the best starting point
is a grammar. Grammars are a very concise way to express the languages you intend to recognize. Not only that, but grammars are excellent documentation that can go into a reference manual and into

parsing code as comments. This pattern gives us a way to build recognizers directly from grammars.

A word of caution: this pattern works for many but not all grammars. The most obvious troublesome grammar construct is *left recursion* (a rule that invokes itself without consuming a token). Left recursion results in an infinite method invocation loop. For example, the following rule yields a parser that does not terminate:

```
r : r X ;
```

Using this design pattern, we'd end up with a function that immediately called itself, leading to an infinite loop:

```
void r() { r(); match(X); }
```

Besides left-recursive rules, there are other grammar constructs that yield *nondeterministic* recursive-descent recognizers. A nondeterministic recognizer cannot decide which path to take. The parsers in Pattern 4, *LL(k) Recursive-Descent Parser*, on page 43 and Pattern 5, *Backtracking Parser*, on page 55, use more and more lookahead to increase the strength of the recognizer. The more powerful the underlying recognition strategy, the easier it is to write a grammar. That is because more powerful parsing strategies allow a larger set of grammars.

Implementation

A grammar, G, is a set of rules from which we generate a class definition (in any object-oriented programming language) containing a method for each rule:

```
public class G extends Parser { // parser definition written in Java
    «token-type-definitions»
    «suitable-constructor»
    «rule-methods»
}
```

Class Parser defines the state a typical parser needs, such as a lookahead token or tokens and an input stream.

Converting Rules

For each rule, r, defined in a grammar, we build a method of the same name:

```
public void r() {
    ...
}
```

The inside of a rule looks exactly like a subrule (a rule embedded within another rule), as we'll see shortly.

Rule references to **r** become method calls: r().

Converting Tokens

Token references for token type **T** become calls to match(T). match() is a support method in Parser that consumes a token if **T** is the current lookahead token. If there is a mismatch, match() throws an exception.

Also, we need to define token type **T** somewhere, either in the parser object or in our lexer object. For every token **T**, we write this:

```
public static final int T = «sequential-integer»;
```

We'll also probably need this:

```
public static final int INVALID_TOKEN_TYPE = 0; // to be explicit
public static final int EOF = -1;                // EOF token type
```

You might wonder why I'm not using the **enum** functionality in Java to represent sets of integers. It's because I always end up wanting to treat them as simple integers.

Converting Subrules

Alternatives become either a switch or an if-then-else sequence, depending on the complexity of the lookahead decision. Each alternative gets an expression that predicts whether that alternative would succeed at the current input location. Consider the following generic subrule:

(«alt1»|«alt2»|..|«altN»)

The control flow looks like this:

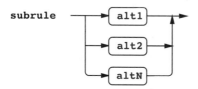

The most general subrule implementation looks like this:

```
if ( «lookahead-predicts-alt1» ) { «match-alt1» }
else if ( «lookahead-predicts-alt2» ) { «match-alt2» }
...
else if ( «lookahead-predicts-altN» ) { «match-altN» }
else «throw-exception» // parse error (no viable alternative)
```

If all of those lookahead expressions only test a single symbol lookahead, we can generate a switch statement, which is usually more efficient:

```
switch ( «lookahead-token» ) {
    case «token1-predicting-alt1» :
    case «token2-predicting-alt1» :
    ...
        «match-alt1»
        break;
    case «token1-predicting-alt2» :
    case «token2-predicting-alt2» :
    ...
        «match-alt2»
        break;
    ...
    case «token1-predicting-altN» :
    case «token2-predicting-altN» :
    ...
        «match-altN»
        break;
    default : «throw-exception»
}
```

As an optimization, we can collapse subrules whose alternatives are token references such as (A|B|C) into sets. Testing the current symbol of lookahead against a set is usually much faster and smaller than a switch.

All recursive-descent recognizers make decisions according to this template. To implement a recognizer, we fill in those lookahead prediction expressions. The nature of the expressions dictates the strength of the strategy. Pattern 2, *LL(1) Recursive-Descent Lexer*, on the next page and Pattern 3, *LL(1) Recursive-Descent Parser*, on page 38 have *LL(1)* decisions, which means their prediction expressions test one symbol of lookahead. Pattern 4, *LL(k) Recursive-Descent Parser*, on page 43 has *LL(k)* decisions whose prediction expressions test *k* symbols of lookahead. Pattern 5, *Backtracking Parser*, on page 55 and Pattern 7, *Predicated Parser*, on page 68 augment *LL(k)* decisions with an arbitrary amount of lookahead and arbitrary user-defined run-time tests, respectively.

Converting Subrule Operators

Optional subrules are easy to convert because all we have to do is remove the default error clause from the subrules in the previous section. If the subrule is optional, there is no possibility of an error. For example, the control flow of optional subrule (T)? looks like this:

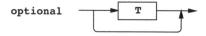

In code, these subrules become conditional statements. For example, (T)? becomes the following:

```
if ( «lookahead-is-T» ) { match(T); } // no error else clause
```

The control flow of one or more (...)+ subrules looks like this:

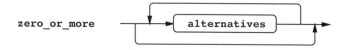

In code, (...)+ subrules become do-while loops:

```
do {
    «code-matching-alternatives»
} while ( «lookahead-predicts-an-alt-of-subrule» );
```

Zero or more (...)* subrules are like optional one-or-more loops. Their control flow looks like this:

zero_or_more

In code, (...)* subrules become while loops:

```
while ( «lookahead-predicts-an-alt-of-subrule» ) {
    «code-matching-alternatives»
}
```

This way, the recognizer can skip over the subrule if the lookahead does not predict an alternative within the subrule.

In the next pattern, we will look at how to build lexers using this grammar-to-recognizer mapping as scaffolding.

☐
2 *LL(1)* Recursive-Descent Lexer

Purpose

Lexers derive a stream of tokens from a character stream by recognizing lexical patterns.

Lexers are also called *scanners*, *lexical analyzers*, and *tokenizers*. As a bonus, this pattern can recognize nested lexical structures such as nested comments (even though languages typically don't have super-complicated lexical structure).

Discussion

The goal of the lexer is to emit a sequence of tokens. Each token has two primary attributes: a *token type* (symbol category) and the text associated with it. In the English language, we've got categories such as verbs and nouns as well as punctuation symbols such as commas and periods. All words within a particular category are said to have the same token type, though their associated text is different.

Let's identify the token types from the list language in Section 2.4, *Tokenizing Sentences*, on page 27. The token type **NAME** represents the identifier category. Then we need token types for the fixed string vocabulary symbols: **COMMA**, **LBRACK**, and **RBRACK**. Lexers also typically deal with whitespace and comments. Because the parser ignores these, we don't bother defining token types for them. We can just have the lexer throw out such character sequences if it finds them between tokens.

To build a lexer by hand, we write a method for each token definition (lexical rule). In other words, token T's definition becomes method T(). These methods recognize the pattern expressed in the associated lexical rule. In programming languages, for example, there are methods to match integers, floating-point numbers, identifiers, operators, and so on. To write the code for the lexer rules, we follow Pattern 1, *Mapping Grammars to Recursive-Descent Recognizers*, on page 29.

To make the lexer look like an enumeration of tokens, it's handy to define a method called nextToken(). nextToken() uses the lookahead character (character under the input cursor) to route control flow to the appropriate recognition method. For example, upon seeing a letter, nextToken() would call a method to recognize the identifier pattern. Here is the core of a typical lexer nextToken() that skips whitespace and comments:

```
public Token nextToken() {
    while ( «lookahead-char»!=EOF ) { // EOF==-1 per java.io
        if ( «comment-start-sequence» ) { COMMENT(); continue; }
        ... // other skip tokens
        switch ( «lookahead-char» ) { // which token approaches?
            case «whitespace» : { consume(); continue; } // skip
            case «chars-predicting-T1» : return T1(); // match T1
            case «chars-predicting-T2» : return T2();
            ...
            case «chars-predicting-Tn» : return Tn();
            default : «error»
        }
    }
    return «EOF-token»; // return token with EOF_TYPE token type
}
```

To use this lexer pattern, we create an instance of a lexer from an input string or stream reader. Our parser object then feeds off this lexer, calling its nextToken() method to extract tokens. The code would look something like this:

```
MyLexer lexer = new MyLexer("«input-sentence»");  // create lexer
MyParser parser = new MyParser(lexer);           // create parser
parser.«start_rule»(); // begin parsing, looking for a list sentence
```

Implementation

As a sample implementation, let's build a lexer for the nested list-of-names grammar shown in Section 2.4, *Tokenizing Sentences*, on page 27. Our goal is a lexer that we can treat like an enumeration. Here is a loop from the test rig that pulls tokens out of the lexer until it returns a token with type EOF_TYPE:

```
parsing/lexer/Test.java
```

```
ListLexer lexer = new ListLexer(args[0]);
Token t = lexer.nextToken();
while ( t.type != Lexer.EOF_TYPE ) {
    System.out.println(t);
    t = lexer.nextToken();
}
System.out.println(t); // EOF
```

We'd like output like this from the list argument:

```
$ java Test '[a, b ]'
<'[',LBRACK>
<'a',NAME>
<',',COMMA>
```

```
<'b',NAME>
<']',RBRACK>
<'<EOF>',<EOF>>
$
```

To implement this, we'll need Token objects, an abstract Lexer for support code, and finally a concrete ListLexer to do the actual work. Let's start by defining tokens to have token type and text properties.

parsing/lexer/Token.java

```java
public class Token {
    public int type;
    public String text;
    public Token(int type, String text) {this.type=type; this.text=text;}
    public String toString() {
        String tname = ListLexer.tokenNames[type];
        return "<'"+text+"',"+tname+">";
    }
}
```

For now, let's skip over the support code, Lexer, to focus on the list language lexer. We need to define token types, and we might as well define them in our lexer:

parsing/lexer/ListLexer.java

```java
public class ListLexer extends Lexer {
    public static int NAME = 2;
    public static int COMMA = 3;
    public static int LBRACK = 4;
    public static int RBRACK = 5;
    public static String[] tokenNames =
        { "n/a", "<EOF>", "NAME", "COMMA", "LBRACK", "RBRACK" };
    public String getTokenName(int x) { return tokenNames[x]; }

    public ListLexer(String input) { super(input); }
    boolean isLETTER() { return c>='a'&&c<='z' || c>='A'&&c<='Z'; }
```

The getTokenName() method helps us generate good error messages and generate readable Token.toString() output.

Following the nextToken() code template, here is the method matching tokens or routes traffic to the appropriate method:

parsing/lexer/ListLexer.java

```java
public Token nextToken() {
    while ( c!=EOF ) {
        switch ( c ) {
            case ' ': case '\t': case '\n': case '\r': WS(); continue;
            case ',' : consume(); return new Token(COMMA, ",");
            case '[' : consume(); return new Token(LBRACK, "[");
```

```
        case ']' : consume(); return new Token(RBRACK, "]");
        default:
            if ( isLETTER() ) return NAME();
            throw new Error("invalid character: "+c);
    }
}
return new Token(EOF_TYPE,"<EOF>");
}
```

To match an identifier, we need to buffer characters while the lookahead character is a letter:

parsing/lexer/ListLexer.java

```
/** NAME : ('a'..'z'|'A'..'Z')+; // NAME is sequence of >=1 letter */
Token NAME() {
    StringBuilder buf = new StringBuilder();
    do { buf.append(c); consume(); } while ( isLETTER() );
    return new Token(NAME, buf.toString());
}
```

If nextToken() finds a whitespace character, it calls WS() to consume all the whitespace without buffering it up or returning a token. Here is WS():

parsing/lexer/ListLexer.java

```
/** WS : (' '|'\t'|'\n'|'\r')* ; // ignore any whitespace */
void WS() {
    while ( c==' ' || c=='\t' || c=='\n' || c=='\r' ) consume();
}
```

On to the support code in our Lexer base class. Here are the necessary fields to maintain state:

parsing/lexer/Lexer.java

```
public abstract class Lexer {
    public static final char EOF = (char)-1; // represent end of file char
    public static final int EOF_TYPE = 1;    // represent EOF token type
    String input; // input string
    int p = 0;    // index into input of current character
    char c;       // current character
```

The constructor records the input string and primes the lookahead by loading the first character into lookahead character c.

parsing/lexer/Lexer.java

```
public Lexer(String input) {
    this.input = input;
    c = input.charAt(p); // prime lookahead
}
```

Method consume() advances the input pointer and sets lookahead character c to the next character in the string. This method also detects when the lexer has run out of input characters, setting the lookahead character to EOF (-1).

parsing/lexer/Lexer.java

```
/** Move one character; detect "end of file" */
public void consume() {
    p++;
    if ( p >= input.length() ) c = EOF;
    else c = input.charAt(p);
}

/** Ensure x is next character on the input stream */
public void match(char x) {
    if ( c == x) consume();
    else throw new Error("expecting "+x+"; found "+c);
}
```

Class Lexer is abstract because it has no code to match tokens. Any concrete subclasses, such as our ListLexer, need to implement the following methods:

parsing/lexer/Lexer.java

```
public abstract Token nextToken();
public abstract String getTokenName(int tokenType);
```

Related Patterns

There is a great similarity between the structure of this lexer and the structure of Pattern 3, *LL(1) Recursive-Descent Parser*. They're both instances of recursive-descent recognizers generated using Pattern 1, *Mapping Grammars to Recursive-Descent Recognizers*, on page 29.

3   *LL(1) Recursive-Descent Parser*

Purpose

This pattern analyzes the syntactic structure of the token sequence of a phrase using a single lookahead token.

This parser belongs to the *LL(1)* top-down parser class in particular because it uses a single token of lookahead (hence the "1" in the name). It's the core mechanism of all subsequent parsing patterns.

Discussion

This pattern shows how to implement parsing decisions that use a single token of lookahead. It's the weakest form of recursive-descent parser but the easiest to understand and implement. If you can conveniently implement your language with this *LL(1)* pattern, you should do so. Pattern 4, *LL(k) Recursive-Descent Parser*, on page 43 uses multisymbol lookahead, which is more powerful but has more complicated infrastructure.

To implement an *LL(1)* recursive-descent parser, we can start by filling in the lookahead expressions from the parsing decisions shown in Pattern 1, *Mapping Grammars to Recursive-Descent Recognizers*, on page 29. To make parsing decisions, the parser tests the current lookahead token against the alternatives' lookahead sets. A lookahead set is the set of tokens that can begin a particular alternative. The parser should attempt the alternative that can start with the current lookahead token. In the next two sections, we'll figure out how to compute lookahead sets and how to detect decisions with more than one viable path.

Computing Lookahead Sets

Formally, we compute lookahead sets using two computations: *FIRST* and *FOLLOW*. In practice, though, it's easier to simply ask ourselves, "What tokens can possibly start phrases beginning at this alternative?" The exact definition of FIRST is a bit much to chew on for our purposes here, but if you're interested, a web search reveals plenty of decent descriptions.[1]

Let's start with the easiest lookahead computation case: an alternative that begins with a token reference. Its lookahead set is just that token. For example, here is a programming language statement rule where each alternative begins with single token reference:

```
stat: 'if' ...    // lookahead set is {if}
    | 'while' ... // lookahead set is {while}
    | 'for' ...   // lookahead set is {for}
    ;
```

---

1. http://www.cs.virginia.edu/~cs415/reading/FirstFollowLL.pdf

If an alternative begins with a rule reference instead of a token reference, the lookahead set is whatever begins any alternative of that rule.

Here is a rule whose first alternative invokes **stat**:

```
body_element
    : stat      // lookahead is {if, while, for}
    | LABEL ':' // lookahead is {LABEL}
    ;
```

The lookahead set for the first alternative is the union of the lookahead sets from **stat**. Lookahead computations only get complicated when we consider empty alternatives. For example, it's not immediately obvious what tokens predict the empty alternative in the following rule:

```
optional_init
    : '=' expr
    | // empty alternative
    ;
```

The lookahead for the first alternative is =. For the empty alternative, the lookahead is the set of tokens following references to **optional_init**. So, let's add some other rules that invoke **optional_init**:

```
decl: 'int' ID optional_init ';' ;
arg : 'int' ID optional_init ;
func_call: ID '(' arg ')' ; // calls arg; ')' included in lookahead
```

In this case, ; follows **optional_init** in **decl** so we know that at least ; is in the set. Rule **arg** also references **optional_init**, but there is no token following it. This means that we have to include whatever follows **arg**. Token) can follow a reference to **arg**, so tokens ';' and ')' can follow a reference to **optional_init**.

Don't worry if you don't fully understand these lookahead computations in detail. Most likely you won't have to compute them yourself; ANTLR likes nothing better than to compute these for you. With this general understanding of lookahead computation in mind, let's consider what happens when the same token predicts more than one alternative.

Deterministic Parsing Decisions

LL parsing decisions work only when the lookahead sets predicting the alternatives are disjoint (the sets have no tokens in common).

For example, here is a rule whose parsing decision is deterministic because the single lookahead token uniquely predicts which alternative to choose:

```
/** Match -3, 4, -2.1 or x, salary, username, and so on */
expr: '-'? (INT|FLOAT) // '-', INT, or FLOAT predicts this alternative
    | ID               // ID predicts this alternative
    ;
```

Upon -, **INT**, or **FLOAT**, rule **expr** knows to predict the first alternative. Upon **ID**, it knows to predict the second.

If the lookahead sets overlap, though, the parser is *nondeterministic*—it cannot determine which alternative to choose. For example, here's a rule that's nondeterministic for an *LL(1)* parser:

```
expr: ID '++'    // match "x++"
    | ID '--'    // match "x--"
    ;
```

The two alternatives begin with the same token (**ID**). The token beyond dictates which alternative phrase is approaching. In other words, **expr** is LL(2). An *LL(1)* parser can't see past the left common prefix with only one symbol of lookahead. Without seeing the suffix operator after the **ID**, the parser cannot predict which alternative will succeed. To handle grammatical constructs like this, either tweak your grammar or use Pattern 4, *LL(k) Recursive-Descent Parser*, on page 43. By left-factoring out the common **ID** left-prefix, we get an *LL(1)* grammar that matches the same language:

```
expr: ID ('++'|'--') ;    // match "x++" or "x--"
```

If you plan on building lots of parsers by hand, it's worth spending time to get good at computing lookahead sets. Otherwise, you can just let a parser generator do it for you.

To see how the lookahead computations fit into the grammar to parser mapping, let's build a parser for the nested list-of-names language in Section 2.4, *Tokenizing Sentences*, on page 27.

Implementation

We're going to build a parser, ListParser, to go with the lexer from Pattern 2, *LL(1) Recursive-Descent Lexer*, on page 33. Here's the grammar again:

parsing/recursive-descent/NameList.g

```
list     : '[' elements ']' ;        // match bracketed list
elements : element (',' element)* ;  // match comma-separated list
element  : NAME | list ;             // element is name or nested list
```

Following the grammar-to-parser mapping we've established, we arrive at the following parser:

parsing/recursive-descent/ListParser.java

```java
public class ListParser extends Parser {
    public ListParser(Lexer input) { super(input); }

    /** list : '[' elements ']' ; // match bracketed list */
    public void list() {
        match(ListLexer.LBRACK); elements(); match(ListLexer.RBRACK);
    }
    /** elements : element (',' element)* ; */
    void elements() {
        element();
        while ( lookahead.type==ListLexer.COMMA ) {
            match(ListLexer.COMMA); element();
        }
    }
    /** element : name | list ; // element is name or nested list */
    void element() {
        if ( lookahead.type==ListLexer.NAME ) match(ListLexer.NAME);
        else if ( lookahead.type==ListLexer.LBRACK ) list();
        else throw new Error("expecting name or list; found "+lookahead);
    }
}
```

Rules **elements** and **element** use lookahead to make parsing decisions. In **elements**, **COMMA** predicts entering the (...)* subrule. In **element**, **NAME** predicts the first alternative, and **LBRACK** predicts the second alternative.

To support this concrete class, we need to build some support code in an abstract Parser class. First, we need two state variables: an input token stream and a lookahead buffer. In this case, we can use a single lookahead variable, token:

parsing/recursive-descent/Parser.java

```java
Lexer input;     // from where do we get tokens?
Token lookahead; // the current lookahead token
```

Alternatively, we could use a big token buffer that holds all tokens. In this way, we could track an index into the token buffer rather than a token field. For this particular implementation of this pattern, we'll assume that we cannot buffer all the input (we might be reading from a socket).

Next, we need methods to compare expected tokens against the lookahead symbol and to consume input.

`parsing/recursive-descent/Parser.java`

```java
/** If lookahead token type matches x, consume & return else error */
public void match(int x) {
    if ( lookahead.type == x ) consume();
    else throw new Error("expecting "+input.getTokenName(x)+
                         "; found "+ lookahead);
}
public void consume() { lookahead = input.nextToken(); }
```

To test our parser, we need a test rig like the following:

`parsing/recursive-descent/Test.java`

```java
ListLexer lexer = new ListLexer(args[0]); // parse command-line arg
ListParser parser = new ListParser(lexer);
parser.list(); // begin parsing at rule list
```

Upon valid input, the test rig emits nothing because we don't have any application-specific code in there. We could easily add actions to track a list of names, for example. Upon error, we want to throw an exception like the following:

```
$ java Test '[a, ]'
Exception in thread "main" java.lang.Error:
  expecting name or list; found <']',RBRACK>
        at ListParser.element(ListParser.java:24)
        at ListParser.elements(ListParser.java:16)
        at ListParser.list(ListParser.java:8)
        at Test.main(Test.java:6)
$
```

Building an *LL(1)* parser is the easiest way to learn about parsers. In practice, though, we really need more than a single token of lookahead. The next pattern describes how to build an *LL(k)* parser for *k>1*.

Related Patterns

See Pattern 2, *LL(1) Recursive-Descent Lexer*, on page 33, Pattern 4, *LL(k) Recursive-Descent Parser*, and Pattern 5, *Backtracking Parser*, on page 55.

---

4   LL(k) Recursive-Descent Parser

Purpose

This pattern analyzes the syntactic structure of the token sequence of a phrase using k>1 lookahead tokens.

An *LL(k)* parser augments the previous pattern with up to a fixed number of lookahead tokens, *k*.

Discussion

The strength of a recursive-descent parser depends entirely on the strength of its lookahead decisions. A single token of lookahead is pretty weak in that we usually have to contort grammars to make them *LL(1)*. By allowing a larger (but still fixed) lookahead buffer, we get a parser strong enough for most computer languages. This includes configuration files, data formats, network protocols, graphics languages, and many programming languages. Some programming languages present tougher challenges, though, for which we'll need a more powerful recognition pattern. Pattern 5, *Backtracking Parser*, on page 55 introduces an extension to this fixed-lookahead recursive-descent recognizer that, in effect, allows arbitrary lookahead.

Having more lookahead is like being able to see farther down multiple paths emanating from a fork in a maze. The farther we can see ahead, the easier it is to decide which path to take. More powerful parsing decisions make it easier to build parsers. We don't have to contort our parsers (or grammars) as much to suit a weak underlying parsing strategy.

In this Discussion section, we're going to figure out why we need more than a single token of lookahead and figure out how to build circular lookahead buffers. In the Implementation section, we'll use that lookahead buffer in an *LL(k)* parser.

Motivating the Need for More Lookahead

To see why we need *k>1* lookahead, let's augment the list-of-names grammar from Section 2.4, *Tokenizing Sentences*, on page 27 to allow assignments as list elements. For example, we want to recognize input such as [a, b=c, [d,e]]. To accommodate this change, we can add an alternative to **element** that matches assignments:

```
list     : '[' elements ']' ;        // match bracketed list
elements : element (',' element)* ;  // match comma-separated list
element  : NAME '=' NAME             // match assignment such as a=b
         | NAME
         | list
         ;
```

The new alternative renders **element** non-*LL(1)* since the first two alternatives start with the same **NAME** token. Now, we need two lookahead tokens to distinguish the alternatives. The grammar is *LL(2)*. Each time we look for an **element**, we need to decide whether it's an assignment or just a name. If the lookahead sequence is **NAME** followed by =, the parsing decision should predict the first alternative (an assignment). Otherwise, the parser should predict the second alternative. For example, the following diagram represents the lookahead available to the parsing decision in **element** for input [a,b=c]:

If we had only an *LL(1)* parser, we'd have to rewrite **element** to look like this:

```
element  : NAME ('=' NAME)?  // match assignment such as a=b or just a
         | list
         ;
```

This (..)? optional subrule version works but is less clear. There are lots of similar situations that occur in real grammars.

Building a Circular Lookahead Buffer

The simplest way to provide lots of parser lookahead is to buffer up all the input tokens. The input cursor can be an integer index, say, p into that buffer. We can execute p++ to consume tokens. The next *k* tokens of lookahead would be tokens[p]..tokens[p+k-1]. This approach works for finite and reasonably small input. This obviously doesn't work for infinite token streams like network sockets.

When we can't buffer up all of the input, we need to make a *k*-sized buffer of tokens. We'll have at most *k* tokens in memory at once. Our index, p, now moves only through the fixed lookahead buffer. To consume a token, we increment p and add a token to the end of the buffer.

The only complication is that the buffer size is fixed so we have to add tokens in a circular fashion: p ranges from =0..*k-1*. A circular buffer is one where indexes that fall off the end wrap to the beginning. In other words, in a circular buffer of, say, three tokens, index 2 is the last valid index. Index p=3 actually wraps to become index 0. Modulo expression p%3 wraps indexes nicely for a buffer of size 3.

Graphically, here is how p moves through the lookahead buffer as the parser consumes tokens from input sentence [a,b=c]:

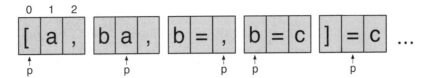

When we start parsing, the lookahead buffer looks like the leftmost diagram where p=0. The second diagram (where p=1) shows the buffer after we've consumed the first [token. We add tokens behind p as we advance. The rightmost diagram shows the state of the lookahead buffer after we've loaded the final] token. p points at =, and so the parser needs to consume three more times before running out of input (those p positions aren't shown).

Implementation

Let's implement the list-of-names language augmented with assignments from the previous section. First we'll build the lookahead infrastructure, and then we'll implement *LL(2)* rule **element**.

To support a fixed lookahead buffer, our Parser support class needs the following fields:

parsing/multi/Parser.java

```
Lexer input;        // from where do we get tokens?
Token[] lookahead;  // circular lookahead buffer
int k;              // how many lookahead symbols
int p = 0;          // circular index of next token position to fill
```

Because different parsers need different amounts of lookahead, the constructor takes a size argument and initializes the lookahead buffer:

parsing/multi/Parser.java

```
public Parser(Lexer input, int k) {
    this.input = input;
    this.k = k;
    lookahead = new Token[k];        // make lookahead buffer
    for (int i=1; i<=k; i++) consume(); // prime buffer with k lookahead
}
```

To consume a token, the parser advances the token index in a circular fashion and adds another token to the buffer.

`parsing/multi/Parser.java`

```
public void consume() {
    lookahead[p] = input.nextToken();   // fill next position with token
    p = (p+1) % k;                       // increment circular index
}
```

To isolate the lookahead mechanism from the parser, it's a good idea to create lookahead methods, LA() and LT(). Method LA() returns lookahead token types up to *k* symbols ahead starting at *k=1*. Recall that token types are integers representing input symbol categories. Method LT() returns the actual lookahead token at a particular lookahead depth.

`parsing/multi/Parser.java`

```
public Token LT(int i) {return lookahead[(p+i-1) % k];} // circular fetch
public int LA(int i) { return LT(i).type; }
public void match(int x) {
    if ( LA(1) == x ) consume();
    else throw new Error("expecting "+input.getTokenName(x)+
                         "; found "+LT(1));
}
```

Only rule **element** needs more than single token of lookahead in our case. Its implementation method tests the first two tokens of lookahead, LA(1) and LA(2), to predict the first alternative:

`parsing/multi/LookaheadParser.java`

```
/** element : NAME '=' NAME | NAME | list ; assignment, NAME or list */
void element() {
    if ( LA(1)==LookaheadLexer.NAME && LA(2)==LookaheadLexer.EQUALS ) {
        match(LookaheadLexer.NAME);
        match(LookaheadLexer.EQUALS);
        match(LookaheadLexer.NAME);
    }
    else if ( LA(1)==LookaheadLexer.NAME ) match(LookaheadLexer.NAME);
    else if ( LA(1)==LookaheadLexer.LBRACK ) list();
    else throw new Error("expecting name or list; found "+LT(1));
}
```

Because the method tests the alternatives in order, the second alternative prediction expression gets away with looking only a single symbol ahead. Also note that a single lookahead, [, uniquely predicts the third alternative. The lookahead depth *k* in *LL(k)* is really a maximum not the exact, fixed amount of lookahead each parsing decision uses.

Our test rig is the same as that in Pattern 3, *LL(1) Recursive-Descent Parser*, on page 38 except that we need to pass in the necessary lookahead depth to the parser constructor.

`parsing/multi/Test.java`

```
LookaheadLexer lexer = new LookaheadLexer(args[0]); // parse arg
LookaheadParser parser = new LookaheadParser(lexer, 2);
parser.list(); // begin parsing at rule list
```

If we pass in a valid list such as [a,b=c,[d,e]], the test rig quietly returns this:

```
$ java Test '[a,b=c,[d,e]]'
$
```

Upon error, however, the parser throws an exception:

```
$ java Test '[a,b=c,,[d,e]]'
Exception in thread "main" java.lang.Error:
 expecting name or list; found <',',,>
        at LookaheadParser.element(LookaheadParser.java:25)
        at LookaheadParser.elements(LookaheadParser.java:12)
        at LookaheadParser.list(LookaheadParser.java:7)
        at Test.main(Test.java:6)
$
```

Related Patterns

This pattern builds on Pattern 3, *LL(1) Recursive-Descent Parser*, on page 38 and uses Pattern 2, *LL(1) Recursive-Descent Lexer*, on page 33 to feed it tokens. Pattern 5, *Backtracking Parser*, on page 55 extends this pattern with arbitrary lookahead.

Up Next

At this point, we've got the most important parsing patterns down. To handle really tough language problems, we'll need to dress up the recursive-descent parser even further. The next chapter defines patterns for arbitrary lookahead and using semantic information to guide the parse.

## Chapter 3

Enhanced Parsing Patterns

In the previous chapter, we looked at the fundamental language recognition patterns. They're sufficient to handle most parsing tasks, but some languages defy even Pattern 4, *LL(k) Recursive-Descent Parser*, on page 43. In this chapter, we'll explore how to crank up the parsing power at the cost of some complexity and run-time efficiency. We'll look at three important specialized parsing patterns:

- Pattern 5, *Backtracking Parser*, on page 55. This pattern adds a speculative parsing facility to recursive-descent parsers. It's useful to have because sometimes it's hard to distinguish between alternatives without simply trying them. A *backtracking* parser attempts alternatives in order until one of them matches the current input. In effect, this supports arbitrarily deep lookahead as opposed to the fixed lookahead of Pattern 4, *LL(k) Recursive-Descent Parser*, on page 43. This pattern is extremely powerful but can be very expensive at run-time.

- Pattern 6, *Memoizing Parser*, on page 62. This pattern dramatically increases speculative parsing performance at the cost of a small amount of memory.

- Pattern 7, *Predicated Parser*, on page 68. Predicated parsers allow us to alter parser control-flow with arbitrary boolean expressions called *semantic predicates*. We can extend any of the parsing patterns in this book with predicates.

These patterns are tedious to implement by hand, but again, it's important to understand how they work. The code generated by parser generators like ANTLR make a lot more sense when you're familiar with the underlying pattern. When debugging parsers, for example, stepping through the code will make much more sense.

You might have seen backtracking and predicated parsers before if you have a computer science background. It's OK to skip this chapter in that case. Memoizing parsers are new enough, though, that you might want to take a look at them. They really make backtracking parsers practical.

Let's begin learning about advanced parsing by figuring out why we sometimes need arbitrary lookahead.

3.1 Parsing with Arbitrary Lookahead

Differentiating some language constructs is easy. For example, in the following **element** rule from the list-of-names language in Section 2.4, *Tokenizing Sentences*, on page 27, a single token of lookahead dictates which alternative to choose:

```
element  : NAME | list ;     // element is name or nested list
list      : '[' elements ']' ; // match bracketed list
...
```

Token **NAME** predicts the first alternative, and [predicts the second because **list** starts with [.

Sometimes, though, the most natural way to express a given language construct does not fit in Pattern 3, *LL(1) Recursive-Descent Parser*, on page 38 or Pattern 4, *LL(k) Recursive-Descent Parser*, on page 43. Such language constructs are typically very similar and only differ on the right side. For example, C++ function definitions and declarations are identical until the parser sees ; or {:

```
void bar() {...} // a function definition
void bar();      // a function declaration (forward declaration)
```

Because C++ function headers can be arbitrarily long, the distinguishing token does not appear at a fixed lookahead position from the left side of the statement. Consequently, Pattern 4, *LL(k) Recursive-Descent Parser*, on page 43 is too weak to distinguish function definitions from declarations using a natural grammar. The natural grammar rule defining C++ function definitions and declarations might look like this:

```
function : def | decl ;
def : functionHead '{' body '}' ; // E.g., "void bar() {}"
decl: functionHead ';'            // E.g., "void bar();"
functionHead : ... ; // E.g., "int (*foo)(int *f[], float)"
```

To distinguish these two constructs starting at the left edge in **function**, we need to scan past the entire function header to the token that follows. Such constructs have always been a drag to parse. In a parser with backtracking machinery, however, it's not too bad (see Pattern 5, *Backtracking Parser*, on page 55). We can make a parsing method for rule **function** that follows this pseudocode:

```
void function() {
    if ( «speculatively-match-def» ) def();
    else if ( «speculatively-match-decl» ) decl();
    else throw new RecognitionError("expecting function");
}
```

The parser can speculatively parse as far ahead as it needs. If the first parsing conditional in function() doesn't match, the parser simply rewinds the input and tries the next alternative.

There is a subtle but important point here. Speculatively matching the alternatives of a rule effectively orders them. The first alternative that matches wins. This is great because we can use ordering to specify precedence. For example, in some cases, two alternatives of a rule can match the same input. With ordered alternatives, there is no ambiguity because the parser consistently chooses the first of two ambiguous alternatives.

By having the parser pay attention to the order of alternatives, we can solve a nasty C++ ambiguity. C++ input T(a) can be both a declaration and an expression (see Chapter 12 in *The Definitive ANTLR Reference* [Par07] for more details). The C++ reference manual says that phrases that look like both should be treated as declarations. In a parser that can backtrack, all we have to do is attempt to match declarations before expressions. Using a syntactic predicate in an ANTLR grammar to invoke backtracking within a specific rule, we'd say this:

```
stat: (declaration)=> declaration // if it looks like declaration, it is
    | expression                   // else it's an expression
    ;
```

Though speculative parsing has a lot of advantages, there are two drawbacks. First, it can make debugging more difficult. When the parser speculatively parses ahead, it's easy to get lost with all of the scanning ahead and rewinding. Second, backtracking can be extremely slow. Fortunately, we can fix the efficiency issue. All we have to do is avoid redundant parsing.

3.2 Parsing like a Pack Rat

Until a backtracking parser finds a winning alternative, it might speculatively parse the same input with the same rule multiple times. Almost by definition, we use backtracking parsers only when we need to distinguish between similar language constructs. If the constructs are similar, the associated grammar likely contains repeated references to the same rule.

In the implementation section of Pattern 5, *Backtracking Parser*, on page 55, we'll augment the list-of-names language to allow parallel assignments like Python does: [a,b]=[c,d]. The **stat** rule needs to backtrack because it cannot distinguish the two alternatives with finite lookahead:

```
stat: list EOF        // try this alternative first
    | list '=' list   // if 1st alternative fails, try this one
    ;
```

Upon input [a,b]=[c,d], **stat** speculatively parses the first alternative, which immediately references **list**. The first alternative will fail, causing a backtracking parser to rewind the input and attempt the second alternative. The second alternative immediately calls **list** again, which is a waste since we already know it matches.

Memoizing allows us to skip the second parse of **list**. **list** can skip ahead to where it left off the last time and then return immediately to **stat**. To make this work, we have to *memoize* (squirrel away) the result of invoking the various parsing methods. Pattern 6, *Memoizing Parser*, on page 62 explains the exact mechanism.

A backtracking strategy allows us to squeeze the maximum power from a top-down parser, and memoization allows us to do this efficiently. In some cases, though, syntax alone won't let us distinguish between sentences. The next section explores how to handle cases where the same phrase means different things depending on its context.

3.3 Directing the Parse with Semantic Information

The parsers we're working with in this book recognize *context-free languages*. A context-free language is a language whose constructs don't depend on the presence of other constructs. Unfortunately, some programming languages have *context-sensitive* phrases. To handle context-sensitive phrases with a context-free parser, we have to predicate alternatives. In effect, a predicate is just a run-time boolean test that says when it's OK to match an alternative. The predicates gate the associated alternatives in and out.

To see why we need predicates, let's look at a context-sensitive phrase within a programming language. C++ is the traditional parsing punching bag, so let's get our gloves on and limber up a bit.

In C++, the expression T(6) is either a function call or a constructor-style typecast depending on whether T is a function or type name. A C++ parser literally does not know how to interpret T(6) without seeing the definition of T. Such a construct is context sensitive and, in this case, ambiguous from a purely syntactic point of view. This ambiguity becomes painfully obvious when you look at the grammar. The following rule is an idealized representation of a C++ expression rule:

```
expr: INTEGER           // integer literal
    | ID '(' expr ')' // function call; AMBIGUOUS WITH NEXT ALT
    | ID '(' expr ')' // constructor-style typecast
    ;
```

Ambiguous grammars lead to *nondeterministic parsers*, parsers that cannot determine which path to take. In this case, the second and third alternatives are identical—the parser could use either. Using Pattern 3, *LL(1) Recursive-Descent Parser*, on page 38, we'd end up with the following method:

```
void expr() {
    // if lookahead is an integer, match an integer
    if (LA(1)==INTEGER) match(INTEGER);
    else if (LA(1)==ID) «match-function-call»
    else if (LA(1)==ID) «match-typecast»      // DEAD CODE!
    else «error»
}
```

The last if statement is dead, unreachable code. Worse, the compiler doesn't warn us about it. This error would only show up during testing.

To solve the problem, we need to augment the final two if-conditions to test what kind of thing T is. By introducing two method calls within the parsing decision itself, we can disambiguate the alternatives:

```
void expr() {
    if ( LA(1)==INTEGER) match(INTEGER);
    else if ( LA(1)==ID && isFunction(LT(1).text) ) «match-function-call»
    else if ( LA(1)==ID && isType(LT(1).text) )     «match-typecast»
    else «error»
}
```

This code follows Pattern 7, *Predicated Parser*, on page 68. Functions isFunction() and isType() answer whether an identifier is a function or type. Their implementation details aren't important for this discussion (we'll learn how to implement them in Chapter 6, *Tracking and Identifying Program Symbols*, on page 131).

At this point, we've covered the four key parsing strategies, so let's summarize what we've learned:

Pattern	When to Apply
Pattern 3, *LL(1) Recursive-Descent Parser*, on page 38	This is the most basic parsing strategy that undergraduate computer science students learn. Start out with this pattern since it'll work for most DSLs.
Pattern 4, *LL(k) Recursive-Descent Parser*, on page 43	If a single token of lookahead can't distinguish between rule alternatives, you need to use this pattern. A more powerful parsing strategy means it's easier to build the parser. You don't need to factor the parser as much to suit weaker parsing decisions.
Pattern 5, *Backtracking Parser*, on the facing page	Some languages are pretty complex with equally complicated grammars. At least a few parsing decisions will be difficult to make with a fixed amount lookahead. When rule alternatives look almost the same, we often have to speculatively parse entire phrases to distinguish them. This is precisely what a backtracking parser does. Use Pattern 6, *Memoizing Parser*, on page 62 to make backtracking efficient.
Pattern 7, *Predicated Parser*, on page 68	Use this pattern when syntax alone is insufficient to make parsing decisions. For example, C++ expression T(6) has multiple interpretations for the same syntax depending on how we defined T. Semantic predicates let us alter the parse based upon run-time information (we can direct by looking up T in a dictionary).

Now, let's learn more about the advanced parsing strategies by diving into their pattern definitions.

> ### ANTLR Warns About Dead Code
>
> One of the problems with writing parsers by hand is that we don't get warnings about unreachable parser regions. Using a parser generator, on the other hand, would provide us with a warning. Here is the ambiguity warning we'd get out of ANTLR for the idealized C++ **expr** rule:
>
> ```
> Decision can match input such as "ID '(' INTEGER ')'"
>     using multiple alternatives: 2, 3
> As a result, alternative(s) 3 were disabled for that input
> ```

5   Backtracking Parser

Purpose

This pattern adds speculative parsing support (arbitrary lookahead) to any recursive-descent recognizer.

Discussion

As we saw in Pattern 1, *Mapping Grammars to Recursive-Descent Recognizers*, on page 29, we can't map all grammars to recursive-descent parsers. Only non-left-recursive grammars work (no rule can directly or indirectly invoke itself without consuming a token). Then Section 3, *Deterministic Parsing Decisions*, on page 40 showed that we can't always get properly functioning (deterministic) parsers even from non-left-recursive grammars. The problem is that fixed lookahead *LL* parsers need the lookahead sets predicting alternatives to be disjoint.

This pattern overcomes this lookahead issue by allowing arbitrary lookahead, which lets us parse much more complicated languages. To look arbitrarily ahead, we need infrastructure to support backtracking. Backtracking also gives us a way to specify the precedence of ambiguous rule alternatives (alternatives that can match the same input). Backtracking parsers, by definition, try the alternatives in order.

The backtracking strategy we'll explore in this pattern supports any parsing mechanism or technique that needs to speculatively match alternatives. For example, ANTLR supports *syntactic predicates* that let you control speculative parsing. Syntactic predicates are grammar fragments that specify the lookahead language predicting an alternative.

Bryan Ford formalized and extended ANTLR's notion of grammars plus syntactic predicates, calling them *Parsing Expression Grammars* (PEGs) *Parsing Expression Grammars: A Recognition-Based Syntactic Foundation* [For04]. In the functional language world, syntactic predicates are called *parser combinators*; see Parsec.[1]

Syntactic predicates and speculative parsing are extremely useful when parsing phrases that look the same from the left edge. Distinguishing between C++ function definitions and declarations is a prime example, as we saw in Section 3.1, *Parsing with Arbitrary Lookahead*, on page 50. Before diving into the guts of a sample implementation, let's look at the basic code templates we need, how to manage the input stream, and then how to handle application-specific actions.

Backtracking Code Templates

The easiest way to implement a backtracking strategy for a parsing decision is to speculatively attempt the alternatives in order until we find one that matches. Upon success, the parser rewinds the input and parses the alternative normally (we'll see why we parse it twice when we discuss actions). Upon failing to match an alternative, the parser rewinds the input and tries the next one. If the parser can't find any matching alternative, it throws a "no viable alternative" exception. Here is a template in pseudocode that implements that strategy:

```
public void «rule»() throws RecognitionException {
    if ( speculate_«alt1»() ) {        // attempt alt 1
        «match-alt1»
    }
    else if ( speculate_«alt2»() ) { // attempt alt 2
        «match-alt2»
    }
    ...
    else if ( speculate_«altN»() ) { // attempt alt N
        «match-altN»
    }
    // must be an error; no alternatives matched
    else throw new NoViableException("expecting «rule»")
}
```

---

1. Daan Leijen. Parsec, A Fast Combinator Parser. http://research.microsoft.com/en-us/um/people/daan/download/parsec/parsec.pdf.

> ### Why Using Exceptions for Parser Control Flow Is OK
>
> There are two common objections to using exceptions to implement backtracking. First, using exceptions for control flow is usually a very bad idea because they act like **goto**s. In the case of the backtracking parser, however, the parser really is detecting syntax errors. We want it to roll back to where it started speculating no matter how deeply nested the method calls are. Exceptions work perfectly for this. Besides, we're throwing exceptions for errors anyway and might as well keep the same mechanism for both. The second issue is that exceptions can be very slow. Fortunately, only the creation of Exception objects is expensive. Throwing and catching them is approximately the same cost as unrolling the stack with a sequence of return instructions. All we need to do is create a single shared exception for use for backtracking.

The speculation methods amount to syntactic predicates and look like this:

```
public boolean speculate_«alt»() {
    boolean success = true;
    mark(); // mark this spot in input so we can rewind
    try { «match-alt» } // attempt to match the alternative
    catch (RecognitionException e) { success = false; }
    release(); // either way, rewind to where we were before attempt
    return success;
}
```

By using these pseudocode templates, we can reuse code templates from Pattern 3, *LL(1) Recursive-Descent Parser*, on page 38. All we need is some machinery to mark and rewind the input stream. The most important change to the usual recursive-descent parsing strategy is that we use syntax errors (thrown exceptions) to guide the parse. In other words, when speculating, a parser does not report syntax errors. Instead, it forces the parser to roll back to where it started speculating. That's what the **try-catch** is for in the speculate_«alt»() code template.

Rewinding the Token Stream

The heart of a backtracking parser lies in its token buffer management. The buffer must handle an arbitrary amount of lookahead and support nested mark and release operations. The easiest way to deal with arbitrary lookahead is simply to buffer up the entire token stream.

That way, the parser's current token index would simply step through the buffer as the parser consumes tokens. This approach works great unless we need to parse an "infinite" token stream. To support infinite token streams or simply to reduce the memory footprint of our parser, we need a lookahead buffer that caches as few tokens as possible.

Our parser can start out with a small fixed buffer size, n. Like Pattern 4, *LL(k) Recursive-Descent Parser*, on page 43, we'll use p as the index of the current token in the lookahead buffer. The difference is that we need to hold more than (fixed) *k* tokens in a backtracking parser. Our goal is to keep n from growing while still holding critical tokens. To do this, we need to reset p to 0 when it falls off the end of the buffer rather than stretching the buffer. We also want lookahead operations (via LT()) to stay within the confines of the lookahead buffer. Visually these two situations look like this:

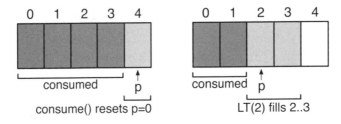

If we request a lookahead token beyond the end of the buffer with LT(), though, we need to stretch the buffer to make room:

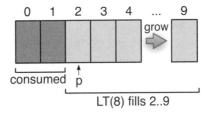

We also need to stretch the buffer while speculating. The parser can never throw out tokens that it speculatively matches. We'll need to reparse those tokens.

The speculate_«*alt*»() code template manages the lookahead buffer with mark() and release() methods. mark() pushes the current token index onto a stack. release() pops the index back off the stack and rewinds p to that position. We need a stack of markers to handle nested backtracking.

By rewinding the input, we are sort of undoing the consume() operations that the parser executes. But, things get a lot trickier when programmers stick application-specific code into the parser.

Dealing with Actions While Backtracking

Application-specific parser actions can have side effects we can't undo such as "launch missiles." There are three choices. Either we disallow actions or disallow actions with side effects, or we parse winning alternatives twice. We'll choose the third alternative. It's the least efficient but the most flexible since we need those programmer-defined actions. They are often the easiest way to implement a language application.

A backtracking parser parses the winning alternative once during speculation and then again during normal alternative matching. To allow actions with side effects in a backtracking parser, all we have to do is gate actions with a test to see whether the parser is speculating:

if (*«not-speculating»*) { *«arbitrary-action»* }

During speculation, all actions are off. Once the parser knows an alternative will match, however, it can match the alternative again "with feeling" to do the actions.

The one caveat to action gating is that there are some actions we must execute during speculation. Tracking variable and method names is critical if we need to guide the parse with such information (see Pattern 7, *Predicated Parser*, on page 68). Actions that must always execute shouldn't have the action gate.

Enough generalities. Let's build a backtracking parser!

Implementation

For this pattern's example, let's augment our list-of-names language to allow parallel assignments like Python does: [a,b]=[c,d]. Here is our usual grammar with a new start rule, **stat**, that adds parallel list assignment:

parsing/backtrack/NameListWithParallelAssign.g

```
stat     : list EOF | assign EOF ;
assign   : list '=' list ;
list     : '[' elements ']' ;          // match bracketed list
elements : element (',' element)* ;   // match comma-separated list
element  : NAME '=' NAME | NAME | list ; //element is name, nested list
```

The parallel assignment construct in **stat** would cause trouble for Pattern 4, *LL(k) Recursive-Descent Parser*, on page 43. Both alternatives begin with a call to **list**. Because **list** can be arbitrarily long, no fixed-lookahead recursive-descent parser can distinguish between **stat**'s alternatives. We need to parse at least an entire **list** plus one token before deciding which alternative will succeed. Following the code templates from the previous section, **stat** looks like this:

parsing/backtrack/BacktrackParser.java

```
/** stat : list EOF | assign EOF ; */
public void stat() throws RecognitionException {
    // attempt alternative 1: list EOF
    if ( speculate_stat_alt1() ) {
        list(); match(Lexer.EOF_TYPE);
    }
    // attempt alternative 2: assign EOF
    else if ( speculate_stat_alt2() ) {
        assign(); match(Lexer.EOF_TYPE);
    }
    // must be an error; neither matched; LT(1) is lookahead token 1
    else throw new NoViableAltException("expecting stat found "+LT(1));
}
```

The speculative parsing support methods look like this:

parsing/backtrack/BacktrackParser.java

```
public boolean speculate_stat_alt1() {
    boolean success = true;
    mark(); // mark this spot in input so we can rewind
    try { list(); match(Lexer.EOF_TYPE); }
    catch (RecognitionException e) { success = false; }
    release(); // either way, rewind to where we were
    return success;
}

public boolean speculate_stat_alt2() {
    boolean success = true;
    mark(); // mark this spot in input so we can rewind
    try { assign(); match(Lexer.EOF_TYPE); }
    catch (RecognitionException e) { success = false; }
    release(); // either way, rewind to where we were
    return success;
}
```

All the other rules follow Pattern 4, *LL(k) Recursive-Descent Parser*, on page 43, so we don't need to look at those here (there's no point in speculating in the other rules if *LL(k)* is sufficient). The only thing left to do is build the support machinery for managing the lookahead buffer.

Our Parser base class tracks the input stream, a stack of markers for mark() and release(), the lookahead buffer itself, and an index for the current token:

parsing/backtrack/Parser.java

```
Lexer input;            // from where do we get tokens?
List<Integer> markers;  // stack of index markers into lookahead buffer
List<Token> lookahead;  // dynamically-sized lookahead buffer
int p = 0;              // index of current lookahead token;
                        // LT(1) returns lookahead[p]
```

The token access and testing methods are very similar to the fixed-lookahead parser versions:

parsing/backtrack/Parser.java

```
public Token LT(int i) { sync(i); return lookahead.get(p+i-1); }
public int LA(int i) { return LT(i).type; }
public void match(int x) throws MismatchedTokenException {
    if ( LA(1) == x ) consume();
    else throw new MismatchedTokenException("expecting "+
                 input.getTokenName(x)+" found "+LT(1));
}
```

The only difference is that LT() treats lookahead as a simple list, not a circular list (there is no modulo operator in the index computation). That implies that there must always be a valid token at index p+i-1 (i tokens ahead). This is where the call to sync() comes in. The sync() method makes sure that the lookahead buffer always has valid tokens from index p to p+i-1:

parsing/backtrack/Parser.java

```
/** Make sure we have i tokens from current position p */
public void sync(int i) {
    if ( p+i-1 > (lookahead.size()-1) ) {        // out of tokens?
        int n = (p+i-1) - (lookahead.size()-1); // get n tokens
        fill(n);
    }
}
public void fill(int n) { // add n tokens
    for (int i=1; i<=n; i++) { lookahead.add(input.nextToken()); }
}
```

To advance through the input stream, the parser calls consume(). The consume() method is the same as in the fixed-lookahead parser except that we clear the lookahead buffer when we hit the end.

parsing/backtrack/Parser.java

```
public void consume() {
    p++;
    // have we hit end of buffer when not backtracking?
    if ( p==lookahead.size() && !isSpeculating() ) {
        // if so, it's an opportunity to start filling at index 0 again
        p = 0;
        lookahead.clear(); // size goes to 0, but retains memory
    }
    sync(1); // get another to replace consumed token
}
```

The marker management methods are simple because all they do is manage the markers stack:

parsing/backtrack/Parser.java

```
public int mark() { markers.add(p); return p; }
public void release() {
    int marker = markers.get(markers.size()-1);
    markers.remove(markers.size()-1);
    seek(marker);
}
public void seek(int index) { p = index; }
public boolean isSpeculating() { return markers.size() > 0; }
```

To learn more about backtracking parsers, take a look at Chapter 14 in *The Definitive ANTLR Reference* [Par07], which explains how ANTLR implements backtracking. Chapters 11 and 12 in that book provide examples and discuss how ANTLR optimizes away a lot of backtracking.

Related Patterns

The pattern described here extends Pattern 3, *LL(1) Recursive-Descent Parser*, on page 38, with arbitrary lookahead and backtracking support. Pattern 6, *Memoizing Parser* shows how to avoid unnecessary reparsing by recording partial parsing results.

6   Memoizing Parser

Purpose

This pattern records partial parsing results during backtracking to guarantee linear parsing performance, at the cost of a small amount of memory.

Memoizing is a form of dynamic programming and lets us avoid reparsing the same input with the same rule. Another name for *memoizing recursive-descent parser* is *packrat parser*, a fabulous term coined by Bryan Ford in *Packrat parsing:: simple, powerful, lazy, linear time, functional pearl* [For02].

Discussion

Without memoization to avoid redundant parsing, backtracking can lead to impractically slow (exponentially complex) parse times. This pattern guarantees linear parse time at the cost of a bit of memory. The extra memory is well worth the gain in parsing speed. I've seen backtracking parse times go from hours to seconds with the introduction of memoization.

Memoization only helps us, though, if we invoke the same rule at the same input position more than once. For example, upon input (3+4);, a backtracking parser derived from the following rule invokes **expr** twice:

```
s    : expr '!' // assume backtracking parser tries this alternative
     | expr ';' // and then this one
     ;
expr : ... ; // match input such as "(3+4)"
```

Rule **s** invokes **expr** to speculatively match the first alternative. **expr** succeeds, but **s** finds that the next input symbol is ; and not !. Rule **s** rewinds the input and tries the second alternative. The parser immediately calls **expr** again and at the same input position. That's a waste of CPU time. To avoid reparsing, all we have to do is remember that **expr** succeeded the last time we tried it at this position.

Rule **expr** can avoid parsing if it succeeded the last time by just pretending to parse. To simulate a successful speculative parse, we skip ahead to where **expr** left off the last time and return immediately.

Oddly enough, we can also avoid parsing with **expr** if it failed the last time. We know it won't match, so we can return immediately. The invoking parser rule will rewind the input to try the next alternative, so we don't have to adjust the input position.

To record partial results, we need a memoizing dictionary for each rule that maps an integer token buffer index to a condition value. There are three possible conditions: *unknown, failed*, or *succeeded*. An *unknown* dictionary result indicates that the associated rule method hasn't parsed at that position before. *Failed* indicates that the parser

> ## Why Packrat Parsing Is Fast
>
> Memoization of parsing results guarantees there is no way to parse the same rule at the same input position more than once. Therefore, parsing speed is bounded by how many rules and how many input tokens there are. Because the number of rules in a grammar is fixed, the dominant component of the speed function is the number of input tokens. Consequently, packrat parsers are guaranteed to have linear performance, albeit with some heavy overhead sometimes. As for memory requirements, the most we can record is a single integer per rule per input position leading also to a linear space complexity. In the worst case, we have to call every rule once for each input position (saving an integer for each invocation). In practice, packrat parser generators must do a great deal of optimization to approach the performance of fixed-lookahead parsers.

failed the last time it tried to parse starting at that input position. Any other result indicates a previously successful parse.

We can represent the *failed* condition with a negative number in the dictionary. The *unknown* condition happens by default when the dictionary has no entry for that input position. The integers zero and greater indicate a previously successful parse. The integer also records the token index one past where the parsing method finished previously. (The position is an index into the lookahead token buffer, not an absolute token position within the input stream.)

To turn Pattern 5, *Backtracking Parser*, on page 55 into a packrat parser, we also need a memoizing method for each rule method. The memoizing method either avoids reparsing or records the success or failure of the normal parsing method. The code template looks like this:

```
/** Map input position to FAILED or previous stop token index.
 *  Missing value implies we've not parsed this rule at that index.
 */
Map<Integer, Integer> «rule»_memo = new HashMap<Integer, Integer>();

public void «rule»() throws RecognitionException {
    boolean failed = false;
    int startTokenIndex = index();
    if ( isSpeculating() && alreadyParsedRule(«rule»_memo) ) return;
    // must not have previously parsed rule at token index; parse it
    try { _«rule»(); }
```

```
        catch (RecognitionException re) { failed = true; throw re; }
        finally {
            // succeed or fail, we must record result if backtracking
            if (isSpeculating())
                memoize(«rule»_memo, startTokenIndex, failed);
        }
    }
}
```

This memoizing method assumes the role of the original rule method.
Other rules that refer to it don't need to change. We can rename the
original parsing rule method to be _«rule».

Implementation

To demonstrate packrat parsing, let's memoize the **list** method from Pattern 5, *Backtracking Parser*, on page 55. Rule **stat** invokes rule **list** multiple times from its left edge during backtracking:

```
stat        : list EOF         // try this alternative first
            | list '=' list    // if 1st alternative fails, try this one
            ;
```

The parser method, _list(), is the same except for the _ prefix:

parsing/memoize/BacktrackParser.java

```java
// match '[' elements ']'
public void _list() throws RecognitionException {
    System.out.println("parse list rule at token index: "+index());
    match(BacktrackLexer.LBRACK);
    elements();
    match(BacktrackLexer.RBRACK);
}
```

To memoize it, we create the following method using the code template
from the previous section:

parsing/memoize/BacktrackParser.java

```java
/** list : '[' elements ']' ; // match bracketed list */
public void list() throws RecognitionException {
    boolean failed = false;
    int startTokenIndex = index(); // get current token position
    if ( isSpeculating() && alreadyParsedRule(list_memo) ) return;
    // must not have previously parsed list at tokenIndex; parse it
    try { _list(); }
    catch (RecognitionException re) { failed = true; throw re; }
    finally {
        //  succeed or fail, must record result if backtracking
        if (isSpeculating()) memoize(list_memo, startTokenIndex, failed);
    }
}
```

We also need to augment the support code in Parser. First, we need a constant to represent failed parsing results:

```
public static final int FAILED = -1;  // parsing failed on last attempt
```

Then, we need to implement alreadyParsedRule() and memoize():

`parsing/memoize/Parser.java`

```
/** Have we parsed a particular rule before at this input position?
 *  If no memoization value, we've never parsed here before.
 *  If memoization value is FAILED, we parsed and failed before.
 *  If value >= 0, it is an index into the token buffer.  It indicates
 *  a previous successful parse.  This method has a side effect:
 *  it seeks ahead in the token buffer to avoid reparsing.
 */
public boolean alreadyParsedRule(Map<Integer, Integer> memoization)
    throws PreviousParseFailedException
{
    Integer memoI = memoization.get(index());
    if ( memoI==null ) return false;
    int memo = memoI.intValue();
    System.out.println("parsed list before at index "+index()+
                       "; skip ahead to token index "+memo+": "+
                       lookahead.get(memo).text);
    if ( memo==FAILED ) throw new PreviousParseFailedException();
    // else skip ahead, pretending we parsed this rule ok
    seek(memo);
    return true;
}


/** While backtracking, record partial parsing results.
 *  If invoking rule method failed, record that fact.
 *  If it succeeded, record the token position we should skip to
 *  next time we attempt this rule for this input position.
 */
public void memoize(Map<Integer, Integer> memoization,
                    int startTokenIndex, boolean failed)
{
    // record token just after last in rule if success
    int stopTokenIndex = failed ? FAILED : index();
    memoization.put(startTokenIndex, stopTokenIndex);
}

public int index() { return p; } // return current input position
```

One final detail: recall that consume() resets lookahead buffer index p to 0 and clears the lookahead buffer when no longer speculating. That means that all the indexes in the memoization dictionaries are no longer valid. We don't need that data anymore anyway. If the parser isn't speculating, then it's committed to a particular alternative.

Memoization data for positions earlier in the input are no longer useful. Here's the critical part of that method:

parsing/memoize/Parser.java

```
// if so, it's an opportunity to start filling at index 0 again
p = 0;
lookahead.clear(); // size goes to 0, but retains memory
clearMemo();        // clear any rule_memo dictionaries
```

To convince ourselves that we're actually avoiding some reparsing, let's make a test rig:

parsing/memoize/Test.java

```
BacktrackLexer lexer = new BacktrackLexer(args[0]); // parse arg
BacktrackParser parser = new BacktrackParser(lexer);
parser.stat(); // begin parsing at rule stat
```

Here is a sample run with input [a,b]=[c,d]:

```
$ java Test '[a,b]=[c,d]'
attempt alternative 1
parse list rule at token index: 0
attempt alternative 2
parsed list before at index 0; skip ahead to token index 5: =
parse list rule at token index: 6
predict alternative 2
parse list rule at token index: 0
parse list rule at token index: 6
$
```

Let's interpret the output. Rule **stat** attempts its first alternative (a simple list followed by **EOF**). It enters memoized list(), which calls _list() and then records a successful parse at token index 0. The first alternative ultimately fails, though, because = follows the list, not **EOF**.

Rule **stat** therefore attempts the second alternative. It calls memoized list() (via **assign**) and finds that the dictionary contains token index 5 for key 0. That means the parser remembers parsing **list** at index 0. More important, the dictionary tells us that the parser left off at index 5 the last time. Instead of parsing, list() can just skip ahead. To finish speculative parsing of the second alternative, the parser matches = (index 5) and then another **list** (index 6). At this point, the parser has convinced itself that the second alternative of **stat** will succeed.

After the speculative parse, the parser knows to match the second alternative. It rewinds and matches the second alternative of **stat** normally (recall that a backtracking parser rematches the alternative to execute any application-specific actions). The last two parse list rule... lines in the output show the parser matching lists on the left and right of the assignment operator.

So, the output shows that adding memoization prevents the parser from performing a redundant computation.

Related Patterns

This pattern extends Pattern 5, *Backtracking Parser*, on page 55 to make it more efficient.

□   ### 7   Predicated Parser

Purpose

This pattern augments any top-down parser with arbitrary boolean expressions that help make parsing decisions.

These boolean expressions are called *semantic predicates* and specify the semantic applicability of an alternative. Predicates that evaluate to false effectively "turn off" a parser decision path. From a grammar point of view, false predicates make alternatives invisible.

Discussion

We need semantic predicates when the parser cannot use syntax alone to make parsing decisions, that is, when the parser cannot distinguish between alternatives without using run-time information. The most common case is when we need to use symbol table information to guide the parse. (See Chapter 6, *Tracking and Identifying Program Symbols*, on page 131.) As we saw in Section 3.3, *Directing the Parse with Semantic Information*, on page 52, C++ expression T(6) can be a function call or typecast depending on whether T is a function or a class.

Predicates are also useful when a parser must recognize multiple versions of an input language. For example, the GCC C compiler adds a number of extensions beyond C. Java 5.0 introduced the **enum** keyword to support enumerated types. To handle multiple language versions with the same parser, we can make a core version that matches the most complete language version. Then, we can predicate parsing decisions to "turn off" various version-dependent language constructs.

Predicated parsing decisions look exactly like those in Section 1, *Converting Subrules*, on page 31. The only difference is the introduction of arbitrary boolean tests after the lookahead tests. Here is the basic decision code template:

```
public void «rule»() throws RecognitionException {
    if ( «lookahead-test-alt1» && «pred1» ) {        // attempt alt 1
        «match-alt1»
    }
    else if ( «lookahead-test-alt2» && «pred2» ) { // attempt alt 2
        «match-alt2»
    }
    ...
    else if ( «lookahead-test-altN» && «predN» ) { // attempt alt N
        «match-altN»
    }
    // must be an error; no alternatives matched
    else throw new NoViableException("expecting «rule»")
}
```

Predicated loop decisions for grammar (...)* and (...)+ subrules look like this:

```
while ( «lookahead-test-for-loop-alts» && «pred» ) {
    «subrule-code-to-match-alts»
}
```

To see how semantic predicates solve a surprisingly nasty parsing problem, let's do battle with C++ again in the Implementation section.

Implementation

C++ allows multiple type specifiers before the variable name, as follows:

```
volatile unsigned long int x; // lots of type specifiers before x
```

But an identifier can also be a type name as in const T y;. To see why that's a problem, let's build a simplified C++ grammar to deal with variable declarations. To match the type specifiers before the **ID** variable name, let's loop around rules **qualifier** and **types**:

```
declaration : (qualifier|type)+ ID ';' ; // E.g., "const int x;"
qualifier   : 'const' | 'volatile' ;
type        : 'int' | 'unsigned' | 'long'| ID ;
```

Unfortunately, the loop in **declaration** can't decide what to do upon seeing **ID**. The loop doesn't know whether to match **ID** now or to leave it to the following **ID** reference. If the loop matches it, the parser interprets **ID** as a type name. By letting the loop exit, the parser interprets **ID** as the variable name. For example, upon T in const T y;, the loop doesn't

know whether T is a type name or a variable name. The loop decision
will match T no matter what:

```
while ( LA(1)==CONST || LA(1)==VOLATILE || LA(1)==INT ||
        LA(1)==UNSIGNED || LA(1)==LONG || LA(1)==ID ) {
    // match qualifier or type;
}
```

The correct solution is to match **ID** inside **type** only if it's a type name.
In an ANTLR grammar, we can prefix the **ID** alternative with a semantic
predicate that checks the lookahead token's status as a type name:

```
type:   'int' | 'unsigned' | 'long'
    |   {isTypeName(LT(1).getText())}? ID // type name
    ;
```

Assume method isTypeName() looks up the lookahead token's text in a
type table. (LT(1) is the current lookahead token.) To do the same thing
manually, we just add a new clause to the (...)+ loop condition from
declaration:

```
while ( LA(1)==CONST || LA(1)==VOLATILE || LA(1)==INT ||
        LA(1)==UNSIGNED || LA(1)==LONG ||
        (LA(1)==ID&&isTypeName(LT(1).getText())) ) {
    // match qualifier or type;
}
```

Now, the parser will only match **ID**s as part of the type qualifiers if they
are type names. The key lesson here is that we need to predicate the
parsing decision with information that is only available at run-time. In
this case, we need context information (is T a type name?) to figure out
how to parse declarations.

Up Next

We've just spent two chapters learning how to build recognizers. We're
ready to move on to the second part of the book. We're going to learn
how to build internal data structures from the input, how to walk those
structures, and how to analyze sentences to check for correctness.

Part II

Analyzing Languages

## Chapter 4

Building Intermediate Form Trees

Before interpreting or translating an input phrase, we have to fully understand that phrase. That means we have to verify its syntax and verify that it makes sense. In the previous part of this book, we learned how to check phrase syntax. In this part of the book, we're going to explore the patterns that help us analyze input phrases.

Only the simplest language applications get away with reading input and directly generating output. Such applications are called *syntax-directed* applications because they can generate output as soon as they recognize a construct. For example, if we wanted to convert a wiki markup format to HTML, we could translate it almost character by character. The key characteristic of syntax-directed applications is that they translate input phrase by phrase using a *single* pass over the input.

Most language applications, however, need to build an *intermediate representation* (IR) or *intermediate form*. The goal of an application's reader component is to fill an IR data structure with elements of interest from the input stream. Some language applications, such as configuration file readers, stop after building an IR. Usually, though, readers are just the first stage in a pipeline of components. That's why the *I* in IR stands for intermediate, not internal.

The needs of the intended application dictate the nature of the IR. For example, if we need to track word occurrences in a document, an unordered set of words works fine. If the order of word occurrence is important, we need to construct a list rather than a set. Generally speaking, though, to get a computer to understand a nontrivial sentence, we have to break it down into a series of operations and operands. That's just the way computers like to do things.

Once we identify the operators and operands among the input tokens, we need to build an IR data structure. For most language applications, that means building a tree data structure. In particular, we'll build an *abstract syntax tree* (AST). ASTs hold the key tokens from the input stream and record grammatical relationships discovered during the parse. ASTs are so central to translator and interpreter design that it's worth spending an entire chapter on them.

ASTs are the *lingua franca* spoken by the various stages in a language application. Each stage performs a computation, rewrites the tree, or creates another data structure before passing the tree along to the next stage. To do their work, the stages need to walk the trees and trigger actions when they encounter specific subtree patterns. As we'll see in the next chapter, tree pattern matching is a pain to do by hand. Fortunately, we can automate tree matching just like we do with flat sentence parsing.

Before we get into tree walking and matching, though, we need to learn everything we can about ASTs. In this chapter, we'll discuss:

- Why we build trees in the first place

- How we should structure ASTs and why

- How to implement ASTs in an object-oriented language

- How to enforce tree structure with an implementation language's static type system

- How to construct ASTs with ANTLR's AST operators and rewrite rules

During our introductory discussion, we'll explore the four most common IR tree patterns and then formally define them:

- Pattern 8, *Parse Tree*, on page 90. Parse trees record how a parser recognizes an input sentence. The interior nodes are rule names, and the leaves are tokens. Although parse trees are less suitable than ASTs for most language applications, parsers can create them automatically.

- Pattern 9, *Homogeneous AST*, on page 94. The most important thing about a tree is its shape, not its node data type. Unless we're writing a lot of code by hand, we can get away with a few or

---

Representing Nested Structures with Trees

A *tree* is a data structure composed of a set of nodes organized into a hierarchy. Each node has a parent and an ordered list of zero, one, or multiple children. The children can be simple nodes or complete subtrees. In computer science, we draw trees with the root node at the top and the branches descending below. Root nodes are analogous to the root directory on a disk. Children are analogous to files and subdirectories.

---

even just one node data type. If all the nodes have the same type, we say that they are homogeneous. With a single node type, there can be no specialty fields to reference child subtrees. Nodes track children with lists of child pointers.

- Pattern 10, *Normalized Heterogeneous AST*, on page 96. Trees with a multitude of node types are called *heterogeneous trees*. Normalized heterogeneous trees use a normalized list of children like homogeneous trees.

- Pattern 11, *Irregular Heterogeneous AST*, on page 99. When we refer to an AST as heterogeneous, we also assume that the nodes have irregular children. Instead of a normalized child list, the nodes have named fields, one per child.

4.1 Why We Build Trees

As we saw in Chapter 2, *Basic Parsing Patterns*, on page 21, being able to recognize an input phrase means being able to identify and extract key input elements. For example, recognizing the English phrase "Rebecca runs to the park" means we know "Rebecca" is the subject, "runs" is the verb, and "to the park" is the object. Language recognition is more complicated than simply picking out the parts of speech, though. The order of those elements counts. In a modern English sentence, for example, the verb usually sits between the subject and the object. It sounds wrong (despite being intelligible) to say "Rebecca to the park runs."[1]

---

1. To a Middle English speaker (the language of Geoffrey Chaucer), however, this might sound more normal, as the main verb could appear at the end of the sentence. We still

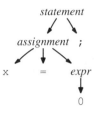

Figure 4.1: x=0; ASSIGNMENT STATEMENT PARSE TREE

Order is not the only important sentence recognition issue. Many languages have subphrases and nested structures. For example, some object-oriented languages allow nested class definitions. An inner class definition is a phrase nested within another phrase (the outer class). So, our IR must record not only the elements of interest but the relationship between them as well. It turns out that trees are the perfect data structure to represent ordered and nested structures. There are two general kinds of trees we're going to look at: *parse trees* and *abstract syntax trees*.

Since we're already familiar with parse trees from Chapter 2, *Basic Parsing Patterns*, on page 21 (sometimes called *syntax trees*), let's look at them first. Parse trees record the sequence of rules a parser applies as well as the tokens it matches. Interior parse tree nodes represent rule applications, and leaf nodes represent token matches.

Parsers don't normally create parse trees, though. Instead, recursive-descent rule method invocations simply trace out the parse tree during the parse. Because the rules for constructing parse trees are simple and regular, though, the parser can automatically construct them in memory. The parse tree acts like an execution trace. See Pattern 8, *Parse Tree*, on page 90.

Given assignment x=0;, our parser might create a parse tree like Figure 4.1. The tree represents the tokens from the assignment as well as its grammatical structure. It has everything we need to know about interpreting the sequence of input symbols as an assignment. The interior nodes organize and identify what roles their children play.

---

have some vestiges of this in sentences like "something wicked this way comes" and "with this ring I thee wed."

Parse trees are nice to look at and help us understand how a parser interpreted an input phrase. But, a parser execution trace isn't really the best IR. Certainly we need to pinpoint the various substructures, but we don't need to name them explicitly. Surprisingly, we don't need the internal rule nodes at all. The next section describes how to construct suitable intermediate form trees using only the tokens.

4.2 Building Abstract Syntax Trees

Rather than simply taking what the parser can give us for free (parse trees), let's take a second to design what we actually want in an IR. The critter that we end up with is called an *abstract syntax tree* (AST).

To figure out what ASTs should look like, let's start with a list of design guidelines. An IR tree should be the following:

- *Dense*: No unnecessary nodes

- *Convenient*: Easy to walk

- *Meaningful*: Emphasize operators, operands, and the relationship between them rather than artifacts from the grammar

The first two points imply that it should be easy and fast to identify patterns in the tree. Language applications that use intermediate trees usually make multiple passes over the trees in order to analyze or build other data structures. The structure of intermediate trees should be brain-dead simple.

The last point implies that the tree structure should be insensitive to changes in the grammar (at least those unrelated to language syntax). During development and maintenance, grammars change all the time. We don't want to let a simple rule name change in the grammar break other components in our application.

OK, using our design guidelines, let's build a suitable tree structure for assignment x=0;. To start, we can strip away the unnecessary nodes from the parse tree in Figure 4.1, on the preceding page. The ; node disappears because semicolons convey no meaning; they exist only to help the parser (and us humans) separate statements.

Believe it or not, we can also get rid of the rule nodes. We know that we fed a statement to the parser so the *statement* root node is unnecessary. What about the *assignment* node, though? We can drop this too because we only need to know what kind of statement we fed in, not what the grammar calls it. The = operator tells us everything we need to know. Computers only care about operators and operands.

By condensing the input to its essential elements, we decouple it from the original syntax. So, for example, assignment syntax boils down to an assignment operator and two operands. Decoupling does two things. First, it gets us closer to the operator-operand model of the CPU. Second, we can have different languages share a common intermediate form. Compiler writers often leverage an existing optimizer and code generator by translating multiple languages to an established IR.

At this point, we've removed all but three nodes: x, =, and 0. The only thing left to figure out is the relationship between those nodes. One thing is certain: We definitely can't get rid of the two-dimensional structure of the tree. A flat tree is a linked list, which is essentially just a copy of the input stream. In that case, the parser would be throwing away everything it learned about sentence structure.

The key idea behind AST structure is that tokens representing operators or operations become subtree roots. All other tokens become operands (children of operator nodes). Finally, we arrive at the AST for x=0;:

Let's examine this AST to see how it fits our design guidelines. There are no unnecessary nodes; the tree is the smallest possible. Without all of those interior rule nodes, walking this AST would be much faster than walking the parse tree. It's easy to identify subtrees because each subtree root uniquely identifies what the subtree does; in this case, the subtree performs an assignment. Lastly, this AST is an abstract representation of an assignment. No matter what assignment looks like in a programming language, we could translate it to this AST.

Now that we've got the basics down, let's think about the relationship between subtrees in more complicated trees.

How ASTs Encode Operator Precedence

There is only one operation in x=0; and, hence, just one subtree in its AST. Assignment x=1+2;, on the other hand, has two operations: an assignment and an addition. We know that there should be two subtrees, one for each operation, but we need to figure out how they fit together.

The answer depends on which operation needs to happen first. The semantics of assignment dictate that the right-side expression be evaluated before the assignment. To encode "x happens before y," we make x lower than y in the tree. In this case, we make the addition subtree a child (an operand) of the assignment subtree:

To perform the assignment, we first need the value of the right child. This mirrors the precedence of the = and + operators (+ has higher precedence).

The same rule applies for operators within the same expression. Operators with higher precedence appear lower in the AST. For example, in expression 3+4*5, the * operator has higher precedence than +. The * subtree is a subtree of the + operator node. If we alter the precedence of the operators in the expression with parentheses, (3+4)*5, the + subtree becomes a child of the * node. Here are the two AST representations:

AST for 3+4*5   AST for (3+4)*5

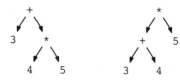

Representing Trees in Text

In future chapters, we'll need a terse, text-based encoding for trees. To arrive at a suitable notation, let's look at these trees as nested function calls:

```
add(3, mul(4,5)); // 3+4*5
mul(add(3,4), 5); // (3+4)*5
```

If we move the (to the left of the function name and replace the function name with the equivalent operator token, we get the following LISP-inspired notation:

```
(+ 3 (* 4 5))    // 3+4*5
(* (+ 3 4) 5)    // (3+4)*5
```

Notation (a b c) means a is the root with children b and c.

At this point, we know what to do with language constructs dealing with operator tokens. Now let's figure out how to create ASTs for nonexecutable language statements such as variable declarations.

Representing Pseudo-operations in ASTs

Not all programming language constructs map directly to executable code. There are even languages without executable statements. For example, DOT[2] is a purely declarative graphics language. We can only define nodes and the relationship between nodes. DOT figures out how to draw the diagram.

To represent such language constructs, we have to invent pseudo-operations. For example, here is a DOT declaration for a node labeled car:

```
node "car" [shape=ellipse, fontsize=14]
```

Because there is no executable operation for this declaration, we can use the node token as a "define node" operator. The property assignments for the declaration are the node's operands. Each property assignment is a subtree of the node:

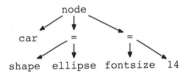

In some cases, there is no reasonable input token to use as a subtree root. We must invent an *imaginary token*, a token for which there is no corresponding input token. For example, variable declarations in languages derived from C usually need an imaginary token. We can use whatever we want, but something like **VARDECL** works well. The AST for int i; would have **VARDECL** at the root and int and i as children. We need something similar for function declarations, class declarations, formal argument declarations, and so on.

OK, so now we know what trees look like and how to map input constructs to AST subtrees. Let's figure out how to represent ASTs in memory. After that, we can build some ASTs using an ANTLR grammar.

---

2. http://www.graphviz.org

Implementing ASTs in Java

In our discussion so far, we've never mentioned the data type or types of the AST nodes. That's because, technically, we need only one data type: a generic tree node with a list of children. What we really care about is the tree structure (relationships between nodes), not necessarily the node implementation type(s) themselves. We could use a single class like the following to represent every node in the tree:

```
public class AST {
    Token token;        // node is derived from which token?
    List<AST> children; // operands
    public AST(Token token) { this.token = token; }
    public void addChild(AST t) {
        if ( children==null ) children = new ArrayList<AST>();
        children.add(t);
    }
}
```

Trees built from a single data type are called *homogeneous trees*. See Pattern 9, *Homogeneous AST*, on page 94. If there is only one data type, you might be wondering how we can distinguish between an addition and an assignment node. We can use a node's token type: t.token.getType() for node t. Each node stores the token from which we created it.

Because there is only a single type, we can use a *normalized child list* representation: List<AST>. Again, we don't care about the type of the children, just that they are nodes or subtrees. We don't even care about naming the fields really. For a + node, we know that the first child, children[0],[3] is the left operand, and the second child, children[1], is the right.

By normalizing the references to the children of every node, it's much easier to provide tree construction and tree-walking support machinery. Later in this chapter, for example, we'll try some of ANTLR's cool tree construction facilities. To use them, though, our trees must have normalized children. In Chapter 5, *Walking and Rewriting Trees*, on page 101, we'll see that it's harder to automatically generate tree visitors for irregular child lists. Just because we use normalized children, though, doesn't mean we can't have different node types.

---

3. The reader will forgive me for using children[i] instead of children.get(i) everywhere for clarity.

In Chapter 8, *Enforcing Static Typing Rules*, on page 181, we'll discuss annotating trees with various bits of information. For example, we might want to annotate expression trees with result types (expression 3+4.0 has result type float). With homogeneous tree nodes, however, adding a evalType field means all nodes (even nonexpression nodes) get the field. We end up including the union of all fields needed by all nodes in the homogeneous AST class definition. This costs memory and makes it hard to figure out which nodes need which fields.

To overcome this weakness, we can build a *heterogeneous tree*, where different kinds of nodes have different types. We'll explore heterogeneous tree nodes with normalized children in Pattern 10, *Normalized Heterogeneous AST*, on page 96. But, the core idea is to use the homogeneous AST class as a base class:

```
public class ExprNode extends AST { DataType evalType; ... }
public class AddNode extends ExprNode { ... }
public class MultNode extends ExprNode { ... }
public class IntNode extends ExprNode { ... }
...
```

One objection to heterogeneous trees with normalized children is that we have to refer to children by position, not by name. For example, we say children[0] and children[1], not, say, left and right. In many cases, having irregular, named fields leads to more readable code. We will explore such trees in more detail later (Pattern 11, *Irregular Heterogeneous AST*, on page 99). In the meantime, here is what ExprNode and AddNode would look like with irregular children:

```
public abstract class AST {
    Token token;
    // missing normalized list of children; subclasses define fields
}
public abstract class ExprNode extends AST { ... }
public class AddNode extends AST {
    ExprNode left, right;        // irregular, named fields
    «fields-specific-to-AddNode»
}
```

By using heterogeneous node types, we can also enforce a bit of structure, as we'll see next.

Enforcing Tree Structure with the Type System

We all make mistakes when writing software. So, if possible, it's a good idea to write code in such a way that it compiles only when we're doing things properly. To avoid creating improperly structured

ASTs, we can co-opt the implementation language's static type system to enforce structure. For example, we could make the constructor for heterogeneous type AddNode take two ExprNode arguments:

```
public AddNode(ExprNode left, ExprNode right) {...}
```

The types of the constructor's arguments make it very clear that addition only works on expressions. We can't use a statement or declaration as an addition operand:

```
// Constructor enforces structure using type system
// COMPILER ERROR: PrintNode is not an ExprNode
a = new AddNode(new IntNode(1), new PrintNode(...));
```

We can enforce many structures easily this way but not all. The VectorNode is a perfect example. To allow an arbitrary number of vector elements, we have to pass in a list:

```
public VectorNode(List<ExprNode> elements) {
    for (ExprNode node : elements) { addChild(node); }
}
```

Unfortunately, this constructor cannot enforce proper structure. We could pass in an empty list, but the grammar requires a least one vector element. There is simply no way to specify cardinality (how many there are) with the type system of commonly used programming languages.

By relying on the implementation language's type system to represent structure, the only sure way to determine the exact order and cardinality of children is to examine how methods use those children. The set of valid data structure organizations is therefore not explicitly described.

Worse, node functionality is spread across multiple node class definition files. The data structure organization is not encapsulated into a single description file. In Chapter 5, *Walking and Rewriting Trees*, on page 101, we see how to formally and tersely describe the set of possible structures with a single tree grammar file. Also note that co-opting a static type system to specify structure is not even an option for dynamically typed languages such as Ruby and Python.

The best way to create ASTs and to verify their structure is with a formal mechanism. In Section 4.4, *Constructing ASTs with ANTLR Grammars*, on page 86, we'll see how to create trees explicitly with tree grammar fragments. Then, in Chapter 5, *Walking and Rewriting Trees*, on page 101, we'll see how to enforce structure and do pattern matching also with tree grammar fragments. But, first, let's get a taste of ANTLR to make that discussion clear.

4.3 Quick Introduction to ANTLR

Once you know how to build lexers and parsers by hand, it's a good idea to use a parser generator to make your life easier. This section gets you started using ANTLR[4] and its grammar DSL. (You can skip to the next chapter if you're already familiar with it.) We're going to build a simple grammar, run it through ANTLR, and write a test rig to exercise the generated lexer and parser.

Let's build a grammar for a simple graphics DSL with a single command for drawing lines. Here's how we'd draw a box 10 units on a side:

`parsing/antlr/box`

```
line from 0,0 to 0,10
line from 0,10 to 10,10
line from 10,10 to 10,0
line from 10,0 to 0,0
```

The syntax of the DSL is a list of **line** commands:

`parsing/antlr/Graphics.g`

```
grammar Graphics;

file : command+ ; // a file is a list of commands

command : 'line' 'from' point 'to' point ;

point : INT ',' INT ; // E.g., "0,10"
```

There are three rules: **file**, **command**, and **point**. The single-quoted strings are tokens representing the keywords in our language. The references to **INT** are references to integer tokens. Here are the lexical rules (minus the implicit rules for matching keywords):

`parsing/antlr/Graphics.g`

```
INT : '0'..'9'+ ; // lexer rule to match 1-or-more digits

/** Skip whitespace */
WS : (' ' | '\t' | '\r' | '\n') {skip();} ;
```

The **WS** rule matches whitespace but immediately throws it away so that the parser doesn't see those characters. That way, the parser doesn't have to check for whitespace between all the rule elements.

---

4. http://www.antlr.org

Running ANTLR on the grammar gets us the lexer and parser classes: GraphicsLexer and GraphicsParser. Make sure antlr-3.2.jar from the main code directory is in your CLASSPATH environment variable and then say:

```
$ java org.antlr.Tool Graphics.g
$ ls
Graphics.g              GraphicsLexer.java      box
Graphics.tokens         GraphicsParser.java
$
```

Or, if you'd prefer to use the JAR file explicitly, invoke Java with the following -cp option, assuming you're in the code/parsing/antlr directory:

```
$ java -cp ../../antlr-3.2.jar org.antlr.Tool Graphics.g
```

The tokens file contains a list of the token types (which we can ignore it for our purposes here). If you take a look at the generated parser, you'll see that the methods of the class follow Pattern 1, *Mapping Grammars to Recursive-Descent Recognizers*, on page 29. For example, here is the core of the generated method for rule **point**:

parsing/antlr/GraphicsParser.java

```
// Graphics.g:8:9: INT ',' INT
match(input,INT,FOLLOW_INT_in_point39);
match(input,9,FOLLOW_9_in_point41);
match(input,INT,FOLLOW_INT_in_point43);
```

The FOLLOW_INT_in_point37 reference is a set of tokens the generated parser uses to automatically resynchronize after syntax errors.

To test the parser, we can use the following main program:

parsing/antlr/Test.java

```
public static void main(String[] args) throws Exception {
    CharStream input = null;
    // Pick an input stream (filename from commandline or stdin)
    if ( args.length>0 ) input = new ANTLRFileStream(args[0]);
    else input = new ANTLRInputStream(System.in);
    // Create the lexer
    GraphicsLexer lex = new GraphicsLexer(input);
    // Create a buffer of tokens between lexer and parser
    CommonTokenStream tokens = new CommonTokenStream(lex);
    // Create the parser, attaching it to the token buffer
    GraphicsParser p = new GraphicsParser(tokens);
    p.file();    // launch parser at rule file
}
```

Since we haven't inserted actions into the grammar to generate output, running the test rig appears to do nothing. But, if we give the program erroneous input, it spits out a syntax error:

```
$ javac *.java      # or, javac -cp ../../antlr-3.2.jar *.java
$ java Test box     # or, java  -cp .:../../antlr-3.2.jar Test box
$ java Test
line to 2,3
line 1:5 mismatched input 'to' expecting 'from'
$
```

Using the DSL of a parser generator saves a huge amount of work. We wrote a 15-line grammar and ANTLR generated more than 500 lines of Java code for us. To learn more, you can visit the website or purchase *The Definitive ANTLR Reference* [Par07]. In the next section, we'll see that ANTLR can also help us build ASTs without resorting to code in a general-purpose programming language.

4.4 Constructing ASTs with ANTLR Grammars

To learn about ANTLR's AST construction mechanism, let's build ASTs for a simple vector math language with addition, multiplication, and dot product.

To design our grammar, we need to look at some sample sentences. Here are some valid vector math statements:

```
x = 1+2
y = 1*2+3
z = [1, 2] + [3, 4]
a = [1, 2] . [3, 4]
b = 3 * [1, 2]
print x+2
```

At the coarsest level, that looks like a series of assignment and print statements. We can express that syntax grammatically as follows:

IR/Vec/VecMath.g

```
statlist : stat+ ;     // match multiple statements
stat: ID '=' expr      // match an assignment like "x=3+4"
    | 'print' expr      // match a print statement like "print 4"
    ;
```

Within the statements, we find various math operators (+, *, and .) and operands (integers, identifiers, and vector literals).

We can describe these expressions grammatically as follows:

`IR/Vec/VecMath.g`

```
expr:    multExpr ('+' multExpr)* ;      // E.g., "3*4 + 9"
multExpr: primary (('*'|'.') primary)* ; // E.g., "3*4"
primary
    :   INT                          // any integer
    |   ID                           // any variable name
    |   '[' expr (',' expr)* ']'     // vector literal; E.g. "[1,2,3]"
    ;
```

To build ASTs, we've got two options. We can add actions to the grammar to manually build trees, or we can use ANTLR's AST construction operators and rewrite rules.

Building trees by hand is easy but tedious. Here are a few rules augmented with tree construction actions (code fragments in curly braces) to give you the flavor:

```
expr returns [AST tr] // expr returns a subtree
    :   a=multExpr {$tr = $a.tr;}
        ( '+' b=multExpr {$tr = new AddNode($tr, $b.tr);} )*

    ;
primary returns [AST tr]
    :   INT {$tr = new IntNode($INT.text);}
    ...
```

AST construction is so important, ANTLR has built-in AST construction support. By setting the output option to AST, ANTLR adds a tree return value to each rule method (like we just did by hand). The tree return value from the start rule represents the root of the entire tree created while parsing. ANTLR also injects code to create an AST node (of type CommonTree) for each input token matched.

Given no instructions to the contrary, ANTLR builds a flat tree (a linked list) of these nodes. Here is the start of our grammar file with the output option set (and the definition of an imaginary token we'll need after that):

`IR/Vec/VecMathAST.g`

```
grammar VecMathAST;
options {output=AST;} // we want to create ASTs
tokens {VEC;} // define imaginary token for vector literal
```

The following rules use ANTLR's AST rewrite notation to specify tree structure:

IR/Vec/VecMathAST.g

```
statlist : stat+ ;                    // builds list of stat trees
stat: ID '=' expr  -> ^('=' ID expr)  // '=' is operator subtree root
    | 'print' expr -> ^('print' expr) // 'print' is subtree root
    ;
```

We use notation ^(...) for tree patterns not (...) in order to distinguish them from grammar subrules. The assignment tree has the same structure we've used so far with the = operator at the root.

Aside from its succinctness and expressivity, ANTLR's formal AST construction mechanism provides another important benefit: this mechanism is language neutral. ANTLR's code generator can generate code in a variety of languages, whereas code blocks we add by hand are language specific.

Sometimes the rewrite notation is inconvenient, particularly with expressions. It's easier to tell ANTLR which tokens are operators using the ^ suffix operator. All other tokens default to operands. Here are the expression rules augmented with AST construction operations (except for the vector literal alternative, which has a rewrite):

IR/Vec/VecMathAST.g

```
expr:   multExpr ('+'^ multExpr)* ;        // '+' is root node
multExpr: primary (('*'^|'.'^) primary)* ; // '*', '.' are roots
primary
    :   INT  // automatically create AST node from INT's text
    |   ID   // automatically create AST node from ID's text
    |   '[' expr (',' expr)* ']' -> ^(VEC expr+)
    ;
```

The ^(VEC expr+) AST rewrite is particularly satisfying. It says create a tree with imaginary token **VEC** at the root and the list of vector elements as children. ANTLR automatically buffers up the trees returned from all **expr** invocations. Referencing expr+ in the tree constructor (tree pattern to the right of ->) says, "Put all the **expr** return values here." To really dive into AST construction, see Chapter 7 of *The Definitive ANTLR Reference* [Par07] or the ANTLR tree construction documentation.[5]

By default ANTLR builds homogeneous trees of type CommonTree, but we can easily tell it to create heterogeneous trees. We can suffix any

---

5. http://www.antlr.org/wiki/display/ANTLR3/Tree+construction

token reference with a fully qualified node class name. For example, here is the **primary** rule augmented with heterogeneous node types:

```
primary
    :   INT<IntNode>    // create IntNode from INT's text
    |   ID<VarNode>     // create VarNode from ID's text
    |   '[' expr (',' expr)* ']' -> ^(VEC<VectorNode> expr+)
    ;
```

ANTLR generates new IntNode(«*INT-token*»); from INT<IntNode>. Without the heterogeneous tree node type, we get adaptor.create(«*INT-token*»);. The adaptor is an instance of the TreeAdaptor interface. The interface acts, in part, as a factory, converting tokens to AST nodes.

The AST constructor to build a subtree representing a vector, ^(VEC expr+), is an example of a tree pattern. What we're really doing here is transforming a linear sequence of tokens into a two-dimensional AST using a grammar-to-tree-grammar rewrite. The key is that we are declaring what the AST should look like, not how to build it. It is analogous to using a grammar to specify syntax rather than building a parser. We'll talk more about this in Chapter 5, *Walking and Rewriting Trees*, on page 101.

In this chapter, we looked at two different ways to structure intermediate representations (parse trees and ASTs) and three different ways to implement ASTs. Each one is useful in different circumstances. The following list summarizes all the pros and cons:

- Pattern 8, *Parse Tree*, on the following page. *Pros*: Parser generators can automatically build these for us. *Cons*: Parse trees are full of noise (unnecessary nodes). They are sensitive to changes in the grammar unrelated to syntax. If a parser generator generates heterogeneous node types, there can be literally hundreds of class definitions.

- Pattern 9, *Homogeneous AST*, on page 94. *Pros*: Homogeneous trees are very simple. *Cons*: It's cumbersome to annotate AST nodes because the single node type has the union of all needed fields. There is no way to add methods specific to a particular kind of node.

- Pattern 10, *Normalized Heterogeneous AST*, on page 96. *Pros*: It's easy to add operator or operand-specific data and methods. *Cons*: Large grammars like Java's need about 200 class definitions to be fully heterogeneous. That's a lot of files to read and write.

- Pattern 11, *Irregular Heterogeneous AST*, on page 99. *Pros*: It's easy to add operator- or operand-specific data and methods. Sometimes code operating on nodes is more readable because the children (operands) have names rather than positions like children[0]. Building tree-walking methods for a small set of heterogeneous nodes is quick and easy. *Cons*: As with Pattern 10, *Normalized Heterogeneous AST*, on page 96, there are lots of AST classes to read and write. Having irregular children makes building external visitors difficult. Most of the time we have to build tree walkers by hand using Pattern 12, *Embedded Heterogeneous Tree Walker*, on page 113.

If you're in doubt about which is best in your situation, choosing Pattern 10, *Normalized Heterogeneous AST*, on page 96 is a safe bet. That said, I tend to use Pattern 9, *Homogeneous AST*, on page 94 because I care most about tree structure, not about node types. If I have to annotate trees, though, I add some distinct node types, thus moving toward a heterogeneous tree.

Now that we've got an overall picture of intermediate representations, let's look at the tree patterns in more detail. After that, we'll tackle tree walking. In future chapters, we'll make heavy use of tree walking to extract information and perform computations.

☐ | 8 | Parse Tree

Purpose

A parse tree describes how a parser recognized an input sentence.

A parse tree is sometimes called a *syntax tree* (as opposed to an abstract syntax tree). Despite not being that useful for building interpreters and translators, I'm including this pattern because parse trees are heavily used by development environments and text rewriting systems.

Discussion

Parse trees record the sequence of rules a parser applies as well as the tokens it matches. Interior parse tree nodes represent rule applications, and leaf nodes represent token matches. Parse trees describe sentence structure by grouping input symbols into subtrees. Subtrees represent

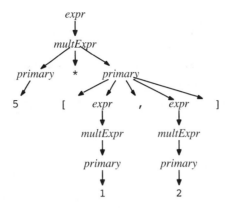

Figure 4.2: PARSE TREE FOR 5*[1,2]

the structure of phrases (sentence fragments). For example, the following parse tree clearly identifies the parts of speech in sentence "the cat runs quickly":

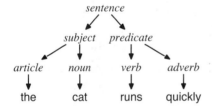

By successfully applying a rule to a phrase, the parser identifies the role it plays in the sentence. So, for example, the parse tree identifies "cat" as a noun and "the cat" as the sentence subject.

Parse trees are specific to a grammar. Here is the core of the grammar for that parse tree:

```
grammar English;
sentence : subject predicate ;
subject : article? noun ;
predicate : verb adverb? ;
...
```

The interior nodes of computer language parse trees also name language substructures. For example, we can see the parse tree for 5*[1,2] in a vector math language in Figure 4.2.

Parse trees are really easy to build by hand and are so regular that tools like ANTLR can automate the process for us. That's the good news. The bad news is that parse trees are extremely inconvenient to walk and transform. Parse trees are full of noise because of all the interior rule nodes. They are also very sensitive to changes in the grammar. For comparison, here is a more appropriate AST structure:

An AST captures just the essential information from the input: all of the input tokens and the appropriate structure. The interior nodes are operators or operations rather than rule names.

Nonetheless, parse trees are still very useful as intermediate representations for some tools and applications. For example, development environments use parse trees to good effect for syntax highlighting and error-checking. A number of text rewriting systems and pretty printing tools also use parse trees as intermediate representations. For these tools, it makes sense because we want to express transformations in the concrete syntax of the language. We want to name the parts of speech when we transform. For example, informally we might say, "When you see an assignment, replace = with :=." Or, in English, "Find all adjectives within sentence subjects." We can refer to parts of speech by using rule names from the grammar if we use parse trees.

Parse trees mirror the function call graphs of a recursive-descent parser, which leads us directly to a construction mechanism.

Implementation

To construct parse trees, we have to add a new interior node to the tree every time we enter a rule. Here's a template for a parser rule method:

```
void «rule»() {
    RuleNode r = new RuleNode("«rule»");
    if ( root==null ) root = r;    // we're the start rule
    else currentNode.addChild(r); // add this rule to current node
    ParseTree _save = currentNode;
    currentNode = r;               // "descend" into this rule
    «normal-rule-code»
    currentNode = _save;           // restore node to previous value
}
```

We also need to track the overall root of the parse tree and the current node:

```
class MyParser extends Parser {
    ParseTree root;           // root of the parse tree
    ParseTree currentNode;    // the current node we're adding children to
    public void match(int x) {          // override default behavior
        currentNode.addChild(LT(1)); // add current lookahead token node
        super.match(x);                 // match as usual
    }
    «rule-methods»
}
```

We override method match() to make it add token leaf nodes as it consumes tokens. The core parsing machinery remains unchanged.

As far as the trees themselves, here is a generic parse tree node:

IR/ParseTree.java

```
import java.util.*;
// Nodes are instances of this class; there's no Node class per se
public abstract class ParseTree {
    public List<ParseTree> children; // normalized child list
    public RuleNode addChild(String value) {
        RuleNode r = new RuleNode(value);
        addChild(r);
        return r;
    }
    public TokenNode addChild(Token value) {
        TokenNode t = new TokenNode(value);
        addChild(t);
        return t;
    }
    public void addChild(ParseTree t) {
        if ( children==null ) children = new ArrayList<ParseTree>();
        children.add(t);
    }
}
```

You can take a look at its subclasses, TokenNode and RuleNode, in the sample code. There's not that much to building parse trees.

9 Homogeneous AST

Purpose

A homogeneous tree implements an abstract syntax tree (AST) using a single node data type and a normalized child list representation.

Discussion

The key idea behind an AST is the operator-operand tree structure, not the node data type. The node data type is really just how we implement ASTs. An AST contains the essence of the input token stream and the relationships between operator and operand tokens.

We don't need to use the type system of our implementation language to distinguish between nodes. Nodes in any AST derive from tokens, so we can use the token type to identify nodes. In fact, homogeneous ASTs are the only convenient choice for non-object-oriented languages like C. To implement Pattern 10, *Normalized Heterogeneous AST*, on page 96, for example, C would have to cut and paste or manually include a reference to the normalized children definition into each node struct definition.

Homogeneous ASTs necessarily use a normalized child representation: List<AST>. This makes it particularly easy to build external visitors (Pattern 13, *External Tree Visitor*, on page 116), which rely on a uniform child list for walking.

Implementation

A homogeneous AST has two key fields: the token from which it was created and a list of children:

`IR/Homo/AST.java`

```
public class AST {      // Homogeneous AST node type
    Token token;        // From which token did we create node?
    List<AST> children; // normalized list of children

    public AST()             { ; } // for making nil-rooted nodes
    public AST(Token token)  { this.token = token; }
    /** Create node from token type; used mainly for imaginary tokens */
    public AST(int tokenType) { this.token = new Token(tokenType); }
```

```
/** External visitors execute the same action for all nodes
 *  with same node type while walking. */
public int getNodeType() { return token.type; }

public void addChild(AST t) {
    if ( children==null ) children = new ArrayList<AST>();
    children.add(t);
}
public boolean isNil() { return token==null; }
```

The isNil() method helps us represent flat lists. A list is a subtree without a root, which we can simulate with a nil root node. A nil node is a node with token==null.

To print out a tree using a text-based encoding (see Section 4.2, *Representing Trees in Text*, on page 79), we need a recursive toStringTree() method. This leaves toString() to convert a single node to text. The following toStringTree() generates strings of the following form: (root child1 child2 ...).

IR/Homo/AST.java

```
/** Compute string for single node */
public String toString() { return token!=null?token.toString():"nil"; }
/** Compute string for a whole tree not just a node */
public String toStringTree() {
    if ( children==null || children.size()==0 ) return this.toString();
    StringBuilder buf = new StringBuilder();
    if ( !isNil() ) {
        buf.append("(");
        buf.append(this.toString());
        buf.append(' ');
    }
    for (int i = 0; i < children.size(); i++) {
        AST t = (AST)children.get(i); // normalized (unnamed) children
        if ( i>0 ) buf.append(' ');
        buf.append(t.toStringTree());
    }
    if ( !isNil() ) buf.append(")");
    return buf.toString();
}
```

The following test code creates and prints the AST for 1+2:

IR/Homo/Test.java

```
Token plus = new Token(Token.PLUS,"+");
Token one = new Token(Token.INT,"1");
Token two = new Token(Token.INT,"2");
```

```
AST root = new AST(plus);
root.addChild(new AST(one));
root.addChild(new AST(two));
System.out.println("1+2 tree: "+root.toStringTree());

AST list = new AST(); // make nil node as root for a list
list.addChild(new AST(one));
list.addChild(new AST(two));
System.out.println("1 and 2 in list: "+list.toStringTree());
```

Here is a sample session:

```
$ java Test
1+2 tree: (+ 1 2)
1 and 2 in list: 1 2
$
```

The next pattern, Pattern 10, *Normalized Heterogeneous AST*, is an extension to this pattern that allows multiple node types while retaining the normalized child list.

Related Patterns

Pattern 10, *Normalized Heterogeneous AST* uses normalized lists of children as well but allows nodes to have different class types.

10 | Normalized Heterogeneous AST

Purpose

This pattern implements an abstract syntax tree (AST) using more than a single node data type but with a normalized child list representation.

Discussion

This pattern is a variation on Pattern 9, *Homogeneous AST*, on page 94. All we're doing differently is distinguishing between nodes with our implementation language's type system. Because this pattern also uses a normalized child list, we can derive heterogeneous nodes using AST from Pattern 9, *Homogeneous AST*, on page 94 as a base class.

This pattern makes the most sense when we need to store node-specific data and plan on using Pattern 13, *External Tree Visitor*, on page 116. The normalized child list makes it much easier to build external visitors. If you need lots of node-specific methods or plan on using Pattern

12, *Embedded Heterogeneous Tree Walker*, on page 113, use Pattern
11, *Irregular Heterogeneous AST*, on page 99 instead. (An embedded
walker has walking methods distributed across the heterogeneous node
type definitions.)

Let's flesh out some of the heterogenous node details from Section 4.2,
Implementing ASTs in Java, on page 81. We added a field, evalType, to
track expression type information (see also Pattern 20, *Computing Static
Expression Types*, on page 184). evalType tracks the type of the value
computed by the expression. For example, the type of 1+2 is integer. We
can put this field into an abstract class:

IR/Normalized/ExprNode.java

```java
public abstract class ExprNode extends AST {
    public static final int tINVALID = 0; // invalid expression type
    public static final int tINTEGER = 1; // integer expression type
    public static final int tVECTOR = 2;  // vector expression type
    /** Track expression type (integer or vector) for each expr node.
     * This is the type of the associated value not the getNodeType()
     * used by an external visitor to distinguish between nodes. */
    int evalType;

    public int getEvalType() { return evalType; }
    public ExprNode(Token payload) { super(payload); }
    /** ExprNode's know about the type of an expression, include that */
    public String toString() {
        if ( evalType != tINVALID ) {
            return super.toString()+"<type="+
                    (evalType == tINTEGER ? "tINTEGER" : "tVECTOR")+">";
        }
        return super.toString();
    }
}
```

Rather than creating a generic node and then adding children to form
a + (addition) subtree, we can use AddNode's constructor:

IR/Normalized/AddNode.java

```java
public class AddNode extends ExprNode {
    public AddNode(ExprNode left, Token addToken, ExprNode right) {
        super(addToken);
        addChild(left);
        addChild(right);
    }
    public int getEvalType() { // ...
```

Note that it's still a good idea to track the + token in the AST node.
This helps with a number of things including producing better error
messages.

Operand node types for integer and vector literals are straightforward subclasses of ExprNode:

IR/Normalized/IntNode.java

```java
public class IntNode extends ExprNode {
    public IntNode(Token t) { super(t); evalType = tINTEGER; }
}
```

IR/Normalized/VectorNode.java

```java
import java.util.List;
public class VectorNode extends ExprNode {
    public VectorNode(Token t, List<ExprNode> elements) {
        super(t); // track vector token; likely to be imaginary token
        evalType = tVECTOR;
        for (ExprNode e : elements) { addChild(e); } // add as kids
    }
}
```

The following test code creates and prints an AST for 1+2.

IR/Normalized/Test.java

```java
Token plus = new Token(Token.PLUS,"+");
Token one = new Token(Token.INT,"1");
Token two = new Token(Token.INT,"2");
ExprNode root = new AddNode(new IntNode(one), plus, new IntNode(two));
System.out.println(root.toStringTree());
```

Here is a sample session:

```
$ java Test
(+ 1<type=tINTEGER> 2<type=tINTEGER>)
$
```

The serialized tree output indicates that the 1 and 2 children have type tINTEGER. Naturally, the result of the addition operation is also an integer, so the root should have type tINTEGER. In Chapter 8, *Enforcing Static Typing Rules*, on page 181, we'll figure out how to do this computation properly. We'll leave it blank for now.

Related Patterns

This pattern defines node types that subclass AST from Pattern 9, *Homogeneous AST*, on page 94. The next pattern, Pattern 11, *Irregular Heterogeneous AST*, on the next page, uses an irregular child list rather than a normalized list like this pattern.

11   # Irregular Heterogeneous AST

□

Purpose

This pattern implements an abstract syntax tree (AST) using more than a single node data type and with an irregular child list representation.

Discussion

This pattern only differs from Pattern 10, *Normalized Heterogeneous AST*, on page 96 in the implementation of its child pointers. Instead of a uniform list of children, each node data type has specific (named) child fields. In this sense, the child pointers are irregular. In some cases, named fields lead to more readable code. For example, methods can refer to left and right instead of, say, children[0] and children[1].

When building trees from scratch, most programmers follow this pattern. It's very natural to name the fields of a class, in this case naming the children of a node. The big downside to using nodes with irregular children is that it's much less convenient to build tree walkers (such as Pattern 13, *External Tree Visitor*, on page 116). This pattern is fine for small projects where the extra gain in readability is worth the small bit of extra work to implement visitors. Larger projects tend to do so much tree walking, though, that the irregular children prove to be a big hassle.

To see where the pain comes from, look again at thetoStringTree() tree printing method shown in Pattern 9, *Homogeneous AST*, on page 94. Because the children of each node look the same, a single toStringTree() works for all nodes. With irregular children, each node has to have its own toStringTree(). There is no way to access a node's children generically. That means duplicating essentially the same logic just to use different field names. In the source code directory, you'll see that both ListNode.java and AddNode.java have node-specific toStringTree() implementations.

Since each node defines its own child fields, the abstract base class HeteroAST doesn't have a normalized list of children:

IR/Hetero/HeteroAST.java

```java
public abstract class HeteroAST {    // Heterogeneous AST node type
    Token token;                     // Node created from which token?
```

Node type AddNode is a typical irregular heterogeneous AST implementation. It has specific named child fields and node-specific methods. In this case, there are methods for printing out the tree structure and computing expression value result types:

IR/Hetero/AddNode.java

```java
public class AddNode extends ExprNode {
    ExprNode left, right; // named, node-specific, irregular children
    public AddNode(ExprNode left, Token addToken, ExprNode right) {
        super(addToken);
        this.left = left;
        this.right = right;
    }
    public String toStringTree() {
        if ( left==null || right==null ) return this.toString();
        StringBuilder buf = new StringBuilder();
        buf.append("(");
        buf.append(this.toString());
        buf.append(' ');
        buf.append(left.toStringTree());
        buf.append(' ');
        buf.append(right.toStringTree());
        buf.append(")");
        return buf.toString();
    }
}
```

The other node type definitions are available in the source directory; they differ only in the child field definitions. There is also a test file in Test.java.

Related Patterns

See Pattern 10, *Normalized Heterogeneous AST*, on page 96.

Up Next

This completes the last tree construction pattern. The next chapter explores how to build tree walkers for these data structures.

## Chapter 5

Walking and Rewriting Trees

In the previous chapter, we learned how to build ASTs, and in the following chapters, we'll start extracting information from them. We're even going to restructure the trees for simplification and translation purposes. For example, we might want to simplify x+0 to x or translate x==y to strcmp(x,y). To support such data extraction and rewriting operations, we'll need to know about tree walking. Tree walking is one of the key processes going on in a large language application.

At first glance, tree walking seems like no big deal. Many of us learned to write simple recursive functions to walk trees fairly early in our programming careers. In real applications, though, tree walking gets surprisingly complicated. There are a number of different variations, sometimes even within the same application.

The variation we choose depends on whether we have the source code for our tree nodes, whether the trees have normalized children, whether the trees are homogeneous or heterogeneous, whether we need to rewrite trees while walking, and even in which order we need to walk the nodes. In this chapter, we're going to explore the four key tree-walking patterns suitable for most language applications:

- Pattern 12, *Embedded Heterogeneous Tree Walker*, on page 113. Heterogeneous AST node classes define walking methods that execute appropriate actions and walk any children. Tree walking code is distributed across potentially hundreds of class files. This is the simplest pattern but the least flexible.

- Pattern 13, *External Tree Visitor*, on page 116. This pattern encapsulates tree walking code (for both homogeneous and heterogeneous ASTs) into a single class definition. It allows us to alter tree-walking behavior without altering AST node definitions. Both the visitor and embedded walker pattern are straightforward but tedious to implement manually.

- Pattern 14, *Tree Grammar*, on page 119. A tree grammar describes the structure of valid ASTs. Just as we can automate parser construction from grammars, we can automate tree visitor construction from tree grammars. Tree grammars work on homogeneous or heterogeneous trees because they rely on node token types rather than node types (like AddNode). Tree grammars explicitly dictate node visitation order like the embedded walker and visitor patterns.

- Pattern 15, *Tree Pattern Matcher*, on page 123. Instead of specifying an entire tree grammar, this pattern lets us focus on just those subtrees we care about. That's useful because different phases of an application care about different parts of the tree. A tree pattern matcher also decouples the order in which we apply tree patterns from the tree patterns themselves. Unlike embedded walkers, visitors, and tree grammars, tree patterns don't specify how to walk the tree. The pattern matching engine dictates the tree traversal strategy. In its simplest form, a pattern matcher repeatedly tries to match patterns against subtrees. When it finds a match, the pattern matcher triggers an action or tree rewrite.

To decide between these design patterns, we need to know how each one works and know their strengths and weaknesses. So, before getting into the patterns themselves, we should take a quick tour of tree walking. It's instructive to see how the weakness of one pattern inspires the development of another. Let's start our tree walking adventure by figuring out the difference between walking and visiting a tree.

5.1 Walking Trees and Visitation Order

When we talk about *visiting* a tree, we mean executing some actions on the nodes of a tree. The order in which we traverse the nodes is important because that affects the order in which we execute the actions. There are three key traversals:

- *Preorder traversal* or *top-down traversal*: + 1 2. Visit a (parent) node before visiting its children.
- *Inorder traversal*: 1 + 2. Visit a node in between visiting children.
- *Postorder traversal* or *bottom-up traversal*: 1 2 +. Visit a node after visiting its children.

Humans can pick out tree traversals by looking at a tree and, perhaps, tapping a pen on the nodes in a particular sequence. To implement this in code, we typically use a tree-walking algorithm called *depth-first search*. A depth-first search starts at the root of a tree or subtree and then recursively walks the children in order.

When a tree walk reaches node *t*, we say that it *discovers* that node. In other words, we discover *t* when execution of our walk() method begins on node *t*. When walk() finishes processing *t* and returns, we say that it has *finished* with *t*.

Visiting a node means to execute an action somewhere between discovering and finishing that node. A particular tree-walking mechanism, such as depth-first search, has a fixed node discovery sequence. But, that same discovery sequence can generate three different tree traversals (node visitation sequences). It all depends on where we put actions in walk().

Let's look at a simple example to see the difference between walking and visiting. With Pattern 11, *Irregular Heterogeneous AST*, on page 99, we can build a tree structure to represent integer addition using classes AddNode and IntNode. For example, here's the AST for 1+2:

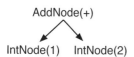

In code, we'd have an abstract class, ExprNode, that represents a generic tree node type and a tree-walking method:

```
/** Abstract class for heterogeneous AST with irregular children
 *  (each node defines their child fields) */
public abstract class ExprNode {
    Token token;        // AST nodes are based on tokens
    public void walk(); // a basic walk operation
}
```

We only have two concrete expression node types in this case: IntNode and AddNode:

```
public class IntNode extends ExprNode {
    public void walk() { ; } // no children; nothing to do
}

public class AddNode extends ExprNode {
    ExprNode left, right; // named, node-specific, irregular children
    public void walk() {
        left.walk();      // walk the left operand subtree
        right.walk();     // walk the right operand subtree
    }
}
```

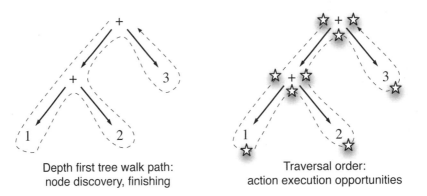

Depth first tree walk path:
node discovery, finishing

Traversal order:
action execution opportunities

Figure 5.1: TREE NODE DISCOVERY VS. TRAVERSAL ORDER

Invoking walk() on the + root node executes AddNode.walk(). This method then invokes walk() on each integer operand (executing IntNode.walk()) from left to right. We discover nodes in this order: + 1 2, which corresponds to a preorder traversal.

Let's analyze how walk() discovers nodes in a slightly larger tree. The AST for expression 1+2+3 appears in the left tree in Figure 5.1, with a dashed line showing walk()'s depth-first search path.

The walk() method starts at the root of a tree and then recursively walks its children in order. So, walk() discovers the root and then descends into the children. It discovers the left child (the + subtree) before discovering the right child (node 3). On the way down, it discovers nodes, and on the way up it finishes nodes. walk() discovers and immediately finishes leaf nodes.

If we look closely at the dashed line, the depth-first search provides multiple opportunities per node to execute actions. The right tree (in Figure 5.1) indicates those locations with stars. We can execute an action upon discovery (the star to the left of the + nodes), in between child discovery (the star below), or upon finishing (the star to the right). For leaf nodes, there is only one action execution opportunity. The complete discovery sequence is + + 1 2 3, which corresponds to a preorder traversal. The finishing sequence is 1 2 + 3 +, which corresponds to a postorder traversal. Executing actions in between child discovery corresponds to an inorder traversal: 1 + 2 + 3.

To obtain a different traversal, we'd alter AddNode.walk() to execute actions before, during, or after walking its children (depending on the application, we might do one, two, or all actions):

```
public void walk() {
    «preorder-action»
    left.walk();
    «inorder-action»
    right.walk();
    «postorder-action»
}
```

For example, to print nodes out in postorder, we'd add a print statement at the end of AddNode's walk().

```
public void walk() {
    left.walk();
    right.walk();
    System.out.println(token); // print "+" token
}
```

And then we'd add a print statement in IntNode (which has only one opportunity to execute an action since it has no children):

```
public void walk() { System.out.println(token); }
```

Tree-walking mechanisms such as this that embed walking code in each heterogeneous node follow Pattern 12, *Embedded Heterogeneous Tree Walker*, on page 113. The beauty of the embedded walker is its simplicity: it's pretty obvious what's going on.

Unfortunately, there are a number of disadvantages. For one, the walking code is distributed across potentially hundreds of node class definition files. That makes it hard to get a feel for the overall tree structure. The main problem, though, is that we can't alter our walking algorithm or add new walking tasks without modifying the node classes. We might not even have the source code for the nodes. Lack of source makes adding new embedded walking methods impossible for most programming languages. A better way is to collect all walking methods into a separate specification, one that is external to the tree classes.

5.2 Encapsulating Node Visitation Code

By collecting all of the tree walking methods from Pattern 12, *Embedded Heterogeneous Tree Walker*, on page 113 into a single class definition, we arrive at Pattern 13, *External Tree Visitor*, on page 116. Our primary goal is to separate our tree-walking code from our tree node definitions. The key advantage of a visitor is that it's external to the objects it walks.

There are a number of ways to achieve this separation, depending on the programming language we use. Languages such as Ruby and Python make short work of the visitor pattern because they can add methods at run-time. Static languages like Java and C++ require some gymnastics.

The first, and most common solution for Java, is to leave a general visit() method in each heterogeneous node definition. But, again, this requires modification of the source code, which we might not have. Take a look at the sample code in the Pattern 13, *External Tree Visitor*, on page 116 for a complete example.

A better solution involves a completely independent visitor that never has to touch the node class definitions. For example, imagine we want to mimic the postorder print actions we saw in the previous section. We could combine the walk() methods from AddNode and IntNode into a single class with a dispatcher method:

```
/** Completely encapsulated and independent node visitor */
public class IndependentPostOrderPrintVisitor {
    /** visitor dispatcher according to argument type */
    public void print(ExprNode n) {
        if ( n.getClass() == AddNode.class ) print((AddNode)n);
        else if ( n.getClass() == IntNode.class ) print((IntNode)n);
        else «error-unhandled-node-type»
    }

    public void print(AddNode n) {
        print(n.left);            // visit left child
        print(n.right);           // visit right child
        System.out.print(n.token); // action in postorder position
    }
    public void print(IntNode n) { System.out.print(n.token); }
}
```

The print() dispatcher method figures out which overloaded method to call according to the run-time argument type (either AddNode or Int-Node). Such a dispatcher method fakes method argument type polymorphism in Java. It's what gives the visitor its independence from the node class definition files. For a large number of node classes, the if-then-else chain would be pretty inefficient, though. It's more efficient to have the dispatcher switch on the node's token type.

```
public void print(ExprNode n) {
    switch ( n.token.type ) { // switch on token type
        case Token.PLUS : print((AddNode)n); break;
        case Token.INT  : print((IntNode)n); break;
        default : «error-unhandled-node-type»
    }
}
```

This visitor pattern is an improvement over the embedded walker, but it too has weaknesses. First, it cries out for some kind of automation. Writing the dispatcher method by hand is tedious. Also, many of the print() methods (for example, all binary operators) are similar or identical. That is just asking for a cut-and-paste error. Fortunately, we can solve this problem by using a Pattern 14, *Tree Grammar*, on page 119, as we'll see in the next section.

The second weakness is more serious. The mechanisms we've described so far execute actions when they see a node of a particular type. In practice, we need to match subtree patterns, not just single node types. We rarely want to match any old **ID** node. Usually we want to match **ID** nodes that are assignment left sides or that are names in method definition subtrees. Writing tree pattern matching code by hand is error prone and unpleasant. The good news is that tree grammars make this easier too.

5.3 Automatically Generating Visitors from Grammars

Rather than writing parsers by hand, we write grammars and have a parser generator like ANTLR generate parsers automatically for us. Similarly, ANTLR can automatically generate tree visitors from tree grammars. That's great because we get to express ourselves in a DSL designed to describe trees. We tell ANTLR *what* the trees look like, and it figures out *how* to walk them. The only wrinkle is describing a two-dimensional tree structure with a grammar.

To parse a two-dimensional structure, we have to serialize the tree to a one-dimensional list of nodes. Then we can use a conventional parser. To serialize, we start with the "flat" text-based tree format from Section 4.2, *Representing Trees in Text*, on page 79 and then replace parentheses with imaginary **UP** and **DOWN** navigation nodes. For example, the text-based form of the AST for 1+2 is (+ 1 2), a preorder traversal with subtrees wrapped in parentheses.

The serialization of (+ 1 2) looks like this:

```
+ DOWN 1 2 UP
```

The navigation nodes simulate the up-and-down movement of a tree walker, forcing a one-dimensional parser to do the same.

Let's figure out what the grammar for our little addition expression trees should look like. Nodes are either integers or addition subtrees whose children are nodes or subtrees. Grammatically we can describe that structure with a single rule:

```
expr : ^('+' expr expr) // E.g., "(+ 1 2)" and "(+ (+ 1 2) 3)"
     | INT               // E.g., 1 and 2
     ;
```

The recursion in the first alternative highlights the self-similar nature of expression trees—the children of an expression operator can also be expressions. The ^ prefix is necessary to distinguish tree constructs from normal subrules.

ANTLR automatically translates tree pattern ^('+' expr expr) to '+' DOWN expr expr UP. ANTLR generates a parser (following Pattern 3, *LL(1) Recursive-Descent Parser*, on page 38) from rule **expr**, which is akin to the following:

```
void expr() {                        // match an expression subtree
    if ( LA(1)==Token.PLUS ) {       // if next token is +
        match(Token.PLUS);
        match(DOWN);                 // simulate down movement
        expr();
        expr();
        match(UP);                   // simulate up movement
    }
    else if ( LA(1)==Token.INT ) { // if next token is INT
        match(Token.INT);            // match single INT node expr
    }
    else «invalid-tree»              // detected malformed tree
}
```

Looking back at our heterogeneous node definitions now (Pattern 11, *Irregular Heterogeneous AST*, on page 99), we see that they actually say sort of the same thing as rule **expr**. An ExprNode is an AddNode or IntNode (because they are subclasses of ExprNode). An AddNode has two ExprNode children (left and right). Rule **expr** makes it clearer what the trees look like, though.

As with any grammar, we can embed actions. To print out a tree in postorder, we add print statements at the end of the two alternatives.

```
expr : ^('+' expr expr) {System.out.println("+");}
     | INT               {System.out.println($INT.text);}
     ;
```

For tree (+ 1 2), the ANTLR-generated tree visitor would print 1 2 +. Rather than creating a visitor function based upon a node type, we tell the parser to execute actions when it comes across a particular tree pattern. Actions at the start of alternative are in node discovery position. Actions at the end of an alternative are in node finishing position. Actions embedded within the alternative happen in between node discovery and finishing.

A tree grammar specifies the complete "syntax" of all valid ASTs for a particular application just as a parser grammar specifies a valid set of sentences. Tree grammars are extremely useful as a form of executable documentation describing the trees generated by a parser.

Not only does the tree grammar describe the set of valid trees, but running an ANTLR-generated visitor over a tree checks its structure. Instead of co-opting the type system to enforce structure during construction like Section 4.2, *Enforcing Tree Structure with the Type System*, on page 82, we can check it later at run-time. Catching structural errors at compile time is great, but we have to walk the trees anyway. We might as well check their structure as we go. Also, the type system isn't always sufficient to prevent invalid tree structures. If we're using a dynamically typed language, we don't even have the option. We have to use a tree grammar to enforce tree structure in that case.

Tree grammars are most useful when we've got lots of work to do on the tree. In other words, they're most useful when we have actions all over the grammar. A good example is a final tree-walking phase that generates source code. (We'll use a tree grammar to emit a subset of C in Section 12.5, *Using a Tree Grammar to Create Templates*, on page 324.) In that case, the tree grammar provides a terse means of specifying a complete visitor and associated code generation actions.

But, many of the intermediate tree-walking phases only care about certain sections or pieces of the tree. It's a burden to build a complete tree grammar when all we care about is, say, collecting information at method and variable definition subtrees. I've often created a prototype tree grammar and then made copies of that grammar for every phase. Unfortunately, this poses a maintenance problem because AST structure can change, particularly during development. I've had to push changes to all grammar copies.

For intermediate tree-walking phases, we need a solution that lets us focus only on the tree patterns we care about for a particular phase. To make this work, we need to separate our tree traversal strategy from pattern matching and action execution. In the next section, we'll explore how to do that with tree pattern matchers (based upon tree grammars).

5.4 Decoupling Tree Traversal from Pattern Matching

Imagine we need to print a list of all assignments to simple variables in a Python program. It would be overkill to create or use an existing full Python parser. The pattern we're looking for is unique. Using regular expressions and UNIX awk, we could filter Python programs looking for assignments with a one-liner:

```
$ awk '/[ \t]+[a-zA-Z]+ =/ {print $1}' < myprog.py # $1 is left of '='
style
x
keymap
pt
...
```

Don't worry about the details (which aren't perfect anyway). The key is that we made a tool consisting of a just one pattern and associated action. We left the details of traversing the input to awk. We really don't care, in this case, if awk walks the input lines forward, backward, or randomly. When awk matches a line to a pattern, it triggers the action. We don't have to specify traversal instructions in the pattern itself. For example, the print $1 action doesn't include code telling awk to walk the remainder of the file.

If you're asking yourself why we would ever entangle pattern matching with traversal, note that embedded walker and external visitor patterns both do it. Take a look at one of the visitor methods we built earlier:

```
public void print(AddNode n) {
    print(n.left);              // visit left child
    print(n.right);             // visit right child
    System.out.print(n.token);  // action in postorder position
}
```

The first two statements specifically tell the visitor to visit the left child and then the right child. That is clearly encoding the tree traversal strategy in the method that matches an AddNode. Forget the first print() call, and the visitor won't walk the left operand subtree of any addition node.

When we only care about some of the subtrees, building a full tree grammar or complete external visitor is overkill. But, only specifying some of the rules or visitor methods won't work. We need a pattern for each subtree and node because the pattern code includes the traversal instructions. We couldn't visit all nodes without a complete tree specification.

The way around this is to decouple the tree traversal strategy from pattern matching. In other words, we want to think about pattern matching and actions separately from how and when we apply those patterns. In fact, we might want to use one set of patterns on the way down the tree and another on the way up.

For example, on the way down, it makes sense to eliminate unreachable code so we don't waste time traversing it. Take the **if** statement. There is no point in descending into an **if**'s statement when the conditional expression is boolean literal false.

In other cases, it makes more sense to do rewrites on the way up. Eliminating multiply-by-zero operations is a good example. We'd like to rewrite expression 4*0*2 to be 0. Its AST looks like this:

We need to reduce the 4*0 subtree to 0 before checking the topmost * node. Otherwise, we won't see it as 0*2 and replace it with 0.

Repeatedly applying rules to subtrees using a separate (usually bottom-up) traversal strategy is called *term rewriting*. A *term* is just a subtree. There are a number of nice tools specifically designed to rewrite terms. ASF+SDF[1] is one of the most popular. Eelco Visser took term writing to a new level by supporting programmable rewriting strategies in his Stratego/XT[2] tool. He also has some useful documentation on Stratego's website about separating tree traversal from transformation patterns if you'd like to learn more about this topic.

These tools require a pure functional programming style, though, which is an uphill struggle for many of us. They don't allow arbitrary actions,

---

1. http://www.meta-environment.org
2. http://strategoxt.org

which can make it harder to integrate transformation phases into existing applications. One term-rewriting tool, Tom,[3] though, acts as an extension to Java.

As we'll see in Pattern 15, *Tree Pattern Matcher*, on page 123, ANTLR can do tree pattern matching also. It uses a depth-first tree walker that invokes tree grammar rules at each node, looking for a match. If a tree pattern doesn't match the current subtree, ANTLR tries another pattern. If it doesn't find one, it walks to a new node in the tree and looks for a matching pattern again.

All the patterns described in this chapter have their place. Which one we use depends on the nature of our task. The following table summarizes their strengths and weaknesses.

Pattern	When to Apply
Pattern 12, *Embedded Heterogeneous Tree Walker*, on the facing page	Embedding walking methods in tree nodes is the simplest mechanism for building a tree walker. It doesn't work so well with 50 or 100 node types because walker functionality is distributed across 50 or 100 files.
Pattern 13, *External Tree Visitor*, on page 116	Visitors encapsulate tree walkers into a single class and allow us to change visitors on the fly. Visitors are useful for collecting information or doing some simple interpretation, such as expression evaluation. They are not well suited to tree pattern matching applications. Visitors simply walk the tree node by node.
Pattern 14, *Tree Grammar*, on page 119	Embedded walkers and visitors are hand-built. ANTLR can generate external tree visitors for us automatically from tree grammars, which are smaller and easier to read. Tree grammars specify the structure of entire trees. They are most effective when we need to execute actions in many or most rules. For example, tree-walking code generators typically need to emit code for every subtree. There are actions strewn throughout the grammar.

---

3. http://tom.loria.fr

Pattern	When to Apply
Pattern 15, *Tree Pattern Matcher*, on page 123	If you're only interested in executing actions on a few subtree patterns, it's a burden to fill out an entire tree grammar (or build a complete visitor, for that matter). All visitors, automatically generated or not, entangle tree traversal instructions with action execution. To walk the entire tree looking for patterns, then, we need to give a complete tree grammar specification. To operate only on a specific subset of an AST structures, we can use a tree pattern matcher.

With this comparison in mind, we're ready to tackle the details of the four tree-walking patterns. To keep a common thread, we'll work with the little vector math language from Section 4.4, *Constructing ASTs with ANTLR Grammars*, on page 86.

12 Embedded Heterogeneous Tree Walker

Purpose

This pattern walks heterogeneous ASTs using a set of recursive methods defined within the node class definitions.

Discussion

As object-oriented programmers, it is natural for us to think about adding tree-walking methods to node definitions. For each task, we'd add a different set of recursive methods. For example, to print trees back to text, we could define an abstract print() method in the root class. To evaluate expressions, we could add an abstract eval() method to the abstract expression class.

This is the easiest tree-walking pattern to understand, but, ultimately, this approach doesn't scale well. Because it distributes tree-walking code across all node definitions, it works best when there are only a few node definitions. More important, we need access to node source code. If we don't have source code (or we need to change tree walker functionality on the fly), we have to use Pattern 13, *External Tree Visitor*, on page 116 instead.

Building an embedded walker means adding a walking method like this (assuming we only need preorder actions):

```
class «NodeName» extends «common-root» {
    public void «walking-method-name»() {
        «preorder-action-for-this-node-or-subtree»
        «walk-any-children»
    }
}
```

The walking methods serve two purposes: first, to execute an action or actions per node and second, to guide the walk through the tree. If a walking method forgets to walk a node's children, those children won't ever be visited.

Implementation

The sample code for this pattern defines heterogeneous AST nodes for the vector math language from Section 4.4, *Constructing ASTs with ANTLR Grammars*, on page 86. The generic root class defines the token payload:

walking/embedded/HeteroAST.java

```
public class HeteroAST {// Heterogeneous AST node type
    Token token;        // This node created from which token?
    public HeteroAST()              { ; }
    public HeteroAST(Token token)   { this.token = token; }
    public String toString()        { return token.toString(); }
}
```

A generic VecMathNode node embeds a walking method called print():

walking/embedded/VecMathNode.java

```
/** A generic heterogeneous tree node used in our vector math trees */
public abstract class VecMathNode extends HeteroAST {
    public VecMathNode() {;}
    public VecMathNode(Token token) { super(token); }
    public void print() { // generic print tree-walker method
        System.out.print(token != null ? token.toString() : "<null>");
    }
}
```

Our vector math language has two general node categories: statements (assignment and print) and expressions. We can use StatNode and ExprNode to group related nodes. The concrete subclasses override print().

For example, here's AssignNode:

`walking/embedded/AssignNode.java`

```java
public class AssignNode extends StatNode {
    VarNode id;
    ExprNode value;
    public AssignNode(VarNode id, Token token, ExprNode value) {
        super(token); this.id = id; this.value = value;
    }
    public void print() {
        id.print();             // walk left child
        System.out.print("=");  // print operator
        value.print();          // walk right child
        System.out.println();
    }
}
```

Notice that print() walks the children in addition to printing the assignment operator.

The print() method in the AddNode operator node is similar:

`walking/embedded/AddNode.java`

```java
public void print() {
    left.print();             // walk left child
    System.out.print("+");    // print operator
    right.print();            // walk right child
}
```

The test rig within the source code directory manually builds a tree holding two statements: an assignment and print statement. For simplicity, it builds trees with code rather than relying on an AST-constructing parser. To launch the embedded walker, the rig calls print() on the root node:

`walking/embedded/Test.java`

```java
statlist.print(); // Launch embedded walker
```

Running the test rig prints the statements:

```
$ java Test
x=3+4
print x*[2, 3, 4]
$
```

The next pattern collects embedded tree-walking methods into a single, external class.

13   External Tree Visitor

Purpose

This pattern encapsulates all tree-walking code associated with a particular task into a single visitor class.

Visitors combine tree walking and action execution code outside the AST node definitions. Consequently, we can change the functionality of the tree walker without having to change the AST class definitions and can even switch visitors on the fly. An external visitor can walk either heterogeneous or homogeneous AST nodes.

Discussion

The visitor pattern is the workhorse of choice for tree walking in most language applications. Ultimately you might get tired of manually building visitors, though, and you might come to rely on either Pattern 14, *Tree Grammar*, on page 119 or Pattern 15, *Tree Pattern Matcher*, on page 123. That said, the key to understanding automatically generated visitors is to know how to build visitors manually.

Visitors use similar code to what we'd find in Pattern 12, *Embedded Heterogeneous Tree Walker*, on page 113. The only difference is that visitors are external to the AST node definitions, giving us a nice separation of concerns. The tree-walking methods live within a single visitor class.

Implementation

There are two ways to implement this pattern. The first is more traditional and relies on the node types themselves. The second relies on the node's token type instead. This section gives examples of both using the AST nodes from the vector math language in Section 4.4, *Constructing ASTs with ANTLR Grammars*, on page 86.

Visitor Switching on Node Type

The traditional implementation of the visitor pattern originally specified in *Design Patterns: Elements of Reusable Object-Oriented Software* [GHJV95] relies on a "double-dispatch" method within each AST node. The double-dispatch method redirects visit() calls on a node to an appropriate method in a visitor servicing that node type. The visitor is like a set of callback methods. To make this work, we need to define the crucial visit() double-dispatch method signature in our generic node:

walking/visitor/VecMathNode.java

```
/** A generic heterogeneous tree node used in our vector math trees */
public abstract class VecMathNode extends HeteroAST {
    public VecMathNode() {;}
    public VecMathNode(Token t) { this.token = t; }
    public abstract void visit(VecMathVisitor visitor); // dispatcher
}
```

Unfortunately, we need to implement visit() in every class (we'll look at its argument type, VecMathVisitor, in a second). Surprisingly, every visit() method is identical. Here it is in AddNode:

walking/visitor/AddNode.java

```
public void visit(VecMathVisitor visitor) { visitor.visit(this); }
```

Calling a node's visit() method immediately redirects (which is why it's called *double-dispatch*) to the associated visitor's method. For example, if n points at an AddNode at run-time, then a method dispatch to n.visit(myVisitor) immediately redispatches to myVisitor.visit((AddNode)n).

Given this double-dispatch mechanism, let's figure out what the visitor itself looks like. The only constraint on the visitor objects is that they implement VecMathVisitor:

walking/visitor/VecMathVisitor.java

```
public interface VecMathVisitor {
    void visit(AssignNode n);
    void visit(PrintNode n);
    void visit(StatListNode n);
    void visit(VarNode n);
    void visit(AddNode n);
    void visit(DotProductNode n);
    void visit(IntNode n);
    void visit(MultNode n);
    void visit(VectorNode n);
}
```

As a sample implementation, let's write a visitor that prints out vector math nodes just like we did in Pattern 12, *Embedded Heterogeneous Tree Walker*, on page 113. The output will be the same, but the mechanism is different.

Here is the start of a PrintVisitor with the code for visiting AssignNode:

walking/visitor/PrintVisitor.java

```java
public class PrintVisitor implements VecMathVisitor {
    public void visit(AssignNode n) {
        n.id.visit(this);
        System.out.print("=");
        n.value.visit(this);
        System.out.println();
    }
```

To print a tree, we invoke visit() on the root node and pass in a visitor:

walking/visitor/Test.java

```java
PrintVisitor visitor = new PrintVisitor();
statlist.visit(visitor); // tell root node to visit with this visitor
```

This visitor implementation requires heterogeneous nodes and, sadly, isn't truly independent of the AST nodes because of the double-dispatch visit() method. The implementation in the next section works on homogeneous nodes as well and is completely independent of the AST node definitions.

Switching on the Token Type to Build Independent Visitors

For language applications, we build trees from tokens. Since we can distinguish between tokens using the token type, we can also distinguish between AST nodes using the token type. By switching on the token type rather than the AST node type, we can avoid the visit() method in each AST node. In its place, we use just one dispatch method inside the visitor:

walking/visitor/IndependentPrintVisitor.java

```java
public void print(VecMathNode n) {
    switch ( n.token.type ) {
        case Token.ID :        print((VarNode)n); break;
        case Token.ASSIGN :    print((AssignNode)n); break;
        case Token.PRINT :     print((PrintNode)n); break;
        case Token.PLUS :      print((AddNode)n); break;
        case Token.MULT :      print((MultNode)n); break;
        case Token.DOT :       print((DotProductNode)n); break;
        case Token.INT :       print((IntNode)n); break;
        case Token.VEC :       print((VectorNode)n); break;
        case Token.STAT_LIST : print((StatListNode)n); break;
        default :
            // catch unhandled node types
            throw new UnsupportedOperationException("Node "+
                    n.getClass().getName()+ " not handled");
    }
}
```

The dispatch method invokes the appropriate overloaded method. For example, here is the visitor method for AddNode:

walking/visitor/IndependentPrintVisitor.java

```
public void print(AddNode n) {
    print(n.left);          // walk left child
    System.out.print("+"); // print operator
    print(n.right);         // walk right child
}
```

To walk an AST, we pass an AST node to the visitor instead of passing the visitor to an AST node. The following snippet from the test rig creates a visitor and then tells it to visit the root node:

walking/visitor/Test.java

```
IndependentPrintVisitor indepVisitor = new IndependentPrintVisitor();
indepVisitor.print(statlist); // tell visitor to print from root
```

This implementation has a number of advantages over an embedded walker. With an external visitor, the method names can be relevant to the task at hand such as print(). A traditional visitor has to name every method visit() because the visitors have to follow the interface. This implementation does not need an interface at all and has a double-dispatch mechanism that is completely encapsulated within the visitor. The only disadvantage is that we lose compile-time checking if we forget a visitor method for a node type. We have to wait until run-time before throwing an UnsupportedOperationException from the dispatch method.

Related Patterns

This pattern effectively collects the tree-walking methods from the nodes discussed in Pattern 12, *Embedded Heterogeneous Tree Walker*, on page 113 and puts them into a single class. ANTLR can automatically build an external visitor from Pattern 14, *Tree Grammar*.

14 Tree Grammar

Purpose

Tree grammars are a terse and formal way of building an external visitor.

Visitors generated from tree grammars are usually called *tree parsers* because they are the two-dimensional analog of conventional parsers.

Discussion

In Section 5.3, *Automatically Generating Visitors from Grammars*, on page 107, we saw that tree grammars look just like conventional parser grammars except that we can match subtree patterns as well. As with parser grammars, we can embed actions to extract information or reorganize the input (a tree, in this case).

In order to convert tree grammars to tree parsers (visitors), we can follow Pattern 1, *Mapping Grammars to Recursive-Descent Recognizers*, on page 29. The only extra mapping we need is for tree structures:

```
// match ^(«root» «children»)
match(«root»);
match(DOWN); // simulate downward movement of a tree walker
«match-children»
match(UP);   // simulate upward movement of a tree walker
```

«root» is usually a token but can be a set of tokens. *«children»* can be any token, any rule, or even a nested tree reference.

ANTLR generates tree walkers from tree grammars that literally act like parsers. For example, the walkers automatically detect tree structure errors and emit error messages (analogous to syntax errors). If we build an invalid tree such as '=' (x 1) instead of ('=' x 1), a tree walker might emit something like this:

```
Printer.g: node from line 1:0 extraneous input 'x' expecting <DOWN>
```

Tree grammars do not care about the implementation language classes used to represent AST nodes (they work with both homogeneous and heterogeneous AST nodes). Instead, they rely on token type differences between AST node token payloads to distinguish different kinds of nodes. So, the tree walker differentiates between node x and node 1 by comparing their **ID** and **INT** token types (as opposed to, say, VarNode and IntNode types).

Once you're comfortable with tree grammars, you'll find them easier to write and more robust than hand-built visitors (Pattern 13, *External Tree Visitor*, on page 116). Tree grammars and visitors are equally powerful; it's really the difference between using a grammar and writing a parser by hand.

Implementation

To compare tree grammars to hand-built visitors, let's implement the same printing functionality as PrintVisitor from Pattern 13, *External Tree*

Visitor, on page 116. The most obvious difference is that PrintVisitor.java is 82 lines, but our functionally equivalent tree grammar is only 25 lines.

The header for our tree grammar tells ANTLR that we'll be using token types from a VecMath.g parser grammar (provided in the source code directory) that builds vector math ASTs. It also says we'll be using homogeneous tree nodes (the default ANTLR CommonTree).

<code>walking/tree-grammar/Printer.g</code>

```
tree grammar Printer; // this grammar is a tree grammar called Printer
options {
    tokenVocab=VecMath;       // use token vocabulary from VecMath.g
    ASTLabelType=CommonTree; // use homogeneous CommonTree for $ID, etc.
}
@members { void print(String s) { System.out.print(s); } }
```

Our trees are lists of statement subtrees, and there are two kinds of statements:

<code>walking/tree-grammar/Printer.g</code>

```
prog:   stat+ ; // match list of statement subtrees
// match trees like ('=' x 1) and ('print' ('+' 3 4))
stat:   ^('=' ID  {print($ID.text+" = ");} expr) {print("\n");}
    |   ^('print' {print("print ");}         expr) {print("\n");}
    ;
```

The print actions occur after the immediately preceding grammar element and before the following element. So, the newline print at the end of each alternative occurs after the tree walker prints the statements. The ANTLR-generated tree walker executes actions as it walks the tree-matching patterns just like a hand-built visitor.

To print out expressions, we provide a subtree pattern for each operator and then the three literals (vectors, integers, and identifiers):

<code>walking/tree-grammar/Printer.g</code>

```
expr:   ^('+' expr {print("+");} expr)
    |   ^('*' expr {print("*");} expr)
    |   ^('.' expr {print(".");} expr)
    |   ^(VEC {print("[");} expr ({print(", ");} expr)* {print("]");})
    |   INT {print($INT.text);}
    |   ID  {print($ID.text);}
    ;
```

Our test rig builds trees from vector math statements read from standard input:

walking/tree-grammar/Test.java

```java
// Create lexer/parser to build trees from stdin
VecMathLexer lex = new VecMathLexer(new ANTLRInputStream(System.in));
CommonTokenStream tokens = new CommonTokenStream(lex);
VecMathParser p = new VecMathParser(tokens);
RuleReturnScope r = p.prog(); // launch parser by calling start rule
// get tree result
CommonTree tree = (CommonTree)r.getTree();
System.out.println(tree.toStringTree()); // print out LISP style
```

The rig then walks the tree it gets back from the parser's start rule:

walking/tree-grammar/Test.java

```java
// serialize tree into node stream
CommonTreeNodeStream nodes = new CommonTreeNodeStream(tree);
Printer tp = new Printer(nodes); // create tree walker
tp.prog();                       // launch by calling start rule
```

You can build this code by running ANTLR on the appropriate grammars and compiling:

```
$ java org.antlr.Tool VecMath.g
$ java org.antlr.Tool Printer.g
$ javac *.java
$
```

The output looks like this:

```
$ java Test < t1   # t1 contains an assignment and print statement
(= x (+ 3 4)) (print (* x (VEC 2 3 4)))
x = 3+4
print x*[2, 3, 4]
$
```

The tree walker, Printer, emits the last two lines.

The source code directory for this pattern includes two AST-building parser grammars, one for creating homogeneous trees and one for creating heterogeneous trees. To support the heterogeneous tree construction, you'll also find heterogeneous AST node definitions. Tree grammar Printer works with either kind of tree.

Related Patterns

We translate tree grammars to tree walkers using Pattern 1, *Mapping Grammars to Recursive-Descent Recognizers*, on page 29 as a base. The resulting walker is a Pattern 13, *External Tree Visitor*, on page 116. The sample code in Pattern 15, *Tree Pattern Matcher* uses tree grammar rules to match subtrees.

15   Tree Pattern Matcher

Purpose

This pattern walks trees, triggering actions or tree rewrites as it encounters tree patterns of interest.

The process of matching and rewriting trees is formally called *term rewriting*.

Discussion

Using a tree pattern matcher differs from using a tree grammar in two important ways:

- We have to specify patterns only for the subtrees we care about.

- We don't need to direct the tree walk.

As we saw in Section 5.4, *Decoupling Tree Traversal from Pattern Matching*, on page 110, a tree pattern matcher is analogous to text rewriting tools such as awk, sed, and perl. We get to focus on input patterns of interest and what to do when we match those patterns. Whichever pattern matcher tool we're using deals with tree walking and when to apply the patterns. In contrast, a tree grammar needs a pattern for each subtree. The grammar rules include traversal instructions just like a hand-built visitor. Without a complete tree specification, a visitor would not discover every node.

Tree pattern matching makes a lot more sense after looking at an example. Let's take a look at a few Boolean simplification rewrite rules using two mature rewriting tools, Meta-Environment[4] (ASF+SDF) and Strat-ego/XT.[5] Both tools use a slightly different syntax than ANTLR for specifying subtrees. They use and(x,y), whereas ANTLR uses ^('and' x y). In this case, and is the root (operator); x and y are its children. Using ASF equations, we can easily specify Boolean simplification rewrites.[6]

---

4. http://www.meta-environment.org
5. http://strategoxt.org
6. http://www.meta-environment.org/Meta-Environment/Documentation

Avoiding Infinite Tree Rewriting Loops

A word of caution about tree rewriting: depending on the tree-walking strategy and the patterns we specify, we can cause infinite loops. Imagine a rule that converts x+0 to x and another rule that converts x to x+0. Repeatedly applying these two patterns would prevent termination of our program.

```
equations
 not(true) = false
 not(false) = true
 and(X, true) = X
 and(true, X) = X
```

Stratego/XT uses a similar syntax. From the documentation,[7] here is how we'd say the same thing:

```
rules
  E : Not(True)        -> False
  E : Not(False)       -> True
  E : And(True, x)    -> x
  E : And(x, True)    -> x
```

The cool thing about Stratego/XT is that it supports programmable rewriting strategies. We can explicitly tell it how to traverse the tree and the order to apply rules. For example, the appropriate strategy for simplifying Boolean subtrees is as follows:

```
strategies
  eval = bottomup(repeat(E))
```

That means it should try to match **E**'s alternatives using a bottom-up traversal over the entire tree. At each subtree, it should repeatedly apply **E** rules until nothing changes.

We can also do tree pattern matching with ANTLR using the **filter** option in a tree grammar. Here are the same Boolean simplification rules using an ANTLR tree grammar rule:

```
e : ^('!' 'true')       -> 'false'  // !true -> false
  | ^('!' 'false')      -> 'true'   // !false -> true
  | ^('&&' 'true' x=.) -> $x       // true && x -> x
  | ^('&&' x=. 'true') -> $x       // x && true -> x
  ;
```

---

7. http://buildfarm.st.ewi.tudelft.nl/releases/strategoxt/strategoxt-manual-unstable-latest/manual

This assumes that '!' and '&&' are the token types for "not" and "logical and". The dot element is a wildcard that matches any node or subtree. The rule specifies a tree pattern to tree pattern mapping. In this case, we are reducing subtrees to single nodes based upon an understanding of Boolean logic.

Like Pattern 14, *Tree Grammar*, on page 119, tree pattern matchers don't rely on the implementation language classes used to represent nodes, so they work on both Pattern 9, *Homogeneous AST*, on page 94 and Pattern 10, *Normalized Heterogeneous AST*, on page 96 trees. They do, however, require normalized children (see Pattern 10, *Normalized Heterogeneous AST*, on page 96 and Pattern 9, *Homogeneous AST*, on page 94). Node-independent tree-walking strategies must access and descend into a node's child list using a common interface. It's the shape of the tree that really matters, not the node implementation types.

The next section provides two full tree rewrite examples and discusses traversal strategy details.

Implementation

Let's get our heads wrapped around tree pattern matching with a few concrete examples (that use ANTLR). First, we'll revisit our vector math language and convert scalar-vector multiplies to vectors (by distributing the scalar-multiply across the vector elements). Second, we'll do a few expression optimizations that compilers typically do.

Don't worry if the details, such as the tree pattern syntax, are a bit much at this point in the book. Your goal is to just to get the gist; you can revisit these examples if you need to do tree rewrites in the future. We'll see plenty of tree pattern matching in future chapters such as Chapter 6, *Tracking and Identifying Program Symbols*, on page 131. There, we'll match subtrees and execute actions rather than doing rewrites (which are a little harder to absorb at first).

Rewriting and Simplifying Scalar-Vector Multiplication

Let's say we want to rewrite the tree for input 4 * [0, 5*0, 3] to be [4*0, 4*5*0, 4*3]. Then, for fun, we want to simplify multiply-by-zero operations, yielding [0, 0, 4*3]. Refer to the transformation sequence in tree form in Figure 5.2, on the following page. The original AST on the left in that figure comes to us courtesy of VecMath.g, an AST-constructing parser grammar used throughout this chapter.

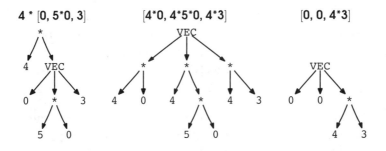

Figure 5.2: SIMPLIFICATION OF 4 * [0, 5*0, 3] VIA AST REWRITING

Tree rewrites in ANTLR consist of a tree pattern to match and a tree pattern to generate. They look like tree grammar fragment to fragment transformations. To multiply a scalar across a vector is a bit tricky, so let's break it down. Here is the tree pattern that matches a scalar multiply whose second operand is a vector subtree:

```
^('*' INT ^(VEC .+))   // '*' at root with 2nd child as vector
```

In a complete tree grammar, we'd have to specify what the vector children looked like because we have to direct the walk. Tree pattern ^(VEC .+) matches any number of child nodes or subtrees under a **VEC** root. To perform the multiply transformation, we need to track the children and include them in the new **VEC** tree (e+=. puts all children into list $e):

walking/patterns/Simplify.g

```
scalarVectorMult : ^('*' INT ^(VEC (e+=.)+)) -> ^(VEC ^('*' INT $e)+) ;
```

The tree rewrite fragment to the right of the -> creates a vector whose children are scalar multiply subtrees. Pattern ^('*' INT $e)+ is a one-or-more loop around a multiply subtree. It makes a new multiply subtree for each element held in list $e.

When we create new multiply subtrees, we sometimes create "multiply by zero" subtrees. To simplify things like 5*0 to 0, we need to replace multiply subtrees where an operand is 0 with 0. Here are the rules we need:

walking/patterns/Simplify.g

```
zeroX : ^('*' a=INT b=INT {$a.int==0}?) -> $a ; // 0*x -> 0
xZero : ^('*' a=INT b=INT {$b.int==0}?) -> $b ; // x*0 -> 0
```

The tree patterns themselves match any integer multiply subtree. The predicates, such as {$a.int==0}?, prevent the alternatives from matching unless one of the integers has a 0 value.

The only thing left to specify is which rule to apply on the way down and which rules to apply on the way up. Rather than add special syntax, ANTLR asks you to define special rules:

walking/patterns/Simplify.g

```
topdown : scalarVectorMult ; // tell ANTLR when to attempt which rule
bottomup: zeroX | xZero ;
```

ANTLR does a depth first search, applying **topdown** rules upon node discovery and **bottomup** rules upon node finishing.

If we did the scalar-vector multiply bottom-up, we'd miss multiply-by-zero opportunities created by distributing the "multiply by 4" across the vector. In a bottom-up traversal, we'd visit the elements of the vector first, then the vector itself, and finally the multiplication above the vector. We would not revisit the vector elements again to reduce 4*0 to 0.

Multiply-by-zero rewrites, on the other hand, can't be done top-down. In subtree (* 4 (* 5 0)), we'd only rewrite the (* 5 0), yielding (* 4 0). Instead, we want reductions to bubble up the expression tree. Using a bottom-up traversal, (* 5 0) becomes 0, and then we rewrite the resulting (* 4 0) subtree to be 0.

To test all this, we first need to have the VecMath parser build us an initial AST from the input. Then, we need to invoke a "down up" rule application strategy on that AST. The downup() method in ANTLR's TreeRewriter class launches the tree walk. Here is a test rig:

walking/patterns/Test.java

```
System.out.println("Original tree: "+t.toStringTree());
// Traverse tree down then up, applying rewrite rules
CommonTreeNodeStream nodes = new CommonTreeNodeStream(t);
Simplify s = new Simplify(nodes);
t = (CommonTree)s.downup(t, true); // walk t, trace transforms
System.out.println("Simplified tree: "+t.toStringTree());
```

Test file t1 contains x = 4 * [0, 5*0, 3]. Running our test rig on it shows the original tree, the intermediate transformations, and the final tree:

```
$ java Test < t1 # t1 is "x = 4 * [0, 0*5, 3]"
Original tree: (= x (* 4 (VEC 0 (* 0 5) 3)))
(* 4 (VEC 0 (* 0 5) 3)) -> (VEC (* 4 0) (* 4 (* 0 5)) (* 4 3))
(* 4 0) -> 0
(* 0 5) -> 0
(* 4 0) -> 0
Simplified tree: (= x (VEC 0 0 (* 4 3)))
$
```

In this example, we needed to apply only one rule for a given subtree. Sometimes, though, we need to repeatedly apply rules to a single subtree until nothing changes. In the next example, we'll look at gradually morphing expression subtrees to get simpler operations.

Applying Optimizations Repeatedly to a Single Subtree

Compiler optimizers try to reduce operations to simpler equivalents in an effort to generate faster code. For example, a compiler might reduce 3+3 to the equivalent 3<<1, which is a fast "shift left by one bit" (multiply by 2). That's a pretty big jump, though, so it might try to convert 3+3 to 2*3 first. Then, it could rewrite the multiply to be a left shift. We can also combine contiguous shifts such as x<<1<<2 into x<<3.

To get the ball rolling, let's provide a rewrite for the addition of identical operands:

walking/patterns/Reduce.g

```
// x+x -> 2*x  (notation INT["2"] creates an INT node with text "2")
xPlusx: ^('+' i=INT j=INT {$i.int==$j.int}?) -> ^(MULT["*"] INT["2"] $j);
```

The {$i.int==$j.int}? predicate ensures that the pattern matches only when the operands are the same.

To replace "multiply by 2" subtrees, we match an integer multiply subtree and use a predicate to verify that the integer operand is 2:

walking/patterns/Reduce.g

```
// 2*x to be x<<1
multBy2
    :   ^('*' x=INT {$x.int==2}? y=.) -> ^(SHIFT["<<"] $y INT["1"])
    |   ^('*' a=. b=INT {$b.int==2}?) -> ^(SHIFT["<<"] $a INT["1"])
    ;
```

Finally, we need to combine adjacent shift operators. The following rule matches a shift subtree whose left child is also a shift subtree. The right operands of the shift operators must be integers in order for us to combine them.

walking/patterns/Reduce.g

```
combineShifts // x<<n<<m to be x<<(n+m)
    :   ^(SHIFT ^(SHIFT e=. n=INT) m=INT)
        -> ^(SHIFT["<<"] $e INT[String.valueOf($n.int+$m.int)])
        ;
```

To specify that ANTLR should apply these rules bottom-up, we list them as alternatives in the **bottomup** rule (there is nothing to do on the way down).

```
bottomup // match these rules bottom-up
    :   xPlusx
    |   multBy2
    |   combineShifts
    ;
```

By default, ANTLR's "down then up" strategy repeatedly applies bottom-up rules until nothing changes. If, for example, we applied the **bottomup** rules only once, we'd leave 3+3 as 2*3 rather than 3<<1.

Let's see our transformations in action using test rig Test2. It differs from Test only in that calls downup() on the tree pattern matcher Reduce.g, not Simplify.g:

```
System.out.println("Original tree: "+t.toStringTree());
CommonTreeNodeStream nodes = new CommonTreeNodeStream(t);
Reduce red = new Reduce(nodes);
t = (CommonTree)red.downup(t, true); // walk t, trace transforms
System.out.println("Simplified tree: "+t.toStringTree());
```

Test file u1 contains x = 2*(3+3). Running Test2 on it shows the original tree, the intermediate reductions, and the final tree (with manually added comments):

```
$ java Test2 < u1 # u1 is "x = 2*(3+3)"
Original tree: (= x (* 2 (+ 3 3)))        # x = 2*(3+3)
(+ 3 3) -> (* 2 3)
(* 2 3) -> (<< 3 1)
(* 2 (<< 3 1)) -> (<< (<< 3 1) 1)
(<< (<< 3 1) 1) -> (<< 3 2)
Simplified tree: (= x (<< 3 2))           # reduced to x = 3 << 2
$
```

If you're curious to learn more about how ANTLR implements tree pattern matching on top of tree grammars, please see TreeParser subclasses TreeFilter and TreeRewriter in package org.antlr.runtime.tree.

Related Patterns

This pattern uses tree grammar fragments (Pattern 14, *Tree Grammar*, on page 119) to match subtrees. Chapter 6, *Tracking and Identifying Program Symbols*, on page 131 and Chapter 8, *Enforcing Static Typing Rules*, on page 181 use tree pattern matchers extensively.

Up Next

In the next chapter, we're going to start analyzing sentences by walking trees using these patterns.

Tracking and Identifying Program Symbols

The previous chapters gave us three critical language implementation skills. We can now write parsers for input sentences, we can make parsers build abstract syntax trees, and we can build tree walkers that visit or rewrite those trees. That means we're almost ready to tackle *semantic analysis*. Semantic analysis is just a fancy way to say we're "sniffing a program to see whether it makes sense." The term *semantics* is synonymous with "meaning."

We'll explore semantic analysis in Chapter 8, *Enforcing Static Typing Rules*, on page 181, but we need to build some infrastructure before we get there. To enforce language semantics, we need to track symbol definitions and be able to identify those symbols later. (A symbol is just a name for a program entity like a variable or method.) It's like keeping track of characters in a novel. Novels introduce characters and then refer to them later. To understand the story, we've got to remember each character and something about their attributes. Killing off a character means there should be no further references to it. Similarly, computer language sentences can define and reference symbols in code blocks. At the end of the code block, the symbols go out of scope.

Language applications track symbols in an abstract data structure called a *symbol table*.

In this chapter, we will define and implement two basic symbol table patterns:

- Pattern 16, *Symbol Table for Monolithic Scope*, on page 141. All symbols exist within a single scope (set of symbols). Simple property files and early BASIC are the best examples.

- Pattern 17, *Symbol Table for Nested Scopes*, on page 146. There are multiple scopes and scopes can nest inside other scopes. C is a typical language that has nested scopes. Scopes start and end at the start and end of language structures such as functions.

Each pattern includes sample code that shows how to populate and query the symbol table. To get the most out of these patterns, we need to learn about representing program symbols, grouping symbols into scopes, and resolving symbols to their definitions.

6.1 Collecting Information About Program Entities

To build a symbol table, we need to formalize what we do implicitly when we read and write software. First, let's figure out how to represent program entities. Take a look at the following C++ code:

```
class T { ... };   // define class T
T f() { ... }      // define function f returning type T
int x;             // define variable x of type int
```

We unconsciously define three *symbols* (program entities) in our head: class T, function f, and variable x. To build a language application, we need to mimic this in software. For those definitions, we need to do something like the following:

```
Type c = new ClassSymbol("T");                    // define class
MethodSymbol m = new MethodSymbol("f", c);        // define method
Type intType = new BuiltInTypeSymbol("int");      // define int type
VariableSymbol v = new VariableSymbol("x", intType); // define var x
```

Those constructors pretty much tell us what we need to know for each symbol. But, to be explicit, each of those symbols has at least the following three key properties:

- *Name*: Symbols are usually identifiers like x, f, and T, but they can be operators too. For example, in Ruby, we can use operators like + as method names.

- *Category*: That is, what kind of thing the symbol is. Is it a class, method, variable, label, and so on. To validate method call f(), for example, we need to know that f is a method, not a variable or class.

- *Type*: To validate operation x+y, for example, we need to know the types of x and y. Dynamically typed languages like Python track type information at run-time. Statically typed languages like C++ and Java track type information at compile time. The programmer usually has to explicitly identify each symbol's type (in some languages, the compiler infers it).

We distinguish program entities via these three parameters. For example, function f that returns a string is obviously different from a variable of type integer called x. In a novel, we might have an elf character (the category) called Sri (the name) that becomes a soldier (the type).

A symbol table implements each symbol category with a separate class, holding the name and type as properties. We can factor out those shared properties into a common Symbol superclass:

```
public class Symbol {
    public String name; // All symbols at least have a name
    public Type type;   // Symbols have types
}
```

VariableSymbol is the simplest program entity category and looks like this:

```
public class VariableSymbol extends Symbol {
    public VariableSymbol(String name, Type type) { super(name, type); }
}
```

Let's turn our attention now to user-defined types like classes and **struct**s. For consistency, let's represent user-defined types like any other program symbol. We can derive BuiltInTypeSymbol and ClassSymbol from Symbol (though they don't need the type field).

To distinguish between user-defined types and other program symbols, it's a good idea to tag types with a Type interface. For example, here's the class that represents built-in types like int and float:

```
public class BuiltInTypeSymbol extends Symbol implements Type {
    public BuiltInTypeSymbol(String name) { super(name); }
}
```

There's not much to interface Type because we're using it only as a tag:

```
public interface Type { public String getName(); }
```

I like to think of interfaces as roles that classes can play. In this case, symbols implementing Type can play the role of a type. Here is a typical (partial) class hierarchy showing the categories subclassing Symbol and types implementing Type:

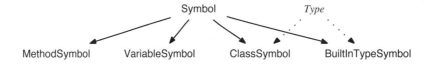

Representing symbols in our symbol table is not too bad. Things only get "interesting" when we have to track those symbols and look them up again.

6.2 Grouping Symbols into Scopes

A scope is a code region with a well-defined boundary that groups symbol definitions (in a dictionary associated with that code region). For example, class scopes group members; function scopes group parameters and local variables. Scope boundaries usually coincide with begin and end tokens such as curly braces (sort of like the "hello" and "good-bye" of a phone conversation). We call this *lexical scoping* because the extent of a scope is lexically delimited. Perhaps a better term is *static scoping* because we can track scopes just by looking at the source code; that is, without executing it. Here's a list of scope characteristics that often differ between languages:

- *Static* vs. *dynamic scoping*: Most languages have static scoping, but some (like classic LISP and PostScript) have dynamic scoping. Think of dynamic scoping as allowing methods to see the local variables of invoking methods.

- *Named scopes*: Many scopes, like classes and methods have names, but global and local scopes don't.

- *Nesting*: Languages usually allow some form of scope nesting. For example, nested code blocks enclosed in curly braces often introduce new scopes. C++ and Java allow nested classes. Languages typically limit nesting to certain combinations. Python allows function definitions within other functions, but Java does not.

- *Contents*: Some scopes allow declarations, some allow statements, and some allow both. C **struct**s only allow declarations. Python's global space allows declarations and executable code.

- *Visibility:*The symbols in a scope might or might not be visible to some other code section. The fields in a C **struct** are visible to any code section. The fields in a class have visibility modifiers such as **public** and **private** that indicate which code sections can reference them. Local variables typically aren't visible to other functions.

To represent a scope, we'll use an interface so that we can tag entities like functions and classes as scopes. For example, a function is a kind of Symbol that also plays the role of a scope. Scopes have pointers to their enclosing scopes (we'll talk about this more later) and can have names. Scopes don't need to track the code region from which we create them. Instead, the AST for the code regions point to their scopes. This makes sense because we're going to look up symbols in scopes according to what we find in the AST nodes.

For now, we only care about the first three methods in interface Scope (we'll learn about resolve() in the next section):

```
public interface Scope {
    public String getScopeName();      // do I have a name?
    public Scope getEnclosingScope();  // am I nested in another?
    public void define(Symbol sym);    // define sym in this scope
    public Symbol resolve(String name); // look up name in scope
}
```

To get the ball rolling, let's see what we can do with a single Scope object.

Monolithic Scopes

Early programming languages such as BASIC had a single global scope. Today, only simple languages like configuration files have a single scope. For example, here's a property file:

```
host=antlr.org            # define properties in single, global scope
port=80                   # a set can act as a symbol table
webmaster=parrt@antlr.org
```

Within a scope, a symbol can only represent a single entity. That means that redefining a property either overwrites the previous value or is an error. Tracking symbols for monolithic scope just means maintaining a set of Symbol objects. As we encounter definitions, we create symbols and add them to the set. Later, we'll look them up again by name. A dictionary that maps symbol names to Symbol objects works best for this. Pattern 16, *Symbol Table for Monolithic Scope,* on page 141 defines the symbol table we'd need to handle languages with a single scope.

Multiple and Nested Scopes

Having multiple scopes lets us reuse the same name in different code regions to identify different program entities. For example, variable name x in the following methods refers to two different variables:

```
void f() { int x;   printf(x); } // this x lives in f's scope
void g() { float x; printf(x); } // this x lives in g's scope
```

To avoid ambiguity, programming languages use context to figure out which symbol we're talking about. Context corresponds to the scope surrounding the symbol and any enclosing scopes. Within the context of method f(), the x argument of printf() resolves to the int local variable. In the context of g(), x resolves to the float variable. At the close of each method, the local variables go out of scope (become invisible).

Programming languages also let us nest one scope within another. Nesting a scope is like allowing someone to pop into your office and ask a question while you're already in a meeting. We return to the meeting after answering the question. To track nested scopes, we push and pop scopes onto a scope stack. As we encounter a new scope, we push it on the scope stack. The top of the stack is called the *current scope*. As we exit a scope, we pop it off the stack, revealing the previous scope as the current scope.

All symbol definitions occur within the current scope. For example, here is some C++ code commented with scope information:

```
❶   // start of global scope
    int x;        // define variable x in global scope
❷   void f() {    // define function f in global scope
      int y;      // define variable y in local scope of f
❸      { int i; } // define variable i in nested local scope
❹      { int j; } // define variable j in another nested local scope
    }
❺   void g() {    // define function g in global scope
      int i;      // define variable i in local scope of g
    }
```

The numbered icons identify the various scopes. The following diagram shows what the scope stack looks like after the definition of each new symbol. The stack grows and shrinks over time (growing upward) as we push and pop scopes.

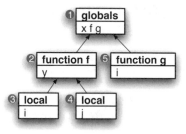

Figure 6.1: SCOPE TREE FOR GLOBAL, FUNCTION, AND LOCAL SCOPES

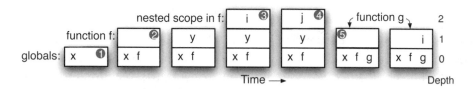

By popping a scope off the scope stack, we're effectively throwing it away. In many cases, though, we're going to need that scope later to check sentences for correctness, generate output, and so on. To keep everything around, we want a data structure called a *scope tree* (a tree of Scope's) that can function like a collection of stacks. In Figure 6.1, we see the scope tree for the previous C++ code. Every path from a node to the scope tree root represents a stack of scopes. For example, node ❹ has implicit scope stack ❹❷❶, and node ❺ has implicit scope stack ❺❶. The levels of the tree correspond to the scope nesting levels. As we move up a level in the tree, we move out a level in the program scopes. Instead of pushing a scope onto a stack, we're going to add a child to a scope tree.

The tree might look a little funny because the nodes point at their parents instead of the reverse. In practice, though, we'll look up symbols by scanning upward toward the root (see the next section).

Building a scope tree boils down to executing a sequence of these operations: push, pop, and def. All of the patterns in this chapter and the next populate symbol tables using these core abstract operations.

- push. At the start of a scope, push a new scope on the scope stack. This works even for complicated scopes like classes. Because we are building scope trees, push is more like an "add child" tree construction operation than a conventional stack push. To make things more concrete, here's an implementation preview:

```
// create new scope whose enclosing scope is the current scope
currentScope = new LocalScope(currentScope);    // push new scope
```

- pop. At the end of a scope, pop the current scope off the stack, revealing the previous scope as the current scope. pop moves the current scope pointer up one level in the tree:

```
currentScope = currentScope.getEnclosingScope(); // pop scope
```

- def. Define a symbol in the current scope. We'll always define symbols like this:

```
Symbol s = «some-new-symbol»;
currentScope.define(s); // define s in current scope
```

Let's look at the sequence of operations we'd need a parser to perform in order to build the scope tree in Figure 6.1, on the previous page. For now, don't worry about what triggers these actions (the pattern implementations go over the details). The most important thing is the order of the operations (for example, to get variables into the right scope, their defs have to appear in between the right push and pop scope operations):

1. push global scope ❶.
2. def variable x in current scope, ❶.
3. def method f in scope ❶ and push scope ❷.
4. def variable y.
5. push local scope ❸.
6. def variable i.
7. pop ❸ revealing ❷.
8. push local scope ❹.
9. def variable j.
10. pop ❹ revealing ❷.
11. pop function f scope ❷ revealing ❶.
12. def method g in scope ❶ and push scope ❺.
13. def variable i.
14. pop function g scope ❺ revealing ❶.
15. pop global scope ❶.

In the next section, we'll see how scope trees make it easy to find the symbols we've squirreled away.

6.3 Resolving Symbols

When we see a reference to symbol x in a program, our brain unconsciously looks for the closest definition. In other words, our brain tries
to *resolve* (identify) which program entity it refers to. If we've only got
one scope, resolving a symbol is easy. Either we find that symbol in
that scope's Symbol dictionary, or we don't. In code, that looks like this:

```
myOnlyScope.resolve(«symbol-name»);
```

Method resolve() does nothing more than look up *«symbol-name»* in the
scope's dictionary.

When there is more than one scope, though, resolving a symbol depends on the location of the symbol reference. In other words, the
same symbol could refer to two different program entities depending
on where the symbol appears in the source code. References in two different scopes see two different scope stacks. A reference's scope stack
is the set of scopes on the path to the root of the scope tree. We call this
stack the *semantic context*.

So, to resolve a symbol reference, we look for it in its semantic context,
starting with the current scope. If resolve() doesn't find the symbol in
the current scope, it asks the enclosing scope if it can find the symbol.
resolve() recursively walks toward the root of the scope tree until it finds
the symbol or runs out of scopes. The algorithm looks like this:

```
public Symbol resolve(String name) {
    Symbol s = members.get(name);   // look in this scope
    if ( s!=null ) return s;        // return it if in this scope
    if ( enclosingScope != null ) { // have an enclosing scope?
        return enclosingScope.resolve(name); // check enclosing scope
    }
    return null; // not found in this scope or there's no scope above
}
```

The enclosingScope variable points to the scope above in the scope tree
(it's a parent pointer). Don't let the recursion bother you. It's just the
most convenient way to express the algorithm. The recursion in resolve()
is essentially equivalent to a loop walking up the enclosingScope chain.

Here's the best part about this algorithm and scope tree combination.
No matter how complicated our scope tree gets, we can always resolve
symbols with the same bit of code:

```
currentScope.resolve(«symbol-name»);
```

The enclosingScope pointer tells resolve() exactly where to look next. Rather than making a clever algorithm that implements all of the look-up rules, we assemble a handy data structure that encodes them.

Let's see how method resolve() gracefully handles two important features of nested scopes: we can see symbols in outer scopes, and we can redefine symbols found in outer scopes. There is a little bit of variability between languages, but let's see how resolve() works on some C++ code:

```
❶   // start of global scope
    int x;          // define variable x in global scope
    int y;          // define variable y in global space
❷   void f() {      // define function f in global scope
      float x;      // redefine x as local variable, hiding outer x
      printf("%f", x); // x resolves to f's local
      printf("%d", y); // y resolves to global
❸     {int z;}      // local scope nested within f's local scope
      printf("%d", z); // z is no longer visible; static analysis ERROR!
    }
```

There are three variable references in f, all in printf calls. The semantic context for the x, y, and z references in f is ❷❶. That means we should look up all symbol references starting in scope ❷. To resolve x, resolve() immediately finds it in ❷. resolve() doesn't find y in the current scope but does find it in enclosing scope ❶. We can't resolve z in the printf, though, because z is defined in ❸. That scope is not in the z reference's semantic context. resolve() returns null in this case, signaling an error.

As you can see, the structure of the scope tree reduces the complexity of symbol resolution to a simple walk up a tree (even when we tackle class inheritance in Chapter 7, *Managing Symbol Tables for Data Aggregates*, on page 155). Throughout the patterns that follow, we'll refer to this abstract reference resolution operation as ref. In total, that gives us four key abstract operations: push, pop, and def to construct scope trees and ref to resolve references in the scope tree. Armed with these operations and a good handle on symbol table management, we're ready to tackle our first two symbol table patterns. Here's a summary of when to apply the patterns:

Pattern	When to Apply
Pattern 16, *Symbol Table for Monolithic Scope*, on the next page	This pattern applies to any language that defines symbols all in one scope.
Pattern 17, *Symbol Table for Nested Scopes*, on page 146	If your language allows multiple scopes or even nested scopes, you'll need this pattern.

As we progress through the symbol table and semantic analysis patterns defined in the next few chapters, we should work with a common language for continuity purposes. Let's use a subset of C++ and call it "Cymbol."[1] We'll start with just variable definition syntax and trivial expressions. Then, we'll add functions, **struct**s, and finally classes. To keep things simple, we'll avoid pointers until absolutely necessary and we'll disregard executable statements (they're not involved in symbol definition).

16 Symbol Table for Monolithic Scope

☐

Purpose

This pattern builds a symbol table for a language with a single, flat scope.

This pattern is suitable for simple programming languages (without functions), configuration files, small graphics languages, and other small DSLs.

Discussion

The primary goal when building a symbol table is to construct a scope tree. In this case, the scope tree is pretty boring since it's a single node (the global scope). The following table indicates how to build the single scope by responding to input constructs. We technically don't need to push and pop scopes for this simple case, but we'll do so for consistency with the other patterns.

Upon	Action(s)
Start of file	push a GlobalScope. def BuiltInType objects for any built-in types such as int and float.
Declaration x	ref x's type (if any). def x in the current scope.
Reference x	ref x starting in the current scope.
End of file	pop the GlobalScope.

---

1. Not to be confused with the Cymbal language (registered trademark) in the AT&T Daytona project; http://www.research.att.com/~daytona/

Let's apply those actions to the following Cymbol declarations:

symtab/monolithic/t.cymbol

```
int i = 9;
float j;
int k = i+2;
```

We'd execute the following sequence: push global scope, def int, def float, ref int, def i, ref float, def j, ref int, def k, ref i, pop global scope. The built-in type definitions are part of symbol table initialization; the parser doesn't trigger those actions because of an input statement. In simple terms, we're creating the global scope and then defining three variables: i, j, and k. To define a variable, we have to look up its type. We also have to look up variables referenced in initialization expressions.

To populate our symbol table, we need objects to represent variables and built-in types. We'll tag type symbols with interface Type and then make our symbol table object play the role of a scope using interface Scope. The class inheritance and interface implementation hierarchy looks like this:

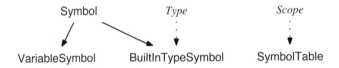

The next section provides a complete Cymbol parser and implementations for these symbol table objects.

Implementation

Because expressions in this version of Cymbol cannot reference variables defined later in the file, we can define and properly reference all symbols in a single pass. We only need a parser and a few actions to demonstrate symbol table management.

For the Cymbol program shown earlier, we need to generate output that convinces us we've properly managed symbols. So, let's try to generate the following (which does not show the def operations for built-in types):

```
$ java Test < t.cymbol
line 1: ref int
line 1: def i
line 2: ref float
line 2: def j
line 3: ref int
line 3: ref to <i:int>   // <i:int> means i has type int
```

```
line 3: def k
globals: {int=int, j=<j:float>, k=<k:int>, float=float, i=<i:int>}
$
```

As we encounter variable definitions, we'll add them to the symbol table and print a message. As we find variable and type references, we'll resolve them and also print a message. Right before terminating, we'll print out the symbols in the symbol table's only scope.

To get started, let's define symbols and then move on to tracking those symbols. Our generic Symbol object has a name and type properties:

```java
public class Symbol { // A generic programming language symbol
    String name;        // All symbols at least have a name
    Type type;
    public Symbol(String name) { this.name = name; }
    public Symbol(String name, Type type) {this(name); this.type = type;}
    public String getName() { return name; }
    public String toString() {
        if ( type!=null ) return '<'+getName()+":"+type+'>';
        return getName();
    }
}
```

This version of Cymbol only has two kinds of symbols: variables and built-in types:

```java
/** Represents a variable definition (name,type) in symbol table */
public class VariableSymbol extends Symbol {
    public VariableSymbol(String name, Type type) { super(name, type); }
}
```

```java
/** A symbol for built in types such int, float primitive types */
public class BuiltInTypeSymbol extends Symbol implements Type {
    public BuiltInTypeSymbol(String name) { super(name); }
}
```

Now we need a dictionary to hold those symbols (it's a single-node tree or a scope stack of depth one). Let's put it in a SymbolTable object. Because it holds the sole dictionary (field symbols), we might as well make SymbolTable itself represent the Scope.

`symtab/monolithic/SymbolTable.java`

```java
import java.util.*;
public class SymbolTable implements Scope { // single-scope symtab
    Map<String, Symbol> symbols = new HashMap<String, Symbol>();
    public SymbolTable() { initTypeSystem(); }
    protected void initTypeSystem() {
        define(new BuiltInTypeSymbol("int"));
        define(new BuiltInTypeSymbol("float"));
    }
    // Satisfy Scope interface
    public String getScopeName() { return "global"; }
    public Scope getEnclosingScope() { return null; }
    public void define(Symbol sym) { symbols.put(sym.name, sym); }
    public Symbol resolve(String name) { return symbols.get(name); }

    public String toString() { return getScopeName()+":"+symbols; }
}
```

At this point, we've got symbols and a symbol table. Let's give them a workout by creating a parser for Cymbol. Cymbol.g defines the Cymbol language, and we're going to insert actions that create symbols, sticks them in the symbol table, and then resolves them.

The details of the grammar aren't important. The take-away is that rules recognizing definitions create Symbol objects and call define(). Rules referencing identifiers invoke resolve() to look them up. Keep in mind that actions execute according to location in the grammar. For example, actions at the end of an alternative execute after the parser matches that construct. Actions use terms like $ID to access the token matched by an **ID** token.

First, we need to add a parameter to the start symbol, **compilationUnit**, so that we can pass in a symbol table:

`symtab/monolithic/Cymbol.g`

```
grammar Cymbol; // my grammar is called Cymbol
// define a SymbolTable field in generated parser
@members {SymbolTable symtab;}
compilationUnit[SymbolTable symtab] // pass symbol table to start rule
@init {this.symtab = symtab;}       // set the parser's field
    :   varDeclaration+ // recognize at least one variable declaration
    ;
```

SymbolTable defines two built-in types that we can look up during variable definitions. Rule **type** looks up the type name and returns it as a Type symbol.

```
type returns [Type tsym]
@after { // $start is the first tree node matched by this rule
    System.out.println("line "+$start.getLine()+": ref "+$tsym.getName());
}
    :   'float' {$tsym = (Type)symtab.resolve("float");}
    |   'int'   {$tsym = (Type)symtab.resolve("int");}
    ;
```

Then, rule **varDeclaration** can create a VariableSymbol with that Type:

```
varDeclaration
    :   type ID ('=' expression)? ';' // E.g., "int i = 2;", "int i;"
        {
        System.out.println("line "+$ID.getLine()+": def "+$ID.text);
        VariableSymbol vs = new VariableSymbol($ID.text,$type.tsym);
        symtab.define(vs);
        }
    ;
```

Expression $type.tsym evaluates to the return value from invoking rule **type**.

And, finally, we have to resolve symbol references. The only place in the grammar where we reference variables is in declaration initialization expressions:

```
primary
    :   ID // reference variable in an expression
        {System.out.println("line "+$ID.getLine()+": ref to "+
         symtab.resolve($ID.text));}
    |   INT
    |   '(' expression ')'
    ;
```

To exercise the symbol table management in our Cymbol grammar, we can use the following test rig:

```
CharStream input = null; // read from filename or stdin
if ( args.length>0 ) input = new ANTLRFileStream(args[0]);
else input = new ANTLRInputStream(System.in);
CymbolLexer lex = new CymbolLexer(input);  // create lexer
CommonTokenStream tokens = new CommonTokenStream(lex);
CymbolParser p = new CymbolParser(tokens); // create parser
SymbolTable symtab = new SymbolTable();    // create symbol table
p.compilationUnit(symtab);                 // launch parser
System.out.println("globals: "+symtab.symbols);
```

Here's how to build the rig, run ANTLR on the Cymbol.g grammar, compile, and run sample input t.cymbol into Test:

```
$ java org.antlr.Tool Cymbol.g
$ javac *.java
$ java Test < t.cymbol
line 1: ref int
...
```

This pattern is a bare-bones symbol table manager. Although it's sufficient for simple DSLs, it mostly serves as a good learning tool for building more realistic symbol tables.

Related Patterns

The next pattern, Pattern 17, *Symbol Table for Nested Scopes*, adds functions and nested scopes to our Cymbol C++ subset.

☐ **17 Symbol Table for Nested Scopes**

Purpose

This pattern tracks symbols and builds a scope tree for languages with multiple, possibly nested scopes.

Programming language functions are a good example of nested scopes. Each function has its own scope that is nested within a global or class scope. Some languages even support nested function definitions or multiple local scopes. Many DSLs have nested scopes as well. The DOT[2] graphics language, for example, has subgraphs within graphs. This pattern handles them all gracefully.

Discussion

To discuss nested scopes, let's add functions to our Cymbol C++ subset. That means we'll need a function (method) Symbol and scopes for globals, parameters, and local variables. Let's take a look at some sample input and identify the various scopes using numbered icons.

---

2. http://www.graphviz.org

```
symtab/nested/t.cymbol
❶  // start of global scope
   int i = 9;
❷  float f(int x, float y)
❸  {
       float i;
❹     { float z = x+y; i = z; }
❺     { float z = i+1; i = z; }
       return i;
   }
❻  void g()
❼  {
       f(i,2);
   }
```

We'll need two more Symbol subclasses to handle functions and local scopes. The following class inheritance and interface implementation hierarchy identifies all the symbol table objects:

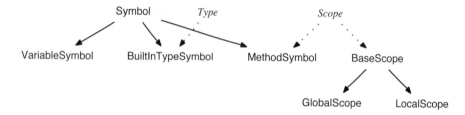

MethodSymbol is both a symbol and a scope. Methods have two scopes actually: one for the parameters (the MethodSymbol itself) and one for its local variables (a LocalScope whose parent is the MethodSymbol).

Now that we know the class names of our symbol table objects, we can make more explicit scope trees than we could before. Previous scope trees (such as Figure 6.1, on page 137) only really showed tree structure. We can see the scope tree for t.cymbol, mentioned earlier, in Figure 6.2, on the next page; it identifies some key object properties. The goal of this pattern is to construct such scope trees.

In Figure 6.3, on the following page, we can see the rules laid out for building a scope tree from nested scopes and resolving symbols in the correct semantic context. The sequence of actions for t.cymbol starts like this: push global scope, def int, def float, ref int, def i, ref float, def f, push f, ref int, def x, ref float, def y, push local scope of f, ref float, def i, and so on.

Notice that we're not making a distinction between global variables, parameters, and local variables in terms of symbol table logic; they are

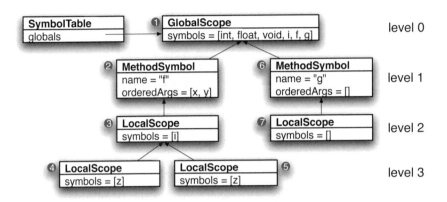

Figure 6.2: SCOPE TREE FOR GLOBAL VARIABLE AND TWO FUNCTIONS

Upon	Action(s)
Start of file	push a GlobalScope. def BuiltInType objects for int, float, void.
Variable declaration x	ref x's type. def x in the current scope.
Method declaration f	ref f's return type. def f in the current scope and push it as the current scope.
{	push a LocalScope as the new current scope.
}	pop, revealing previous scope as current scope.
End of method	pop the MethodSymbol scope (the parameters).
Reference x	ref x starting in the current scope. If not found, look in the immediately enclosing scope (if any).
End of file	pop the GlobalScope.

Figure 6.3: RULES FOR BUILDING A SCOPE TREE FOR NESTED SCOPES AND POPULATING IT WITH SYMBOLS

all VariableSymbol objects. The only difference between them is the scope in which we define them. For example, we define the parameters for f by executing def operations after pushing f's method scope and before pushing its local scope.

Now that we've got the big picture, let's see how to use these rules in practice to manage a symbol table for nested scopes.

Implementation

For our particular implementation, we're going to trigger scope tree construction actions while walking an AST created from the input source code. We could trigger actions directly in the parser as we did in Pattern 16, *Symbol Table for Monolithic Scope*, on page 141, but working on an AST is more flexible. In Pattern 19, *Symbol Table for Classes*, on page 167, we'll need to make multiple passes over the input so we might as well get used to them now.

Starting from the sample implementation source code in the previous pattern, we need to do the following to add functions and nested scopes:

1. *Augment syntax to support functions.* We need to augment grammar Cymbol.g to support function definitions, function calls, return statements, and nested code blocks.

2. *Build an AST.* We will use AST construction rules in the parser grammar.

3. *Define new symbol table objects.* To support scopes, we'll need an abstract BaseScope and two concrete implementations: GlobalScope and LocalScope. BaseScope implements interface Scope. Finally, we'll need MethodSymbol that plays double duty as a Symbol and a Scope (for parameters).

4. *Walk the AST to populate the symbol table and resolve variable and method references.* Using tree pattern matching rules, we'll trigger actions according to Figure 6.3, on the preceding page.

In this pattern and Pattern 18, *Symbol Table for Data Aggregates*, on page 161, we'll combine symbol definition and resolution into a single tree walk. In Pattern 19, *Symbol Table for Classes*, on page 167, we'll separate them into two tree-walking phases to support forward references. (Methods can call methods defined later in the class.)

Before getting into all the gory details, let's assume for the moment that we've got everything set up to build ASTs from source code. Because

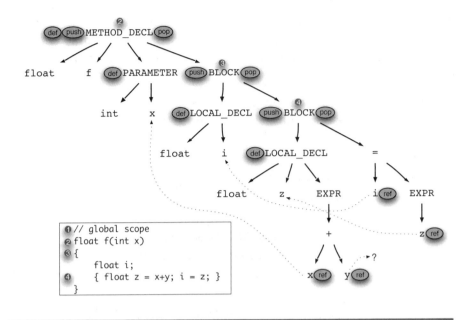

Figure 6.4: AST FOR FUNCTION WITH NESTED SCOPES

all the magic happens with the AST, let's look at the AST of a simple function and annotate it with action execution and scope icons. In Figure 6.4, we can see where and when in the AST we need to execute push, pop, def, and ref actions. (Actually, we're ignoring built-in type lookups to reduce clutter.) Those actions appearing on the left of an AST node trigger as we discover nodes (on the way down) and those appearing on the right trigger as we finish nodes (on the way up). The dotted lines point from variable reference sites to declaration sites in the AST (note that the y reference has no corresponding definition).

To create a scope tree then, all we have to do is a depth-first walk of the AST, executing actions in the pre- and/or postorder position. We push as we descend and pop as we ascend. When we see a symbol, we define or resolve it in the current scope.

On to our implementation—the following sections summarize the software in the source code directory for this pattern.

Adding Function Syntax and Building ASTs

To add functions to Cymbol, we'll add rules **methodDeclaration** and **formalParameters** to Cymbol.g. Beyond the syntax, we have to add AST construction rules. For example, here is the previous **varDeclaration** rule augmented with an AST construction rule:

symtab/nested/Cymbol.g

```
varDeclaration
    :   type ID ('=' expression)? ';' -> ^(VAR_DECL type ID expression?)
    ;
```

The rule now yields **VAR_DECL**-rooted subtrees with a type, an identifier, and an optional initialization expression as children. Method declarations yield **METHOD_DECL**-rooted subtrees:

symtab/nested/Cymbol.g

```
methodDeclaration
    :   type ID '(' formalParameters? ')' block
        -> ^(METHOD_DECL type ID formalParameters? block)
    ;
```

Parsing and AST construction are not the primary focus here, so let's move on to building the scope tree.

Building the Scope Tree

The rules we defined earlier for building scope trees (in Figure 6.3, on page 148) are of the form "upon an input construct *foo*, execute action *bar*." The most direct implementation is a set of tree pattern-action pairs. For example, at the starting { of a code block, we need to push a new scope. At the ending } of a block, we need to pop that same scope off. The phrases "at the start" and "at the end" are synonymous with "on the way down" and "on the way up" the AST. Here are the tree pattern matching rules that handle pushing and popping local scopes:

symtab/nested/DefRef.g

```
enterBlock
    :   BLOCK {currentScope = new LocalScope(currentScope);}// push scope
    ;
exitBlock
    :   BLOCK
        {
        System.out.println("locals: "+currentScope);
        currentScope = currentScope.getEnclosingScope();    // pop scope
        }
    ;
```

The rules match the same **BLOCK** node but do different actions (push vs. pop) depending on whether we are discovering or finishing that node. We control which rules to execute on the way down vs. on the way up by listing them in the special **topdown** or **bottomup** rules:

```
topdown : enterBlock | enterMethod | ... ;
bottomup : exitBlock | exitMethod | ... ;
```

To manage method scopes, we create a method symbol and push it on the way down. On the way back up, we don't need to look inside the method subtree, so we match just the **METHOD_DECL** root. Here are the rules that deal with method definition subtrees:

`symtab/nested/DefRef.g`

```
enterMethod // match method subtree with 0-or-more args
    :   ^(METHOD_DECL type ID .*)
        {
        System.out.println("line "+$ID.getLine()+": def method "+
                    $ID.text);
        Type retType = $type.tsym; // rule type returns a Type symbol
        MethodSymbol ms = new MethodSymbol($ID.text,retType,
                                    currentScope);
        currentScope.define(ms); // def method in globals
        currentScope = ms;       // set current scope to method scope
        }
    ;
exitMethod
    :   METHOD_DECL
        {
        System.out.println("args: "+currentScope);
        currentScope = currentScope.getEnclosingScope();// pop arg scope
        }
    ;
```

You might be wondering where we create the local scopes for methods. Rule **enterBlock** creates them automatically for us since method ASTs contain **BLOCK** subtrees (see Figure 6.4, on page 150).

Populating the Symbol Table

Now that we've got the proper scope tree structure, we just have to fill the scopes with symbols as we walk the AST. Fortunately, all definitions do the same thing: create the appropriate Symbol and then call Scope.define().

Here is the rule to define any kind of variable:

```
symtab/nested/DefRef.g
```

```
varDeclaration // global, parameter, or local variable
    :   ^((ARG_DECL|VAR_DECL) type ID .?)
        {
        System.out.println("line "+$ID.getLine()+": def "+$ID.text);
        VariableSymbol vs = new VariableSymbol($ID.text,$type.tsym);
        currentScope.define(vs);
        }
    ;
```

Field currentScope is always set to the current scope. Our tree pattern matcher always defines symbols within the current scope.

Let's do the opposite now and find those definitions in the scope tree.

Resolving Variable and Method References

In Chapter 8, *Enforcing Static Typing Rules*, on page 181, we'll be looking up symbols all the time to do type checking and so on. To give you a taste, here is a rule that looks up all identifiers that appear in expressions:

```
symtab/nested/DefRef.g
```

```
idref
    :   {$start.hasAncestor(EXPR)}? ID
        {
        Symbol s = currentScope.resolve($ID.text);
        System.out.println("line "+$ID.getLine()+": ref "+s);
        }
    ;
```

The hasAncestor() predicate permits rule **idref** to match an **ID** only when it sits somewhere under an **EXPR** node.

Let's give it the old smoke test. The test rig in the source code directory builds an AST from the source code and then walks the AST using ANTLR's built-in downup() strategy:

```
symtab/nested/Test.java
```

```
CommonTree t = (CommonTree)r.getTree(); // get tree result from parser
CommonTreeNodeStream nodes = new CommonTreeNodeStream(t);
nodes.setTokenStream(tokens);
SymbolTable symtab = new SymbolTable(); // make global scope, types
DefRef def = new DefRef(nodes, symtab); // use custom constructor
def.downup(t); // trigger symtab actions upon certain subtrees
System.out.println("globals: "+symtab.globals);
```

To build all this, run ANTLR on the grammars and compile:

```
$ java org.antlr.Tool Cymbol.g DefRef.g
$ javac *.java
$
```

Here is what the output looks like when we run the test rig against the Cymbol source code in Figure 6.4, on page 150:

```
$ java Test < t2.cymbol
line 2: def method f
line 2: def x
line 4: def i
line 5: def z
line 5: ref <x:int>
line 5: ref null                    // y is not defined, resolves to null
line 5: ref <z:float>
line 5: assign to <i:float>
locals: [z]
locals: [i]
args: method<f:float>:[<x:int>]
globals: [int, float, void, f]
$
```

Related Patterns

This pattern serves as the foundation for Pattern 18, *Symbol Table for Data Aggregates*, on page 161 and Pattern 19, *Symbol Table for Classes*, on page 167.

Up Next

Now that you're comfortable with nested scopes, you could build most of the symbol table infrastructure to track symbols for C. The only involved concept we haven't covered is the **struct** data aggregate. We'll remedy that in the next chapter.

Chapter 7

Managing Symbol Tables
for Data Aggregates

In the previous chapter, we learned the basics about symbol table management. We looked at defining symbols, grouping them into scopes, and organizing those scopes into scope trees. Scope trees are crucial because their structure encodes the rules for looking up symbols. Resolving a symbol means looking for it in the current scope or any scope on the path to the root of the scope tree.

In this chapter, we're going to learn about another kind of scope called a *data aggregate scope*. Like any other scope, it contains symbols and has a place within the scope tree. The difference is that code outside of a data aggregate scope can access the members inside using an expression such as user.name. We're going to cover data aggregate scopes for both non-object-oriented and object-oriented languages:

- Pattern 18, *Symbol Table for Data Aggregates*, on page 161. This pattern tells us how to define and access the fields of simple data aggregates such as C **struct**s.
- Pattern 19, *Symbol Table for Classes*, on page 167. This pattern tells us how to deal with data aggregates that have superclasses and that allow function definitions as well as fields.

structs and classes are pretty similar in that both are simultaneously Symbols, user-defined types, and scopes. The biggest difference is that class scopes have a superclass scope as well as the usual enclosing scope. To resolve symbols, we'll need to modify our algorithm slightly to chase the proper parent pointer in the scope tree. We also need to make an extra pass over the AST to deal with forward references.

The reason we're studying symbol tables so extensively is that they are the bedrock of most language applications. Almost every nontrivial language application needs to resolve symbols to unique program entities. Even a simple report generator that prints out call sites to a particular method can't do so without a proper symbol table. More complicated applications such as interpreters and translators need to check a program's validity, which involves comparing variable and method types (as we'll see in the next chapter). After this chapter, you'll have all the tools you need to build a symbol table for everything from simple data formats to programming languages.

Before jumping into the patterns, though, let's walk through some examples and discuss how class inheritance complicates our lives. As in the previous chapter, we'll use a subset of C++. Even though we're fixated on one specific language, the patterns apply to most programming languages in common use.

7.1 Building Scope Trees for Structs

struct scopes behave just like local scopes from a scope tree construction point of view. They are just another node in the scope tree. That means we'll have StructSymbol nodes as well as LocalScope, MethodSymbol, and GlobalScope nodes. The scope tree for the following sample program appears in Figure 7.1, on the next page:

```
symtab/aggr/t.cymbol
```

```
❶  // start of global scope
❷  struct A {
     int x;
❸    struct B { int y; };
     B b;
❹    struct C { int z; };
     C c;
   };
   A a;

❺  void f()
❻  {
❼    struct D {
       int i;
     };
     D d;
     d.i = a.b.y;
   }
```

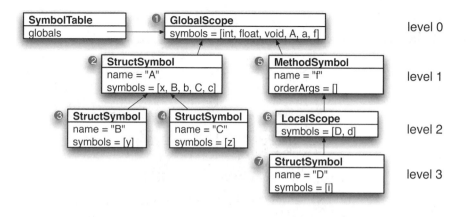

Figure 7.1: SCOPE TREE FOR NESTED DATA AGGREGATES

As before, the numbered icons identify scopes in the code with the associated node in the scope tree. As you can see, the scope tree looks like any other tree we've seen so far. StructSymbol nodes have symbol dictionaries and enclosing scope (parent) pointers.

From within a **struct** scope, we resolve symbols by scanning upward in the scope tree like any other nested scope. Because **struct**s have no embedded executable expressions, the only symbols we can look up are type names. For example, the first field of A references type int. We look for int starting in scope ❷. Scope A does not have it so we look to the enclosing scope, global scope ❶. We do the same thing for the second field, B b;. Since we define type B right before that field declaration, we find B in scope A right away.

We also have to resolve symbols within **struct** scopes from the outside. In other words, a language application might have to figure out which field «*expr*».x refers to. In the previous code, that would mean resolving expressions d.i and a.b.y in f. The general (recursive) rule for resolving «*expr*».x is to determine the type of «*expr*» and then look up x in that scope. Looking toward the root from function f's local scope ❻, the scope stack is ❻❺❶. To resolve d.i, we look up d in that semantic context and find that d has type scope D. D is also the scope in which we resolve i. Similarly, for a.b.y, we look up a and find its type to be A. Looking up b in A yields another scope: B. Finally, we look up field y in B.

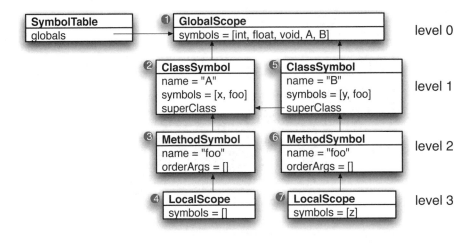

Figure 7.2: SCOPE TREE FOR CLASSES A AND B

There's only one complication with the member access operator. We need to restrict member resolution so it only looks in a specific (**struct**) scope. Member access expressions are like scope overrides. They say exactly in which scope to look for a field. Say we tried to resolve d.a from within function f. D has no a field, but we shouldn't look into D's enclosing scope. Instead, we should report "no such field." If we let it continue looking into D's enclosing scope (f), d.a would eventually resolve to global variable a. That's clearly not right. So, as you'll see in Pattern 18, *Symbol Table for Data Aggregates*, on page 161, we need two different resolve methods: one for looking up isolated symbols like d and another for resolving member access expressions like d.i.

7.2 Building Scope Trees for Classes

Classes are like **struct**s that they can inherit members from another class (the superclass). That means classes have two parent scopes: the usual enclosing scope (physical location) and a superclass scope. To resolve symbols, sometimes we'll chase the enclosing scope pointer, and sometimes we'll chase the superclass pointer. Let's get started by looking at the scope tree for the following Cymbol code (see Figure 7.2).

```
symtab/class/AB.symbol
```

```
❶  // start of global scope
❷  class A {
   public:
    int x;
❸   void foo()
❹   { ; }
   };
❺  class B : public A {
    int y;
❻   void foo()
❼   {
       int z = x + y;
    }
   };
```

The enclosing scope pointers point upward (as in Pattern 18, *Symbol Table for Data Aggregates*, on page 161), but the superclass pointers point horizontally. They point horizontally because all (non-nested) classes live at the same scope level. Because there are two pointers emanating from each ClassSymbol node, classes actually conjure up multiple scope stacks instead of just one. For example, the local scope of method foo in class B could use scope stack ❼❻❺❷❶ or stack ❼❻❺❶.

The language definition dictates which stack to use. Per the usual object-oriented language conventions, we'll use the first stack. That choice means we want to look up the inheritance chain before looking in the global scope. In Pattern 19, *Symbol Table for Classes*, on page 167, we'll introduce method getParentScope() to Scope that returns the appropriate scope (enclosing or superclass). Method resolve() will call getParentScope() to figure out where to look next.

Resolving Member Access Expressions

As with **struct**s, we also have to resolve member access expressions differently than isolated symbol lookups. If we don't find an isolated symbol in the surrounding class or its superclass(es), we look it up in the global scope. When referring to members from outside that class, though, we shouldn't see global variables. For example, a.g referenced in main() in the following should be illegal because g is a global variable:

```
int g;               // global variable g
class A {
public:
 int x;
 void foo() { g = 1; } // can see global g
};
```

```
int main() {
  A a;
  a.x = 3; // no problem; x is the field of A
  a.g = 3; // ERROR! Should not see global variable g
```

So, unadorned g in method foo of class A resolves OK, but a.g makes no sense. To treat these two situations differently, we need to add a resolveMember() method to ClassSymbol. Isolated symbol references use resolve() as before, but a.g must use resolveMember() to look up g in A.

Dealing with Forward References

Classes also allow *forward references*. A forward reference is a reference to a method, type, or variable defined later in the input file. For example, in the next code fragment, method foo references field x that is defined after the method.

symtab/class/forward.cymbol

```
class A {
  void foo() { x = 3; } // forward reference to field x
  int x;
};
```

To handle these forward references, we could try to scan ahead looking for future definitions, but there's an easier way. We can make two passes over the input, one to define symbols and another to resolve them. So, a definition pass would define A, foo, and x. Then a reference pass would scan the input again, finding x in A's member dictionary (scope) without trouble. We'll use a two-pass approach (over an AST) in Pattern 19, *Symbol Table for Classes*, on page 167.

Unfortunately, the two pass approach introduces a problem. We don't want to allow forward references outside of classes (at least according to Cymbol's semantics since it's a C++ subset). In the following code, we don't want the x and y references in method main to see the definitions that appear after the assignment statement.

symtab/class/global-forward.cymbol

```
❶ // globals
❷ int main()
❸ {
    x = y; // shouldn't see global x or local y; ERROR!
    int y;
  }
  int x;
```

To recognize illegal forward references, we can use a trick involving token indexes. If a symbol reference resolves to a local or global symbol, the reference's token index must come after the definition's token index (assuming we're buffering up all tokens from the input string). In this case, the x and y token references in main appear *before* the x and y tokens in the variable declarations. That means we have two illegal forward references, and we should report an error. If the definition and reference tokens are in the proper order, all is well.

At this point, we've got enough of the big picture to follow the patterns in this chapter. Here's a table that summarizes when to apply them.

Pattern	When to Apply
Pattern 18, *Symbol Table for Data Aggregates*	Use this pattern if you need to support data aggregates like C **struct**s or Pascal **record**s or SQL **table**s.
Pattern 19, *Symbol Table for Classes*, on page 167	Use this pattern to build symbol tables for object-oriented languages smacking of Java or C++.

OK, let's dig in and learn about tracking symbols and building scope trees for data aggregates.

18 Symbol Table for Data Aggregates

Purpose

*This pattern tracks symbols and builds a scope tree for data aggregates such as C's **struct**s.*

Discussion

To manage **struct** scopes, we'll build a scope tree and define symbols just like we did in Pattern 17, *Symbol Table for Nested Scopes*, on page 146. The only difference lies in symbol resolution. Member access expressions like a.b can see fields inside a **struct**.

In Section 7.1, *Building Scope Trees for Structs*, on page 156, we examined the scope tree for some sample Cymbol **struct** definitions. The goal of this pattern is to describe the rules and mechanism for building that

Upon	Action(s)
Start of file	push a GlobalScope. def BuiltInType objects for int, float, void.
Variable declaration x	ref x's type. def x as a VariableSymbol object in the current scope. This works for globals, **struct** fields, parameters, and locals.
struct declaration S	def S as a StructSymbol object in the current scope and push it as the current scope.
Method declaration f	ref f's return type. def f as a MethodSymbol object in the current scope and push it as the current scope.
{	push a LocalScope as the new current scope.
}	pop, revealing the previous scope as the current scope. This works for **struct**s, methods, and local scopes.
Variable reference x	ref x starting in the current scope. If not found, look in the immediately enclosing scope if any.
Member access «*expr*».x	Compute the type of «*expr*» using the previous rule and this one recursively. Ref x only in that type's scope, not in any enclosing scopes.
End of file	pop the GlobalScope.

Figure 7.3: RULES FOR BUILDING A SCOPE TREE FOR DATA AGGREGATES, POPULATING IT WITH SYMBOLS, AND RESOLVING SYMBOLS

scope tree and filling the nodes (scopes) with symbols. To get started, we need a new kind of scope tree node called StructSymbol to represent **struct**s. Here's the complete symbol table class hierarchy for this pattern:

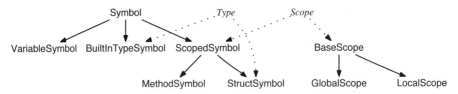

Now that we've got two scoped symbols, it's a good idea to factor out their common functionality into ScopedSymbol and derive both Struct-Symbol and MethodSymbol from it.

To build the scope tree using those objects and to resolve symbols, follow the rules in Figure 7.3, on the preceding page. The rules tell us exactly what to do at each significant input construct, but there are a number of ways to implement the actions. In the next section, we're going to build an AST using an ANTLR grammar and then walk it to define and resolve symbols. If you want, you can leave the sample implementation until you're actually in the process of implementing your own language.

Implementation

The implementation of Pattern 17, *Symbol Table for Nested Scopes*, on page 146 provides most of the implementation we need for this pattern, so we can use it as a foundation. Here is a road map to add **struct**s to our Cymbol language:

- *Add syntax and AST construction rules for struct definitions and member access expressions.* To focus on the symbol table aspects, we'll assume that this part just works. Check out Cymbol.g in the source code directory for AST construction details.

- *Define new symbol table objects.* We need to add StructSymbol. To do so, we'll refactor the class hierarchy, introducing a ScopedSymbol base class. We'll derive MethodSymbol from it as well.

- *Add pattern matching rules to define struct scopes.* As we did for local and function scopes in Pattern 17, *Symbol Table for Nested Scopes*, on page 146, we'll trigger push and pop scope operations for **struct** definitions.

- *Add pattern matching rules to resolve member access expressions.*

Let's start with the symbol table objects. The main change to the symbol table objects is the addition of StructSymbol:

`symtab/aggr/StructSymbol.java`

```
public class StructSymbol extends ScopedSymbol implements Type, Scope {
    Map<String, Symbol> fields = new LinkedHashMap<String, Symbol>();
    public StructSymbol(String name,Scope parent) {super(name, parent);}
    /** For a.b, only look in fields to resolve b, not up scope tree */
    public Symbol resolveMember(String name) { return fields.get(name); }
    public Map<String, Symbol> getMembers() { return fields; }
    public String toString() {
        return "struct "+name+":{"+
               stripBrackets(fields.keySet().toString())+"}";
    }
}
```

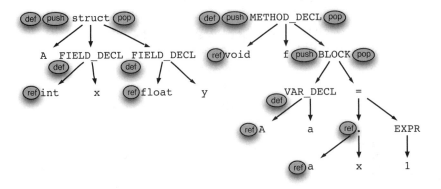

Figure 7.4: AST for struct and function definition

According to the scope tree construction rules, we create a StructSymbol for each **struct** we encounter. We're walking an AST to trigger actions, so let's look at a sample AST. The AST for the following Cymbol code appears in Figure 7.4.

symtab/aggr/t2.cymbol

```
❶   // start of global scope
❷   struct A {
        int x;
        float y;
    };
❸   void f()
❹   {
        A a; // define a new A struct called a
        a.x = 1;
    }
```

Upon seeing the struct node, we create a StructSymbol for A and push it as the current scope. After processing the entire struct subtree, we pop that scope off to reveal the global scope as the current scope. Here are the relevant tree pattern rules from DefRef.g:

symtab/aggr/DefRef.g

```
enterStruct // match as we discover struct nodes (on the way down)
    : ^('struct' ID .+)
      {
      System.out.println("line "+$ID.getLine()+": def struct "+$ID.text);
      StructSymbol ss = new StructSymbol($ID.text, currentScope);
      currentScope.define(ss); // def struct in current scope
      currentScope = ss;       // set current scope to struct scope
      }
    ;
```

```
exitStruct // match as we finish struct nodes (on the way up)
    :   'struct' // don't care about children, just trigger upon struct
        {
        System.out.println("fields: "+currentScope);
        currentScope = currentScope.getEnclosingScope();     // pop scope
        }
    ;
```

To access members of a **struct** like a.x, we trigger two ref operations. The first ref operation looks up a to figure out what type it is. The second ref then resolves x within a's scope (upon seeing the . node). To match (possibly nested) member access expressions, we can use the following recursive rule:

```
member // E.g., "a", "a.b", "a.b.c", and so on
    : ^('.' member ID)
    | ID
    ;
```

The problem is we can't just ask the pattern matcher to look for that pattern because a plain **ID** node like a also matches. We don't want this rule to match, say, the **ID** of a function definition.

To control expression tree walking, we need a tree grammar, not a tree pattern matcher. But, we need tree pattern matching for other language constructs. We can combine the two approaches by using pattern matching to find **EXPR** root nodes and assignments. From there, we can invoke tree grammar rule **member**. In this way, rule **member** isn't triggered as part of the tree pattern matching (we won't put it in the special **topdown** or **bottomup** rules). We'll learn more about this in Pattern 20, *Computing Static Expression Types*, on page 184. Here is the **member** rule now fleshed out with actions:

`symtab/aggr/DefRef.g`

```
member returns [Type type] // expr.x; E.g., "a", "a.b", "a.b.c", ...
    : ^('.' m=member ID)
        {
        StructSymbol scope=(StructSymbol)$m.type;// get scope of expr
        Symbol s = scope.resolveMember($ID.text);// resolve ID in scope
        System.out.println("line "+$ID.getLine()+": ref "+
                        $m.type.getName()+"."+$ID.text+"="+s);
        if ( s!=null ) $type = s.type;          // return ID's type
        }
    | ID                                         // resolve, return type
        {
        Symbol s = currentScope.resolve($ID.text);
        System.out.println("line "+$ID.getLine()+": ref "+$ID.text+"="+s);
        if ( s!=null ) $type = s.type;
        }
    ;
```

Rule **member**'s primary function is to compute the type of member access expressions. To do so, it needs to resolve all the symbols within an expression. Given *«expr».x*, **member** need's *«expr»*'s type because it must look up x with the scope of *«expr»*. Take a look at the action for the isolated **ID** node. It looks up the symbol and returns its type. If that **ID** is the child of a member access subtree as in the AST for a.b, then we'll use a's type to look up b. The action for the . member access operator assumes that the type for a is also a scope. It then looks up b in that scope. It returns the type of b in case a.b is part of a larger expression such as a.b.c.

The test rig in the source code directory is the same as in Pattern 17, *Symbol Table for Nested Scopes*, on page 146. It builds an AST from the source code and then walks the AST using DefRef's downup() strategy. Building the test rig is, again, just a matter of running ANTLR on the grammars and compiling. Here is the output from the test rig when run against †2.cymbol:

```
$ java org.antlr.Tool Cymbol.g DefRef.g
$ javac *.java
$ java Test < t2.cymbol
line 2: def struct A
line 3: def x
line 4: def y
fields: struct A:{x, y}
line 7: def method f
line 9: def a
line 10: ref a=<local.a:struct A:{x, y}>
line 10: ref A.x=<A.x:global.int>
line 10: assign to type int
locals: [a]
args: <global.f():global.void>
globals: [int, float, void, A, f]
$
```

Now that we know how to handle data aggregates, we're ready to tackle classes. The scope trees for classes are a bit more complicated than for **struct**s because we have to track class inheritance. Also, because of forward references, we need to split apart the DefRef.g pattern matcher used in this pattern. We'll do a definition pass over the AST and then a resolution pass.

Related Patterns

This pattern builds on Pattern 17, *Symbol Table for Nested Scopes*, on page 146. Pattern 19, *Symbol Table for Classes*, on the facing page extends this pattern to support classes.

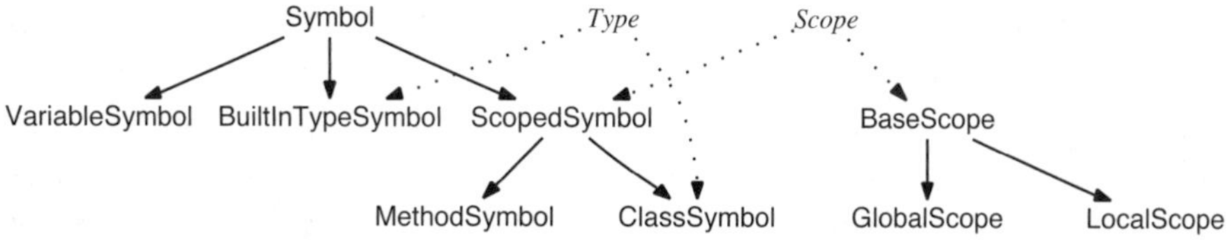

Figure 7.5: CLASS HIERARCHY FOR A SYMBOL TABLE MANAGING CLASSES

19 | Symbol Table for Classes

Purpose

This pattern tracks symbols and builds a scope tree for non-nested classes with single inheritance.

Discussion

Classes are data aggregates that allow method members and that can inherit members from superclasses. Methods within classes can see global variables in the object-oriented version of our Cymbol language (since Cymbol is a subset of C++). To support these language semantics, we need to tweak the scope trees we used for **struct**s in Pattern 18, *Symbol Table for Data Aggregates*, on page 161. We'll replace StructSymbol nodes with ClassSymbol nodes and have them point at their superclasses as well as their enclosing scopes (recall Figure 7.2, on page 158). All the symbol table objects this pattern needs appear in Figure 7.5.

Object-oriented languages like Cymbol also support forward references to symbols defined later in the file. Rather than trying to augment our single AST pass with code to "see into the future," this pattern uses a two-pass approach. We'll define symbols in the first pass and resolve symbol references in the second pass over the AST.

Unfortunately, separating the two phases introduces a data communication issue. To resolve symbol references, we need to know the current scope but that's computed only in the definition phase. So, we need to pass information from the definition to the resolution phase. The logical place to stash information is in the AST representation of the input. (It's much more efficient to walk an AST multiple times than the original token stream.)

The definition phase tracks the current scope as usual and records it in the associated AST nodes. For example, a { node records the associated LocalScope. As we define symbols, we might as well record the resulting Symbol objects in the AST too. The resolution phase can then look in the tree for scope information and symbol definitions. As we resolve symbol references, we'll also shove that into the AST. Any future tree phases would most likely use the symbol pointers for analysis or translation.

To make this clearer, let's carry the following small Cymbol method through both phases to see what the AST and scope tree look like:

symtab/class/t.cymbol

```
❶   // globals
❷   int main()
❸   {
      int x;
      x = 3;
    }
```

In Figure 7.6, on the facing page, we can see the AST and scope tree after the definition phase. To avoid cluttering the diagram, the diagram only shows pointers to and from the AST for x's definition and reference. During the definition phase, we create a VariableSymbol and make the definition's **ID** node point at that symbol. We also make a back pointer from that symbol to the **ID** node using the VariableSymbol's def field.

The definition phase also sets a scope field for some of the AST nodes (shown via numbered icons to avoid cluttering the diagram with more arrows). It's crucial that we set the scope for the variable definition's type node (int) and the x reference in the assignment. The resolution phase needs the scope in order to resolve those symbols.

The resolution phase now has everything it needs to properly resolve all symbol references. During this phase, we update the symbol field of two AST nodes and update the type field of the VariableSymbol, as shown in Figure 7.7, on page 170. As we revisit x's variable declaration subtree, we resolve its type and make that node point at the BuiltInTypeSymbol. When we see the x reference in the assignment, we resolve it and make that node point at the VariableSymbol.

To support checks for illegal forward references, the def field of the VariableSymbol is important. At the x reference in main's assignment, we want to check the relative position of x's definition. To get x's position, we can follow the symbol pointer into the symbol table from the AST. Then, we can follow the def pointer back into the AST to the defini-

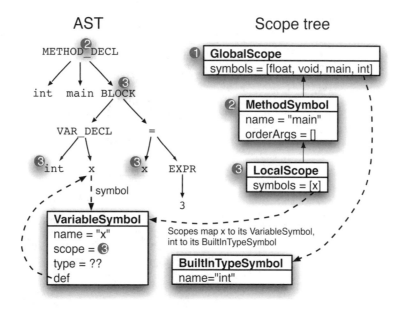

Figure 7.6: AST AND SCOPE TREE SHOWING LINKS FOR X AFTER DEFINI-TION PHASE

tion for that symbol. In this case, the definition for x comes before the reference, so it's OK.

Now that we know what the symbol table objects are, what the scope trees look like, and how to deal with forward references, we can lay out the rules for the definition and resolution passes. See Figure 7.8, on page 171, as well as Figure 7.9, on page 172.

The actions in Figure 7.9, on page 172, perform a lot of abstract ref operations, but the details of symbol resolution aren't shown. Our basic strategy remains the same as we saw in Section 6.3, *Resolving Symbols*, on page 139. We look for the symbol in the current scope's dictionary. If found, we return it. If not found, we recursively look upward in the scope tree:

```
public Symbol resolve(String name) {
    Symbol s = members.get(name);       // look in this scope
    if ( s!=null ) return s;            // return it if in this scope
    if ( getParentScope() != null ) { // do we have a super or enclosing?
        return getParentScope().resolve(name); // check super/enclosing
    }
    return null; // not found in this scope or above
}
```

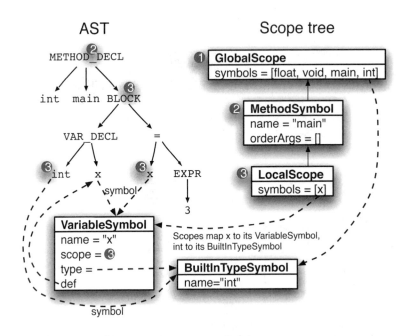

Figure 7.7: AST AND SCOPE TREE SHOWING LINKS FOR X AFTER RESOLU-
TION PHASE

The only difference you'll notice is that we call getParentScope(), not getEnclosingScope() as we did before. ClassSymbol objects have two parent pointers, one for the superclass and one for the enclosing scope. Which one we follow on the way up the scope tree depends on what kind of scope we're looking at. getParentScope() factors out this decision into the various kinds of symbols that implement Scope. Here are the relevant methods in Scope that define upward pointers in the scope tree:

```
symtab/class/Scope.java
```

```
/** Where to look next for symbols; superclass or enclosing scope */
public Scope getParentScope();
/** Scope in which this scope defined. For global scope, it's null */
public Scope getEnclosingScope();
```

For all scopes except ClassSymbol, getParentScope() returns the enclosing scope. getParentScope() in classes returns the superclass pointer, so we follow the superclass chain. If there is no superclass, then we follow the enclosing scope chain like any other scope.

Upon	Action(s)
Start of file	push a GlobalScope. def BuiltInType objects for int, float, void.
Identifier reference x	Set x's scope field to the current scope (the resolution phase needs it).
Variable declaration x	def x as a VariableSymbol object, sym, in the current scope. This works for globals, class fields, parameters, and locals (wow). Set sym.def to x's **ID** AST node. Set that **ID** node's symbol to sym. Set the scope field of x's type AST node to the current scope.
Class declaration C	def C as a ClassSymbol object, sym, in the current scope and push it as the current scope. Set sym.def to the class name's **ID** AST node. Set that **ID** node's symbol to sym. Set the scope field of C's superclass' AST node to the current scope.
Method declaration f	def f as a MethodSymbol object, sym, in the current scope and push it as the current scope. Set sym.def to the function name's **ID** AST node. Set that **ID** node's symbol to sym. Set the scope field of f's return type AST node to the current scope.
{	push a LocalScope as the new current scope.
}	pop, revealing previous scope as current scope.
End of file	pop the GlobalScope.

Figure 7.8: Definition phase rules for building a scope tree for classes and populating it with symbols

Upon	Action(s)
Variable declaration x	Let t be the **ID** node for x's type. ref t, yielding sym. Set t.symbol to sym. Set x.symbol.type to sym; in other words, jump to the VariableSymbol for x via the AST node's symbol field and then set its type field to sym.
Class declaration C	Let t be the **ID** node for C's superclass. ref t, yielding sym. Set t.symbol to sym. Set C's superclass field t sym.
Method declaration f	Let t be the **ID** node for f's return type. ref t, yielding sym. Set t.symbol to sym. Set the type field of the MethodSymbol for f to sym.
Variable reference x	ref x, yielding sym. Set x.symbol to sym.
this	Resolve to the surrounding class scope. Set the symbol field of this's **ID** node to the surrounding class scope.
Member access «*expr*».x	Resolve «*expr*» to a particular type symbol, esym, using these rules. ref x within esym's scope, yielding sym. Set x.symbol (x's **ID** node) to sym.

Figure 7.9: RESOLUTION PHASE RULES FOR UPDATING THE AST AND SYMBOL TABLE FOR CLASSES

The addition of this little "knob" makes resolve() work correctly for all symbol references (types, classes, methods, and variables) in the presence or absence of classes. In Figure 7.10, on the facing page, we see how the algorithm walks up the scope tree according to reference location. The behavior mirrors what we've come to expect in object-oriented languages.

Resolving member access expressions, «*expr*».x, is almost the same. The only difference is symbol resolution should stop looking at the root of the class hierarchy. It shouldn't look in the global scope. Here is the algorithm for resolving members:

```
public Symbol resolveMember(String name) {
    Symbol s = members.get(name);
    if ( s!=null ) return s;
    // if not here, check superclass chain only
    if ( superClass != null ) {
        return superClass.resolveMember(name);
    }
    return null; // not found
}
```

Symbol Reference	Resolution Algorithm Scope Tree Walk
x in method	Look first in the enclosing local scope(s), then into the method scope, and then into the enclosing class scope. If not found in the enclosing class, look up the class hierarchy. If not found in the class hierarchy, look in the global scope.
x in field definition initialization expression	Look in the surrounding class scope. If not found in that class, look up the class hierarchy. If not found in the class hierarchy, look in the global scope.
x in global scope	Look in the surrounding global scope.

Figure 7.10: HOW RESOLVE() WALKS UP THE SCOPE TREE FOR CLASSES

The rules and resolution algorithms we've just gone through tell us everything we need to know in order to build a symbol table for an object-oriented language with single inheritance. They also tell us how to resolve symbols properly, taking into account the class hierarchy and enclosing scope chains. You can skip the following implementation section if you're primarily interested in the principles behind symbol table management. Because the sample implementation is complete, the discussion is a bit long. When you're ready to really dig into the details of building an object-oriented language, though, you should read through it and examine the code in a development tool.

Implementation

For our sample object-oriented Cymbol implementation, we'll use Pattern 18, *Symbol Table for Data Aggregates*, on page 161 as a foundation, so let's just talk about how this implementation extends that one. The biggest difference is that we'll make two passes over the AST per the pattern discussion. Here's our implementation road map:

- Extend the Cymbol language grammar to allow class definitions. We'll also add the notion of a "main" method. These are more or less straightforward grammar extensions. We'll assume that the grammar correctly builds ASTs for classes.
- Define a custom CymbolAST node that tracks scope and symbol pointers for each identifier node.

- Add field def (type CymbolAST) to Symbol that points from the symbol table into the AST. def points at the **ID** node associated with the Symbol.
- Add method getParentScope() to Scope, and alter resolve() methods to use this instead of getEnclosingScope(). We still need getEnclosingScope() for push and pop operations, though.
- Replace StructSymbol with a suitable ClassSymbol.
- Break the single-pass DefRef.g into two passes, Def.g and Ref.g, that define symbols and resolve symbol references, respectively. This is necessary to support forward references.

Let's start by describing the new properties we'll need in the various objects and then look at building scope trees and resolving symbols.

To hold bookkeeping fields for our two pass approach, we need a specialized AST node. Beyond the properties of the usual ANTLR Common-Tree object, we need scope and symbol fields (Test.java shows how to create a custom TreeAdaptor that tells ANTLR to build CymbolAST nodes):

`symtab/class/CymbolAST.java`

```java
public class CymbolAST extends CommonTree {
    public Scope scope;   // set by Def.g; ID lives in which scope?
    public Symbol symbol; // set by Ref.g; point at def in symbol table
    public CymbolAST(Token t) { super(t); }
}
```

We also need the symbol table objects to point back into the AST at their definition **ID** nodes via def:

`symtab/class/Symbol.java`

```java
public class Symbol { // A generic programming language symbol
    String name;       // All symbols at least have a name
    Type type;
    Scope scope;       // All symbols know what scope contains them.
    CymbolAST def;     // points at ID node in tree
```

To represent the Cymbol language class hierarchy, each ClassSymbol needs a superClass field:

`symtab/class/ClassSymbol.java`

```java
public class ClassSymbol extends ScopedSymbol implements Scope, Type {
    /** This is the superclass not enclosingScope field. We still record
     *  the enclosing scope so we can push in and pop out of class defs.
     */
    ClassSymbol superClass;
    /** List of all fields and methods */
    public Map<String,Symbol> members=new LinkedHashMap<String,Symbol>();
```

Per the pattern discussion, we need to define getParentScope(). By default, it just returns the enclosing scope:

`symtab/class/ScopedSymbol.java`

```
public Scope getParentScope() { return getEnclosingScope(); }
```

For classes, the parent scope depends on whether it has a superclass:

`symtab/class/ClassSymbol.java`

```
public Scope getParentScope() {
    if ( superClass==null ) return enclosingScope; // globals
    return superClass; // if not root object, return super
}
```

With this infrastructure in place, we can build the two tree phases that define and resolve symbols.

Populating the Symbol Table in Phase 1

The goal of our first tree-walking phase is to build a scope tree and populate it with all classes, methods, and variables (globals, fields, parameters, and locals). Let's put our definition tree phase in Def.g.

As in the other patterns, we need both top-down and bottom-up actions to track the current scope. The source code identifies the scopes with tokens such as nested curlies. We push and pop the current scope according to these symbols. The current scope has nothing to do with the class hierarchy. So, the scope pop action looks just like in the other patterns:

```
currentScope = currentScope.getEnclosingScope();    // pop scope
```

To execute actions upon symbol definitions, tree matcher **Def** has patterns for classes, methods, and variables. Here is the rule to match and define classes:

`symtab/class/Def.g`

```
enterClass
    :   ^('class' name=ID (^(EXTENDS sup=ID))? .)
        { // def class but leave superclass blank until ref phase
        System.out.println("line "+$name.getLine()+
                           ": def class "+$name.text);
        // record scope in AST for next pass
        if ( $sup!=null ) $sup.scope = currentScope;
        ClassSymbol cs = new ClassSymbol($name.text,currentScope,null);
        cs.def = $name;          // point from symbol table into AST
        $name.symbol = cs;       // point from AST into symbol table
        currentScope.define(cs); // def class in current scope
        currentScope = cs;       // set current scope to class scope
        }
    ;
```

This is analogous to the rule for matching and defining structs but performs two other important operations. First, **enterClass** sets the scope for the superclass identifier node (we'll use this scope to look it up in the resolution phase). Second, it doubly links the class name's **ID** AST node with the associated ClassSymbol object (using AST field symbol and ClassSymbol field def). This builds the dashed lines we see in Figure 7.6, on page 169; these are for the x child of VAR_DECL. There are similar actions to set the scope for method return types and variable types in **enterMethod** and **varDeclaration**. Otherwise, those rules are the same as in Pattern 18, *Symbol Table for Data Aggregates*, on page 161.

We also need to set the scope field for identifiers within expressions so we can resolve them in the next phase. We can't just make a rule that matches identifiers, though. It would trigger the scope setting action at inappropriate times. For example, if class B derives from A, we want to look up superclass A starting in the global scope rather than in class B itself. To limit our scope-setting rule to only those identifiers within expressions and assignments, we can add a semantic predicate to the pattern:

symtab/class/Def.g

```
/** Set scope for any identifiers in expressions or assignments */
atoms
@init {CymbolAST t = (CymbolAST)input.LT(1);}
    :   {t.hasAncestor(EXPR)||t.hasAncestor(ASSIGN)}? ('this'|ID)
        {t.scope = currentScope;}
    ;
```

The predicate ensures that rule **atoms** triggers only when the identifier has an ancestor in the tree of EXPR or ASSIGN.

Now that we've built the scope tree and annotated the AST, we can build the resolution phase.

Resolving Symbol References in Phase 2

The first goal of our second phase is to resolve all type references: variable types, return types, and class superclasses. Once we know the type, we need to update the associated symbol table objects. In other words, upon int x, we need to resolve int to get its BuiltInTypeSymbol. Then we need set the type field of x's VariableSymbol to that BuiltInTypeSymbol. These are the dashed lines pointing at the int symbol shown in Figure 7.7, on page 170.

The second goal of our resolution phase is to resolve the identifiers within expressions and on the left side of assignments. To do this, we'll use a full tree grammar for expressions rather than simple tree pattern matching. As we'll see in Pattern 20, *Computing Static Expression Types*, on page 184, we need to control tree walking to compute expression types. To stop the pattern matcher at the root of an expression or assignment, we use the following rules:

`symtab/class/Ref.g`

```
assignment  : ^( '=' expr expr ) ;
resolveExpr : ^( EXPR expr ) ;
```

Rules **assignment** and **resolveExpr** invoke **expr**, but the tree pattern matcher does not try to match **expr** against subtrees because we don't mention rule **expr** in the **topdown** or **downup** rules. Rule **expr** is a complete tree grammar rule describing the syntax of an expression tree:

`symtab/class/Ref.g`

```
/** Compute types for identifiers and member access.
 *  Ignore actions for others; we don't need for this pattern example.
 */
expr returns [Type type]
    :   member {$type = $member.type;} // E.g., "a.b"
    |   ^(CALL expr)
    |   ^('+' expr expr)
    |   id      {$type = $id.type;}     // E.g., "a", "this"
    |   INT
    ;
```

Rule **expr** returns the type of the expression subtree it matched. We need expression types so that we can resolve member access expressions. To look up b in a.b, we need to know the type (class) of a. Here is the rule that handles member access operations:

`symtab/class/Ref.g`

```
member returns [Type type]
    :   ^('.' m=expr ID) // E.g., "a", "a.b", "a.b.c", ...
        {
        ClassSymbol scope = (ClassSymbol)$m.type;
        Symbol s = scope.resolveMember($ID.text);
        $ID.symbol = s;
        System.out.println("line "+$ID.getLine()+
            ": resolve "+$m.text+"."+$ID.text+" to "+s);
        if ( s!=null ) $type = s.type;
        }
    ;
```

Note that we use resolveMember(), not the generic resolve(), because we only want to look up member references in the class hierarchy. resolve() looks in the global scope after the class hierarchy.

To handle isolated identifiers, we have to react to two different patterns, as shown in the following rule (invoked from **expr**):

symtab/class/Ref.g

```
id returns [Type type]
    :   ID
        {
        // do usual resolve(ID) then check for illegal forward references
        $ID.symbol = SymbolTable.resolveID($ID);
        if ( $ID.symbol!=null ) $type = $ID.symbol.type;
        }
    |   t='this'  {$type = SymbolTable.getEnclosingClass($t.scope);}
    ;
```

For **ID** nodes, we resolve them as usual but then check for illegal forward references. We can factor that code out of the grammar into our SymbolTable class:

symtab/class/SymbolTable.java

```
public static Symbol resolveID(CymbolAST idAST) {
    Symbol s = idAST.scope.resolve(idAST.getText());
    System.out.println("line "+idAST.getLine()+": resolve "+
                        idAST.getText()+" to "+s);
    if ( s.def==null ) return s; // must be predefined symbol
    // if resolves to local or global symbol, token index of definition
    // must be before token index of reference
    int idLocation = idAST.token.getTokenIndex();
    int defLocation = s.def.token.getTokenIndex();
    if ( idAST.scope instanceof BaseScope &&
        s.scope instanceof BaseScope &&
        idLocation < defLocation )
    {
        System.err.println("line "+idAST.getLine()+
            ": error: forward local var ref "+idAST.getText());
        return null;
    }
    return s;
}
```

Rule **id** also matches keyword this, which refers to the current object. So, its type is the surrounding class. Because the this reference could be buried in a deeply nested local scope, we need to look upward in the enclosing scope chain until we find the class scope.

symtab/class/SymbolTable.java

```
/** 'this' and 'super' need to know about enclosing class */
public static ClassSymbol getEnclosingClass(Scope s) {
    while ( s!=null ) { // walk upwards from s looking for a class
        if ( s instanceof ClassSymbol ) return (ClassSymbol)s;
        s = s.getParentScope();
    }
    return null;
}
```

There are a few other details in Ref.g, but we've covered the important points.

Finally, let's give our symbol table manager a workout. The test rig builds an AST from the source code and then walks it using Def's and Ref's downup() strategies:

symtab/class/Test.java

```
CommonTreeNodeStream nodes = new CommonTreeNodeStream(cymbalAdaptor, t);
nodes.setTokenStream(tokens);
SymbolTable symtab = new SymbolTable(); // init symbol table
Def def = new Def(nodes, symtab);       // create Def phase
def.downup(t);                          // Do pass 1
System.out.println("globals: "+symtab.globals);
nodes.reset(); // rewind AST node stream to root
Ref ref = new Ref(nodes);               // create Ref phase
ref.downup(t);                          // Do pass 2
```

Let's run the test rig on inherit.cymbol (the numbered icons identify the various scopes):

symtab/class/inherit.cymbol

```
❶   // start of global scope
❷   // implicit class Object { int hashCode() {...} }
❸   class A {
    public:
     int x;
❹   void foo()
❺   { ; }
❻   void bar()
❼   { ; }
    };
❽   class B : public A {
     int y;
❾   void foo()
❿   {
       this.x = this.y;
       bar(); // invoke A::bar()
     }
    };
```

The output we get is as follows:

```
$ java org.antlr.Tool Cymbol.g Def.g Ref.g
$ javac *.java
$ java Test < inherit.cymbol
line 3: def class A
line 5: def x
line 6: def method foo
locals: []
args: A.foo()
line 8: def method bar
locals: []
args: A.bar()
members: class A:{x, foo, bar}
line 11: def class B
line 12: def y
line 13: def method foo
locals: []
args: B.foo()
members: class B:{y, foo}
globals: [int, float, void, A, B]
line 3: set A
line 5: set var type <A.x:global.int>
line 6: set method type <A.foo():global.void>
line 8: set method type <A.bar():global.void>
line 11: set B super to A
line 12: set var type <B.y:global.int>
line 13: set method type <B.foo():global.void>
line 15: resolve this.x to <A.x:global.int>
line 15: resolve this.y to <B.y:global.int>
line 16: resolve bar to <A.bar():global.void>
$
```

Notice how, for example, the fields in assignments like this.x = this.y resolve correctly (to A.x and B.y because of inheritance).

Related Patterns

This pattern extends and alters the source code from Pattern 18, *Symbol Table for Data Aggregates*, on page 161.

Up Next

This completes a two-chapter sequence on building symbol tables for the four basic language scoping patterns. At this point, we've got the necessary infrastructure to start asking questions about the source code. In the next chapter, we'll figure out how to enforce static typing rules for languages like C++, Java, and C#.

Chapter 8

Enforcing Static Typing Rules

We derive the meaning of a sentence from both its structure (syntax) and the particular vocabulary symbols it uses. The structure says what to do, and the symbols say what to do it to. For example, in phrase print x, the syntax says to print a value, and the symbol x says which value to print. Sometimes, though, we write code that make no sense even if the syntax is correct. Such programs violate a language's semantic rules.

Languages typically have lots and lots of semantic rules. Some rules are run-time constraints (*dynamic semantics*), and some are compile-time constraints (*static semantics*). Dynamic semantic rules enforce things like "no division by zero" and "no array index out of bounds." Depending on the language, we can enforce some rules statically such as "no multiplication of incompatible types."

Where to draw the line between static and dynamic rules is up to the language designer. For example, Python is *dynamically typed*, which means that programmers do not specify the types of program values (nor can the compiler infer every type). The Python interpreter enforces all the semantic rules at run-time. C++ is the opposite extreme. Anything goes at run-time, but C++ is *statically typed*. We have to specify the types of all program values. Some languages enforce the same rule statically and then again dynamically to guard against hostile programs. For example, Java does type checking at compile-time as well as at run-time. Both statically and dynamically typed languages are called *type safe* if they disallow operations on incompatible types.

Because statically typed languages are so common, we are going to devote an entire chapter to enforcing static type safety (those readers interested only in implementing dynamically typed languages such as

Python and Ruby can skip this chapter). Here are the patterns we'll discuss:

- Pattern 20, *Computing Static Expression Types*, on page 184. To guarantee type safety, the first thing we've got to do is compute the types of all expressions and expression elements. We assume that the operands of a binary arithmetic operation have the same type. There is no automatic promotion of arithmetic values. Most languages do automatically promote arithmetic values, but technically type computation and promotion are two different operations. That's why we'll look at them separately in this pattern and the next.

- Pattern 21, *Automatic Type Promotion*, on page 193. This pattern demonstrates how to promote operands to have the same or otherwise compatible types. For example, in the expression 3+4.5, we expect the language to automatically promote integer 3 to a floating-point value.

- Pattern 22, *Enforcing Static Type Safety*, on page 201. Once we know the types of all expressions, we can enforce type safety. This amounts to checking for operand-operator and assignment type compatibility.

- Pattern 23, *Enforcing Polymorphic Type Safety*, on page 208. The notion of type compatibility is a little bit looser in object-oriented languages. We have to deal with polymorphic assignments. We can, for example, assign a Manager object reference (pointer) to an Employee reference: e = m;. Polymorphic means that a reference can point at multiple types. In contrast, assignments in non-object-oriented languages must be between identical types. This pattern explains how to check for polymorphic type compatibility.

Before jumping into the patterns, we need to agree on a specific language that we can use as a common thread throughout this chapter. There's no way we can describe all possible semantic rules for all languages, so we'll have to focus on a single language. Using C as a base is a good choice because it's the progenitor of the statically typed languages commonly in use today (C++, C#, and Java). For continuity, we'll augment our Cymbol language from Chapter 6, *Tracking and Identifying Program Symbols*, on page 131 (with some more operators to make it interesting).

Cymbol has the following features (when in doubt, assume C++ syntax and semantics):

- There are **struct**, function, and variable declarations.

- The built-in types are **float, int, char, boolean,** and **void.** Along with built-in type **boolean,** we have true and false values.

- There are no explicit pointers (except in Pattern 23, *Enforcing Polymorphic Type Safety,* on page 208), but there are one-dimensional arrays: int a[];. Like C++, we can initialize variables as we declare them: int i = 3;. Also like C++, we can declare local variables anywhere within a function, not just at the start like C.

- There are **if, return,** assignment, and function call statements.

- The operators are +, -, *, /, <, >, <=, >=, !=, ==, !, and unary -. Beyond the usual expression atoms like integers and identifiers, we can use function calls, array references, and struct/class member accesses.

We're going to enforce a number of type safety rules. In a nutshell, all operations and value assignments must have compatible operands. In Figure 8.2, on page 202, we see the exact list of semantic type rules. Furthermore, we're going to check symbol categories. The type of expressions on the left of the . member access operator must be of type **struct.** Identifiers in function calls must be functions. Identifiers in array references must be array symbols.

Now we just have to figure out how to implement those rules. All the patterns in this chapter follow the same general three-pass strategy. In fact, they all share the first two passes. In the first pass, a Cymbol parser builds an AST. In the second pass, a tree walker builds a scope tree and populates a symbol table. Pattern 20, *Computing Static Expression Types,* on the following page is the third pass over the AST and computes the type of each expression. Pattern 21, *Automatic Type Promotion,* on page 193 augments this third pass to promote arithmetic values as necessary. We'll assume valid input until Pattern 22, *Enforcing Static Type Safety,* on page 201. In that pattern, we'll add type checking to the third tree pass to enforce our semantic rules.

In practice, you might squeeze the second and third or the first and second passes into a single pass for efficiency. It might even be possible to reduce this to a single pass that parses, defines symbols, computes types, and checks type compatibility. Unless run-time speed is critical, though, consider breaking complicated language applications down into as many bite-size chunks as possible.

Here's a quick summary of when to apply the patterns:

Pattern	When to Apply
Pattern 20, *Computing Static Expression Types*	This pattern is a component of any type safety checker such as Pattern 22, *Enforcing Static Type Safety*, on page 201 and Pattern 23, *Enforcing Polymorphic Type Safety*, on page 208.
Pattern 21, *Automatic Type Promotion*, on page 193	Automatically promoting types is also really just a component of a type checker. If your language doesn't support automatic promotion (like ML), you don't need this pattern.
Pattern 22, *Enforcing Static Type Safety*, on page 201	You'll need this pattern if you're parsing a non-object-oriented programming language such as C.
Pattern 23, *Enforcing Polymorphic Type Safety*, on page 208	Use this pattern if you're dealing with an object-oriented language such as C++ or Java.

OK, let's get to it. Don't worry if the process of computing and checking types seems complicated. We'll take it slowly, component by component. In fact, static type analysis for C and its descendents is not too bad. The following patterns break the problem down into easy-to-digest pieces.

20 Computing Static Expression Types

Purpose

This pattern explains how to statically compute the type of expressions in languages with explicit type declarations like C.

You'll be able to extrapolate from this pattern everything you'd need to build a static type analyzer for C, C++, Java, or C#. Every compiler for

Subexpression	Result Type
true, false	**boolean**.
Character literal	**char**.
Integer literal	**int**.
Floating-point literal	**float**.
id	The declared type of the variable identified by *id*.
!«*expr*»	**boolean**.
-«*expr*»	The result type is the same as «*expr*»'s type.
«*expr*».*id*	The declared type of the field identified by *id*.
a[«*expr*»]	The declared array element type. For example, a[i] has type **float** if a has declaration float a[].
f(«*args*»)	The declared return type of function f.
«*expr*» *bop* «*expr*»	Since both operands have the same type, we can simply choose the type of the left operand as a result type; *bop* is in {+, -, *, /}.
«*expr*» *relop* «*expr*»	**boolean** where *relop* is in {<, >, <=, >=}.
«*expr*» *eqop* «*expr*»	**boolean** where *eqop* is in {!=, ==}.

Figure 8.1: CYMBOL EXPRESSION TYPE COMPUTATION RULES

those languages implements an extended version of this pattern. So, do static bug analyzers such as FindBugs[1] and Coverity.[2]

Discussion

Type computation is an extremely broad topic. To make things more concrete, we'll focus on the type computation rules for Cymbol itemized in Figure 8.1.

Computing the type of an expression is a matter of computing the type of all elements and the result type of all operations.

---

1. http://findbugs.sourceforge.net
2. http://coverity.com/html/prevent-for-java.html

For example, to compute the type of f(1)+4*a[i]+s.x, we proceed as follows:

Subexpression	Result Type
1	int
f(1)	int
4	int
i	int
a[i]	int
4*a[i]	int
f(1)+4*a[i]	int
s	struct S
s.x	int
f(1)+4*a[i]+s.x	int

These computations are pretty dull because we're assuming the operands are all the same type. Technically, we could stop computing the
type after encountering first operand: f(1). The entire expression result
type has to be integer because f returns an integer. In practice, though,
two things can happen: we might need to promote a simpler type like
char to int and sometimes programmers make mistakes (operand types
can be incompatible). This pattern just sets up the proper action plan
for the next two patterns. We'll graft type promotion and type checking
onto this pattern later.

Implementation

The general strategy we'll use is to parse a Cymbol program into an AST
and then walk that tree twice. The first tree walk defines symbols, and
the second walk resolves symbols and computes expression types. The
first two passes come from Pattern 18, *Symbol Table for Data Aggregates*, on page 161, so we can focus on the final type resolution and
computation tree walk.

Once we have an AST and a populated symbol table (courtesy of Cym-
bol.g and Def.g), we can describe the type computation rules as tree
pattern-action pairs. The actions compute types and annotate the AST
with them. Using Pattern 13, *External Tree Visitor*, on page 116, we
could walk the tree looking for the patterns. We have to be careful,
though, how we match expression elements. For example, we have to
consider isolated identifiers and identifiers in array references differently. In ANTLR notation, that means we can't simply make a tree pattern rule like this:

```
id : ID {«action»} ;
```

To encode context information, we need Pattern 14, *Tree Grammar*, on page 119 rather than a set of isolated tree patterns. That said, we don't want to resort to a full tree grammar because we care only about expressions in this pattern. To get the best of both worlds, we can use Pattern 15, *Tree Pattern Matcher*, on page 123 to look for **EXPR** root nodes and then invoke a type computation rule to traverse the expression subtree:

`semantics/types/Types.g`

```
bottomup // match subexpressions innermost to outermost
    :   exprRoot // only match the start of expressions (root EXPR)
    ;


exprRoot // invoke type computation rule after matching EXPR
    :   ^(EXPR expr) {$EXPR.evalType = $expr.type;} // annotate AST
    ;
```

This way we only have to specify the type computation rules and can totally ignore the AST structure outside of expressions.

The meat of our implementation is rule **expr**, which computes the subexpression types:

`semantics/types/Types.g`

```
expr returns [Type type]
@after { $start.evalType = $type; } // do after any alternative
    :   'true'      {$type = SymbolTable._boolean;}
    |   'false'     {$type = SymbolTable._boolean;}
    |   CHAR        {$type = SymbolTable._char;}
    |   INT         {$type = SymbolTable._int;}
    |   FLOAT       {$type = SymbolTable._float;}
    |   ID {VariableSymbol s=(VariableSymbol)$ID.scope.resolve($ID.text);
            $ID.symbol = s; $type = s.type;}
    |   ^(UNARY_MINUS a=expr)   {$type=symtab.uminus($a.start);}
    |   ^(UNARY_NOT a=expr)     {$type=symtab.unot($a.start);}
    |   member      {$type = $member.type;}
    |   arrayRef    {$type = $arrayRef.type;}
    |   call        {$type = $call.type;}
    |   binaryOps   {$type = $binaryOps.type;}
    ;
```

The first few alternatives encode the type computation rules with inline actions for the literals and identifiers. The $ID.scope.resolve($ID.text) expression deserves some explanation. $ID.text is the text of the identifier that we need to look up with resolve(). resolve() needs the identifier's context (surrounding scope), which our definition phase conveniently stashed as the **ID** AST node's scope field. Expression $start refers to the first node matched by enclosing rule **expr**.

The tree grammar handles the more complicated patterns via a few small helper rules in SymbolTable such as uminus() and unot():

semantics/types/SymbolTable.java

```
public Type uminus(CymbolAST a) { return a.evalType; }
public Type unot(CymbolAST a)    { return _boolean; }
```

Rule **expr** also annotates the root of the subexpression subtree with the type it computes (via $start.evalType = $type;). Because a static type analyzer is normally just a component of a larger language application, we need to store type information somewhere rather than throwing it out. We'll store the type in field evalType of a customized AST node, CymbolAST:

semantics/types/CymbolAST.java

```
public class CymbolAST extends CommonTree {
    public Scope scope;   // set by Def.g; ID lives in which scope?
    public Symbol symbol; // set by Types.g; point at def in symbol table
    public Type evalType; // The type of an expression; set by Types.g
```

Continuing on with the type computation rules, here is how to compute the type of a member access operation:

semantics/types/Types.g

```
member returns [Type type]
    :   ^('.' expr ID)          // match expr.ID subtrees
        { // $expr.start is root of tree matched by expr rule
        $type = symtab.member($expr.start, $ID);
        $start.evalType = $type; // save computed type
        }
    ;
```

Notice that the left side of the operation can be any expression according to the grammar. This handles cases such as functions that return **struct** values as in f().fieldname. The member() method in the SymbolTable looks up the field within the scope of the expression on the left side:

semantics/types/SymbolTable.java

```
public Type member(CymbolAST expr, CymbolAST field) {
    StructSymbol scope=(StructSymbol)expr.evalType; // get scope of expr
    Symbol s = scope.resolveMember(field.getText());// resolve ID in scope
    field.symbol = s;  // make AST point into symbol table
    return s.type;     // return ID's type
}
```

It retrieves the type of the expression via the evalType AST field. evalType is set as a side effect of calling rule **expr** in **member** and must point at a StructSymbol.

The next rule computes types for array references. It also delegates the type computation to SymbolTable (the actions for these rules will get bigger in the following patterns; it's a good idea to tuck them out of the way as methods in another class):

semantics/types/Types.g

```
arrayRef returns [Type type]
    :   ^(INDEX ID expr)
        {
        $type = symtab.arrayIndex($ID, $expr.start);
        $start.evalType = $type; // save computed type
        }
    ;
```

The type of an array reference is just the element type of the array (the index isn't needed):

semantics/types/SymbolTable.java

```
public Type arrayIndex(CymbolAST id, CymbolAST index) {
    Symbol s = id.scope.resolve(id.getText());
    VariableSymbol vs = (VariableSymbol)s;
    id.symbol = vs;
    return ((ArrayType)vs.type).elementType;
}
```

Function calls consist of the function name and an optional list of expressions for the arguments. The **call** rule collects all this information and passes it to a helper in SymbolTable:

semantics/types/Types.g

```
call returns [Type type]
@init {List args = new ArrayList();}
    :   ^(CALL ID ^(ELIST (expr {args.add($expr.start);})*))
        {
        $type = symtab.call($ID, args);
        $start.evalType = $type;
        }
    ;
```

The type of a function call is the return type of the function (we'll ignore the argument types until we do type promotion and type checking):

semantics/types/SymbolTable.java

```
public Type call(CymbolAST id, List args) {
    Symbol s = id.scope.resolve(id.getText());
    MethodSymbol ms = (MethodSymbol)s;
    id.symbol = ms;
    return ms.type;
}
```

Finally, we come to the binary operators (binary in the sense that they have two operands). It turns out that we'll ultimately need to deal separately with the arithmetic, relational, and equality operators. For consistency with future patterns, we'll trigger different helper methods:

semantics/types/Types.g

```
binaryOps returns [Type type]
@after { $start.evalType = $type; }
    :   ^(bop a=expr b=expr)   {$type=symtab.bop($a.start, $b.start);}
    |   ^(relop a=expr b=expr) {$type=symtab.relop($a.start, $b.start);}
    |   ^(eqop a=expr b=expr)  {$type=symtab.eqop($a.start, $b.start);}
    ;
```

Because we assume that the operand types of arithmetic operators are identical, there is no computation to do. We can just arbitrarily pick the type of the left operand. The relational and the equality operators always yield **boolean** types:

semantics/types/SymbolTable.java

```
public Type bop(CymbolAST a, CymbolAST b)   { return a.evalType; }
public Type relop(CymbolAST a, CymbolAST b) { return _boolean; }
public Type eqop(CymbolAST a, CymbolAST b)  { return _boolean; }
```

To put everything together, we need to build an AST and then perform two tree walks:

semantics/types/Test.java

```
// CREATE PARSER AND BUILD AST
CymbolLexer lex = new CymbolLexer(input);
final TokenRewriteStream tokens = new TokenRewriteStream(lex);
CymbolParser p = new CymbolParser(tokens);
p.setTreeAdaptor(CymbolAdaptor);  // create CymbolAST nodes
RuleReturnScope r = p.compilationUnit();   // launch parser
CommonTree t = (CommonTree)r.getTree();    // get tree result

// CREATE TREE NODE STREAM FOR TREE PARSERS
CommonTreeNodeStream nodes = new CommonTreeNodeStream(t);
nodes.setTokenStream(tokens);          // where to find tokens
nodes.setTreeAdaptor(CymbolAdaptor);
SymbolTable symtab = new SymbolTable();

// DEFINE SYMBOLS
Def def = new Def(nodes, symtab); // pass symtab to walker
def.downup(t); // trigger define actions upon certain subtrees

// RESOLVE SYMBOLS, COMPUTE EXPRESSION TYPES
nodes.reset();
Types typeComp = new Types(nodes, symtab);
typeComp.downup(t); // trigger resolve/type computation actions
```

After the tree walks, we have annotated all nodes within expressions with two pointers. symbol points at its symbol definition in the symbol table, and evalType points at the node's computed type. To print out our handiwork, we can use Pattern 13, *External Tree Visitor*, on page 116 to trigger a method calledshowTypes() on each expression node. To get a bottom-up, innermost to outermost traversal, we use a postorder walk:

semantics/types/Test.java

```java
// WALK TREE TO DUMP SUBTREE TYPES
TreeVisitor v = new TreeVisitor(new CommonTreeAdaptor());
TreeVisitorAction actions = new TreeVisitorAction() {
    public Object pre(Object t) { return t; }
    public Object post(Object t)  {
        showTypes((CymbolAST)t, tokens);
        return t;
    }
};
v.visit(t, actions); // walk in postorder, showing types
```

Method showTypes() just prints out subexpressions and their types for nodes with non-null evalType fields:

semantics/types/Test.java

```java
static void showTypes(CymbolAST t, TokenRewriteStream tokens) {
    if ( t.evalType!=null && t.getType()!=CymbolParser.EXPR ) {
        System.out.printf("%-17s",
                          tokens.toString(t.getTokenStartIndex(),
                                          t.getTokenStopIndex()));
        String ts = t.evalType.toString();
        System.out.printf(" type %-8s\n", ts);
    }
}
```

Let's run the following sample Cymbol file through our test rig:

semantics/types/t.cymbol

```
struct A {
  int x;
  struct B { int y; };
  struct B b;
};
int i=0; int j=0;
void f() {
  struct A a;
  a.x = 1+i*j;
  a.b.y = 2;
  boolean b = 3==a.x;
  if ( i < j ) f();
}
```

Here's how to build the test rig and run it on t.cymbol (it's the same for all patterns in this chapter):

```
$ java org.antlr.Tool Cymbol.g Def.g Types.g
$ javac *.java
$ java Test t.cymbol
0                    type int
0                    type int
a                    type struct A:{x, B, b}
a.x                  type int
1                    type int
i                    type int
j                    type int
i*j                  type int
1+i*j                type int
a                    type struct A:{x, B, b}
a.b                  type struct B:{y}
a.b.y                type int
2                    type int
3                    type int
a                    type struct A:{x, B, b}
a.x                  type int
3==a.x               type boolean
i                    type int
j                    type int
i < j                type boolean
f()                  type void
$
```

This pattern identifies the basic type computations for expression elements and operations. It's fairly restrictive in that operand types within a single operation must be identical such as integer plus integer. Still, we've created the basic infrastructure needed to support automatic promotion such as adding integers and floats. The next pattern defines the rules for arithmetic type promotion and provides a sample implementation. Its implementation builds upon the source code in this pattern.

Related Patterns

This pattern uses Pattern 18, *Symbol Table for Data Aggregates*, on page 161 to build a scope tree and populate the symbol table. It uses Pattern 13, *External Tree Visitor*, on page 116 to print out type information. Pattern 21, *Automatic Type Promotion*, on the next page, Pattern 22, *Enforcing Static Type Safety*, on page 201, and Pattern 23, *Enforcing Polymorphic Type Safety*, on page 208 build upon this pattern.

21 | Automatic Type Promotion

□

Purpose

This pattern describes how to automatically and safely promote arithmetic operand types.

Discussion

The goal of automatic type promotion is to get all operands of a single operation to be of the same type or compatible types. That's just how computer CPU instructions want their operands. Unfortunately, that's fairly inconvenient from a programming point of view. We often want to use a variety of types within the same operation such as 3+'0'. Most programming languages would, for example, interpret 3+'0' as 3+(int)'0'.

A language application can convert between types at will as long as it doesn't lose information. For example, we can convert 4 to 4.0 but can't convert 4.5 to integer 4 without losing information. We call such automatic conversion *promotion* because we can *widen* types without problem but can't *narrow* them in general.

There is a simple formula that expresses the valid type-to-type promotions. First, order and number the arithmetic types from narrowest to widest. Then, we can automatically promote $type_i$ to $type_j$ as long as $i < j$. In our C++ subset Cymbol language, the ordered arithmetic type list is as follows: **char**, **int**, and **float**. That means we can automatically convert **char** to **int** and **float** as well as **int** to **float**.

Compiler semantic analyzers use static type analyzers to figure out which elements and subexpressions to promote. Typically, they modify an intermediate representation tree to incorporate value promotion nodes. Translators can usually get away with just annotating their tree and checking for promotions later during code generation, which is a lot easier than altering the tree.

Besides expressions, static type analyzers have to promote values in assignments, return statements, function call arguments, and array index expressions. For example, in float f = 1;, the programmer shouldn't have to manually promote 1 to a floating-point value. Similarly, in a['z'], we'd expect a type analyzer to promote 'z' to an integer.

To implement arithmetic type promotion, we need two functions. The first returns the result type given an operator and two operand types. The second tells us whether we need to promote an operand for a particular operator and destination type.

To compute operation result types, we need a function that takes two operand types and an operator as parameters:

resultType($type_1$, *op*, $type_2$)

For example, adding a character and an integer yields an integer:

resultType(**char**, "+", **int**) == **int**

The operator is as important as the operand types. Comparing a **char** and an **int** yields a **boolean** not an **int**:

resultType(**char**, "<", **int**) == **boolean**

Comparing boolean operands for equality is OK but not for less-than and the other relational operators:

resultType(**boolean**, "==", **boolean**) == **boolean**

resultType(**boolean**, "<", **boolean**) == **void**

A result type of **void** indicates the operation is illegal, which we'll exploit in Pattern 22, *Enforcing Static Type Safety*, on page 201.

We need one more function. The resultType function says what the operation result type is but does not directly tell us whether we need to promote either of the operands. For that, we need the following function:

promoteFromTo(*type*, *op*, *destination-type*)

It tells us whether we need to promote an operand type to another type for a given operator. For example, we know from resultType that adding a character and an integer yields an integer. An operand type of **char** and a destination type of **int** for addition indicates we need to promote the **char** to **int**:

promoteFromTo(**char**, "+", **int**) == **int**

For the right operand, though, we don't need a promotion:

promoteFromTo(**int**, "+", **int**) == null

A promotion result of null means "no promotion necessary" not "invalid promotion."

Let's compute the result type and promote operands as necessary for expression 'a'+3+4.2. If we added type casts to make the promotions explicit, we'd write (float)((int)'a'+3)+4.2. (Our Cymbol C++ subset doesn't have doubles, so we'll use **float**.) To store the results of functions result-Type and promoteFromTo, we annotate the AST nodes:

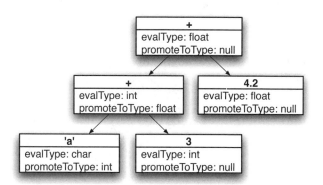

Each node knows its evaluation type and promotion type (if any). For example, the node for 'a' evaluates to **char** but promotes to **int** for the addition operation (its parent). The 3 node evaluates to **int** and doesn't need a promotion. The result of the lower addition operation is also **int** but needs a promotion to **float**.

The next section describes exactly how to implement functions resultType and promoteFromTo in Java and how to fold automatic type promotion into the sample Cymbol implementation from Pattern 20, *Computing Static Expression Types*, on page 184.

Implementation

When confronted with this type promotion problem for the first time, I wrote out all the type promotion cases with a series of if-statements. It was slow and fragile. I finally figured out that assigning a type index would reduce that mess to a few comparisons. Ultimately, I boiled everything down to a few table lookups using operand types as indexes. For each operator, I made a table that told me how to map any two operand types to a result type. Aside from being extremely efficient, the tables make it easy to see the valid operand types and promotions.

To implement Cymbol's result type tables in Java, let's start with the type indexes:

```
semantics/promote/SymbolTable.java
```

```java
// arithmetic types defined in order from narrowest to widest
public static final int tUSER = 0; // user-defined type (struct)
public static final int tBOOLEAN = 1;
public static final int tCHAR = 2;
public static final int tINT = 3;
public static final int tFLOAT = 4;
public static final int tVOID = 5;
```

Then we need to define the types. For example, here's the built-in type for **int**:

```java
public static final BuiltInTypeSymbol _int =
    new BuiltInTypeSymbol("int", tINT);
```

With those definitions in place, we can flesh out our result type table for the arithmetic operators. (The type tables for equality and relational operators are similar except every entry in the table is **boolean**):

```
semantics/promote/SymbolTable.java
```

```java
/** Map t1 op t2 to result type (_void implies illegal) */
public static final Type[][] arithmeticResultType = new Type[][] {
    /*            struct boolean char    int      float,  void */
    /*struct*/  {_void, _void,  _void,  _void,   _void,  _void},
    /*boolean*/ {_void, _void,  _void,  _void,   _void,  _void},
    /*char*/    {_void, _void,  _char,  _int,    _float, _void},
    /*int*/     {_void, _void,  _int,   _int,    _float, _void},
    /*float*/   {_void, _void,  _float, _float,  _float, _void},
    /*void*/    {_void, _void,  _void,  _void,   _void,  _void}
};
```

To compute the result of an arithmetic operation on a character and an integer, evaluate arithmeticResultType[tCHAR][tINT]. The result type is Type _int. The type promotion table works the same way. promoteFrom-To[tCHAR][tINT] gives _int, but promoteFromTo[tINT][tINT] gives null. Because of the semantics of Cymbol, we can get away with a single promotion table. It works not only for the operators but also for checking parameter types, array index types, and so on. For example, a['z'] needs to promote 'z' to an integer.

Here's the table:

```
/** Indicate whether a type needs a promotion to a wider type.
 *  If not null, implies promotion required.  Null does NOT imply
 *  error--it implies no promotion.  This works for
 *  arithmetic, equality, and relational operators in Cymbol.
 */
public static final Type[][] promoteFromTo = new Type[][] {
    /*            struct  boolean  char    int     float,   void */
    /*struct*/   {null,   null,    null,   null,   null,    null},
    /*boolean*/  {null,   null,    null,   null,   null,    null},
    /*char*/     {null,   null,    null,   _int,   _float,  null},
    /*int*/      {null,   null,    null,   null,   _float,  null},
    /*float*/    {null,   null,    null,   null,   null,    null},
    /*void*/     {null,   null,    null,   null,   null,    null}
};
```

Let's fold these type computation tables into the code we built for Pattern 20, *Computing Static Expression Types*, on page 184. The first thing we need to do is alter the operator result type support methods in SymbolTable. For a specified type table, the following method computes the result type. It annotates the AST with operand promotion types as a side effect.

```
public Type getResultType(Type[][] typeTable, CymbolAST a, CymbolAST b) {
    int ta = a.evalType.getTypeIndex(); // type index of left operand
    int tb = b.evalType.getTypeIndex(); // type index of right operand
    Type result = typeTable[ta][tb];    // operation result type
    // promote left to right or right to left?
    a.promoteToType = promoteFromTo[ta][result.getTypeIndex()];
    b.promoteToType = promoteFromTo[tb][result.getTypeIndex()];
    return result;
}
```

The three support methods called from rule **binaryOps** now call getResultType() with the appropriate type table:

```
public Type bop(CymbolAST a, CymbolAST b) {
    return getResultType(arithmeticResultType, a, b);
}
public Type relop(CymbolAST a, CymbolAST b) {
    return getResultType(relationalResultType, a, b);
}
public Type eqop(CymbolAST a, CymbolAST b) {
    return getResultType(equalityResultType, a, b);
}
```

Method arrayIndex() is the same as before except we promote the index to an integer if necessary:

semantics/promote/SymbolTable.java

```
public Type arrayIndex(CymbolAST id, CymbolAST index) {
    Symbol s = id.scope.resolve(id.getText()); // resolve variable
    VariableSymbol vs = (VariableSymbol)s;
    id.symbol = vs;                           // annotate AST
    Type t = ((ArrayType)vs.type).elementType; // get element type
    int texpr = index.evalType.getTypeIndex();
    index.promoteToType = promoteFromTo[texpr][tINT]; // promote index?
    return t;
}
```

For method calls, we have to promote argument expressions to the type specified in the function's formal parameter list:

semantics/promote/SymbolTable.java

```
/** For g('q',10), promote 'q' to int, 10 to float
 *  Given int g(int x, float y) {...} */
public Type call(CymbolAST id, List args) {
    Symbol s = id.scope.resolve(id.getText());
    MethodSymbol ms = (MethodSymbol)s;
    id.symbol = ms;
    int i=0;
    for (Symbol a : ms.orderedArgs.values() ) { // for each arg
        CymbolAST argAST = (CymbolAST)args.get(i++);
        // get argument expression type and expected type
        Type actualArgType = argAST.evalType;
        Type formalArgType = ((VariableSymbol)a).type;
        int targ = actualArgType.getTypeIndex();
        int tformal = formalArgType.getTypeIndex();
        // do we need to promote argument type to defined type?
        argAST.promoteToType = promoteFromTo[targ][tformal];
    }
    return ms.type;
}
```

We also need some rules in Types.g to handle variable initialization, return statements, and assignment:

semantics/promote/Types.g

```
decl:   ^(VAR_DECL . ID (init=.)?) // call declinit if we have init expr
        {if ( $init!=null && $init.evalType!=null )
            symtab.declinit($ID, $init);}
    ;
ret :   ^('return' v=.) {symtab.ret((MethodSymbol)$start.symbol, $v);} ;
assignment // don't walk exprs, just examine types; '.' is wildcard
    :   ^('=' lhs=. rhs=.) {symtab.assign($lhs, $rhs);}
    ;
```

Those rules delegate to helper methods in SymbolTable:

`semantics/promote/SymbolTable.java`

```java
public void declinit(CymbolAST id, CymbolAST init) {
    int te = init.evalType.getTypeIndex(); //promote expr to decl type?
    int tdecl = id.symbol.type.getTypeIndex();
    init.promoteToType = promoteFromTo[te][tdecl];
}
public void ret(MethodSymbol ms, CymbolAST expr) {
    Type retType = ms.type; //promote return expr to function decl type?
    Type exprType = expr.evalType;
    int texpr = exprType.getTypeIndex();
    int tret = retType.getTypeIndex();
    expr.promoteToType = promoteFromTo[texpr][tret];
}
public void assign(CymbolAST lhs, CymbolAST rhs) {
    int tlhs = lhs.evalType.getTypeIndex(); // promote right to left?
    int trhs = rhs.evalType.getTypeIndex();
    rhs.promoteToType = promoteFromTo[trhs][tlhs];
}
```

At this point, we've augmented our tree walker to deal with both expressions and statements that might need type promotions. Further, we've annotated our ASTs with these results. To check our work, we need to see those annotations. Rather than printing out the trees, let's print the original source code back out augmented with type casts as necessary. Our goal is to read in a Cymbol file such as this:

`semantics/promote/t.cymbol`

```
float a[];
int d[];
int c = 'z'+1      // check variable init (no promote on int)
void f() {
    a[0] = 4*'i'; // promote char to int to float
    a[1] = d[0];  // promote int element to float
    a['x'] = 1;   // check array index promotion
    g('q',10);    // arg promotion
}
int g(int x, float y) { return 'k'; } // promote 'k' to int
```

and print it back out with explicit casts:

```
float a[];
int d[];
int c = (int)'z'+1;    // check variable init (no promote on int)
void f() {
    a[0] = (float)(4*(int)'i'); // promote char to int to float
    a[1] = (float)d[0];         // promote int element to float
    a[(int)'x'] = (float)1;     // check array index promotion
    g((int)'q',(float)10);      // arg promotion
}
int g(int x, float y) { return (int)'k'; } // promote 'k' to int
```

To tweak the original source code, we need a bit of magic. There are two approaches. One way involves walking the AST with a clever visitor or tree grammar that knows how to map subtrees to output text. That's a lot of work and can't easily reproduce the original formatting. It's simpler to just to insert type casts directly into the original source code text buffer at the right spot and then print it out.

The only negative is efficiency. It takes a lot of data movement to insert a string into the middle of the character buffer. For a large buffer and lots of insertions, that's prohibitively expensive.

There's a way to do this efficiently using ANTLR's TokenRewriteStream. (We'll see it again in Section 13.5, *Tweaking Source Code*, on page 354 and Section 13.6, *Adding a New Type to Java*, on page 355.) It records all the insertion commands and then "executes" them as it prints the buffer back out. Using Pattern 13, *External Tree Visitor*, on page 116, the test rig invokes method insertCast() for every node with non-null promoteToType:

`semantics/promote/Test.java`

```
/** Insert a cast before tokens from which this node was created. */
static void insertCast(CymbolAST t, TokenRewriteStream tokens) {
    String cast = "("+t.promoteToType+")";
    int left =  t.getTokenStartIndex(); // location in token buffer
    int right = t.getTokenStopIndex();
    Token tok = t.token;                    // tok is node's token payload
    if ( tok.getType() == CymbolParser.EXPR ) {
        tok = ((CymbolAST)t.getChild(0)).token;
    }
    if ( left==right ||
         tok.getType()==CymbolParser.INDEX ||
         tok.getType()==CymbolParser.CALL )
    { // it's a single atom or a[i] or f(); don't use (...)
        tokens.insertBefore(left, cast);
    }
    else { // need parens
        String original = tokens.toString(left, right);
        tokens.replace(left, right, cast+"("+original+")");
    }
}
```

Except for error checking, we now have a static type analyzer! In the next pattern we'll add type checking and a few other semantic checks because we can't assume valid input.

Related Patterns

Automatic arithmetic type promotion goes hand in hand with result type computations, Pattern 20, *Computing Static Expression Types*, on page 184. Pattern 22, *Enforcing Static Type Safety* builds upon this pattern to emit error messages.

---

22   Enforcing Static Type Safety

Purpose

This pattern statically detects incompatible types in expressions and statements.

You can extrapolate from this pattern everything you'd need to build a type safety checker for any statically typed language with explicit declarations like C. Tools such as compilers that translate or otherwise analyze a statically typed language need this pattern.

Discussion

A static type checker adds type compatibility checks to Pattern 21, *Automatic Type Promotion*, on page 193 (which is, in turn, based upon Pattern 20, *Computing Static Expression Types*, on page 184). We're going to enforce the type compatibility checks described in Figure 8.2, on the following page.

In a nutshell, type compatibility means two things:

- An operation must be defined for the operand types it's applied to.
  resultType($operandtype_1$, op, $operandtype_2$) != **void**

- If we're looking for a value of type t, the value must be of type t or promotable to t.

  value-type==destination-type||value-promoted-type==destination-type.

  This ensures that we don't copy data between incompatible types. We can call this computation canAssignTo.

While we're at it, we might as well enforce the following symbol category rules as well:

- In x.y, x must be a **struct**.

1. **if** conditionals must evaluate to a **boolean** value.
2. Array reference indexes must be integers.
3. The left and right sides of an assignment must have compatible types.
4. Function call arguments and formal function declarations must have compatible types.
5. **return** expressions and function return types must be compatible.
6. The two operands of a binary arithmetic operation must have compatible types.
7. The operand of unary operators must have an appropriate type.

Figure 8.2: THE TYPE COMPATIBILITY RULES CYMBOL ENFORCES

- In f(), f must be a function symbol.
- In a[...], a must be an array symbol.

To implement type safety, we need to add resultType checks, canAssignTo checks, or both. In the next section, we'll add them to the helper methods of SymbolTable.

Implementation

Adding type checks to Pattern 21 is not particularly difficult, but it requires widespread changes. To make it easier to digest, we'll break the problem down into manageable chunks. Let's start with the expression operators.

Checking Expression Operand Types

To check for compatible operand types, all we've got to do is watch for a **void** result type. The getResultType() method is the same except for the error check:

`semantics/safety/SymbolTable.java`

```
public Type getResultType(Type[][] typeTable, CymbolAST a, CymbolAST b) {
    int ta = a.evalType.getTypeIndex(); // type index of left operand
    int tb = b.evalType.getTypeIndex(); // type index of right operand
    Type result = typeTable[ta][tb];    // operation result type
    if ( result==_void ) {
        listener.error(text(a)+", "+
                       text(b)+" have incompatible types in "+
                       text((CymbolAST)a.getParent()));
    }
```

```
    else {
        a.promoteToType = promoteFromTo[ta][tb];
        b.promoteToType = promoteFromTo[tb][ta];
    }
    return result;
}
```

The text() method computes the original source code from which we created the subtree. getResultType() works for relational and equality operators as well as the binary arithmetic operators like plus and multiply. The only difference is that the result type of relational and equality operators is always boolean:

semantics/safety/SymbolTable.java

```
public Type relop(CymbolAST a, CymbolAST b) {
    getResultType(relationalResultType, a, b);
    // even if the operands are incompatible, the type of
    // this operation must be boolean
    return _boolean;
}
public Type eqop(CymbolAST a, CymbolAST b) {
    getResultType(equalityResultType, a, b);
    return _boolean;
}
```

The unary operators explicitly check for particular types:

semantics/safety/SymbolTable.java

```
public Type uminus(CymbolAST a) {
    if ( !(a.evalType==_int && a.evalType==_float) ) {
        listener.error(text(a)+" must have int/float type in "+
                        text((CymbolAST)a.getParent()));
        return _void;
    }
    return a.evalType;
}
public Type unot(CymbolAST a) {
    if ( a.evalType!=_boolean ) {
        listener.error(text(a)+" must have boolean type in "+
                        text((CymbolAST)a.getParent()));
        return _boolean; // even though wrong, assume result boolean
    }
    return a.evalType;
}
```

For member access expressions, we only have to check that the left operand evaluates to a **struct**.

Here is the check from member():

`semantics/safety/SymbolTable.java`

```
Type type = expr.evalType;
if ( type.getClass() != StructSymbol.class ) {
    listener.error(text(expr)+" must be have struct type in "+
                    text((CymbolAST)expr.getParent()));
    return _void;
}
```

Array indexing has two semantic hazards to check. We need to verify that the identifier is in fact an array and that the index expression is an integer or promotable to an integer:

`semantics/safety/SymbolTable.java`

```
public Type arrayIndex(CymbolAST id, CymbolAST index) {
    Symbol s = id.scope.resolve(id.getText());
    id.symbol = s;                              // annotate AST
    if ( s.getClass() != VariableSymbol.class || // ensure it's an array
         s.type.getClass() != ArrayType.class )
    {
        listener.error(text(id)+" must be an array variable in "+
                        text((CymbolAST)id.getParent()));
        return _void;
    }
    VariableSymbol vs = (VariableSymbol)s;
    Type t = ((ArrayType)vs.type).elementType;    // get element type
    int texpr = index.evalType.getTypeIndex();
    // promote the index expr if necessary to int
    index.promoteToType = promoteFromTo[texpr][tINT];
    if ( !canAssignTo(index.evalType, _int, index.promoteToType) ) {
        listener.error(text(index)+" index must have integer type in "+
                        text((CymbolAST)id.getParent()));
    }
    return t;
}
```

The canAssignTo() method determines whether a value is compatible with a destination type (based upon its evaluated type and promoted type if needed):

`semantics/safety/SymbolTable.java`

```
public boolean canAssignTo(Type valueType,Type destType,Type promotion) {
    // either types are same or value was successfully promoted
    return valueType==destType || promotion==destType;
}
```

This method is the key type compatibility checker. The following sections use it a lot to analyze method calls and assignments.

Checking Method Calls and Return Values

Method calls have three semantic hazards. First, we have to check that the identifier is a function name, and second, we have to check that the argument expression types are compatible with the formally declared function parameters:

`semantics/safety/SymbolTable.java`

```
public Type call(CymbolAST id, List args) {
    Symbol s = id.scope.resolve(id.getText());
    if ( s.getClass() != MethodSymbol.class ) {
        listener.error(text(id)+" must be a function in "+
                        text((CymbolAST)id.getParent()));
        return _void;
    }
    MethodSymbol ms = (MethodSymbol)s;
    id.symbol = ms;
    int i=0;
    for (Symbol a : ms.orderedArgs.values() ) { // for each arg
        CymbolAST argAST = (CymbolAST)args.get(i++);
        // get argument expression type and expected type
        Type actualArgType = argAST.evalType;
        Type formalArgType = ((VariableSymbol)a).type;
        int targ = actualArgType.getTypeIndex();
        int tformal = formalArgType.getTypeIndex();
        // do we need to promote argument type to defined type?
        argAST.promoteToType = promoteFromTo[targ][tformal];
        if ( !canAssignTo(actualArgType, formalArgType,
                            argAST.promoteToType) ) {
            listener.error(text(argAST)+", argument "+
                            a.name+":<"+a.type+"> of "+ms.name+
                            "() have incompatible types in "+
                            text((CymbolAST)id.getParent()));
        }
    }
    return ms.type;
}
```

Finally, we have to check that return expression types are compatible with the declared function return type. Here is the check from ret():

`semantics/safety/SymbolTable.java`

```
if ( !canAssignTo(exprType, retType, expr.promoteToType) ) {
    listener.error(text(expr)+", "+
        ms.name+"():<"+ms.type+"> have incompatible types in "+
        text((CymbolAST)expr.getParent()));
}
```

Passing parameters and return statement values are implicit assignments. Let's deal with explicit assignments next.

Checking Assignments and Declaration Initializers

To check assignments for type safety, we verify that the right-side expression is compatible with the type of the left side (we're copying data from the right to the left). Here's the check from assign():

semantics/safety/SymbolTable.java

```
if ( !canAssignTo(rhs.evalType, lhs.evalType, rhs.promoteToType) ) {
    listener.error(text(lhs)+", "+
                   text(rhs)+" have incompatible types in "+
                   text((CymbolAST)lhs.getParent()));
}
```

Variable declarations with initialization expressions are also assignments. We have to check that the initialization expression type is compatible with the declaration type. Here's the check from declinit():

semantics/safety/SymbolTable.java

```
if ( !canAssignTo(init.evalType, declID.symbol.type,
                  init.promoteToType) ) {
    listener.error(text(declID)+", "+
        text(init)+" have incompatible types in "+
        text((CymbolAST)declID.getParent()));
}
```

The only thing left to check is that if-conditionals are booleans.

Checking That if-Conditionals Are Booleans

To check if-conditionals, we need to add a rule to our tree pattern matcher Types.g that triggers helper method ifstat() upon if-statement:

semantics/safety/Types.g

```
ifstat : ^('if' cond=. s=. e=.?) {symtab.ifstat($cond);} ;
```

The helper method ensures that the type of the condition is boolean:

semantics/safety/SymbolTable.java

```
public void ifstat(CymbolAST cond) {
    if ( cond.evalType != _boolean ) {
        listener.error("if condition "+text(cond)+
                       " must have boolean type in "+
                       text((CymbolAST)cond.getParent()));
    }
}
```

With these changes, we get some nice error messages from the test rig. For example, the following test file exercises the safety checks for operand types, array indexes, conditionals, function call arguments, and function return values.

```
semantics/safety/t.cymbol
```

```
void f() {
    char c = 4;                 // <char> = <int>                    ERROR
    boolean b;
    int a[];
    if ( 3 ) c='a';             // if ( <int> ) ...                  ERROR
    c = 4+1.2;                  // <char> = <float>                  ERROR
    b = !c;                     // !<char>                           ERROR
    int i = c < b ;             // <char> < <boolean>                ERROR
    i = -b;                     // -<boolean> (must be int/float) ERROR
    g(9);                       // g(<int>) but needs <char>         ERROR
    a[true] = 1;                // <array>[<boolean>] = <int>        ERROR
}
int g(char c) { return 9.2; } // return <float> needs <int>        ERROR
```

From t.cymbol, we get this output (it's missing the output related to the
type of each subexpression):

```
$ java Test t.cymbol
c:<char>, 4:<int> have incompatible types in char c = 4;
if condition 3:<int> must have boolean type in if ( 3 ) c='a';
c:<char>, 4+1.2:<float> have incompatible types in c = 4+1.2;
c:<char> must have boolean type in !c
c:<char>, b:<boolean> have incompatible types in c < b
i:<int>, c < b:<boolean> have incompatible types in int i = c < b ;
b:<boolean> must have int/float type in -b
i:<int>, -b:<void> have incompatible types in i = -b;
9:<int>, argument c:<char> of g() have incompatible types in g(9)
true:<boolean> index must have integer type in a[true]
9.2:<float>, g():<int> have incompatible types in return 9.2;
...
$
```

Test file u.cymbol checks that we use **struct**s properly and that we use
function symbols in function calls:

```
semantics/safety/u.cymbol
```

```
struct A { int x; };
struct B { int y; };
void f() {
  struct A a;
  struct B b;
  a = b;              // <struct A> = <struct B>         ERROR
  int i;
  int c = i.x;        // <int>.x                         ERROR
  c = a + 3 + a[3];   // <struct> + <int> + <struct>[]   ERROR
  c();                // <int>()                         ERROR
}
```

We get the following error messages:

```
$ java Test u.cymbol
a:<struct A:{x}>, b:<struct B:{y}> have incompatible types in a = b;
i:<int> must be have struct type in i.x
c:<int>, i.x:<void> have incompatible types in int c = i.x;
a:<struct A:{x}>, 3:<int> have incompatible types in a + 3
a must be an array variable in a[3]
a + 3:<void>, a[3]:<void> have incompatible types in a + 3 + a[3]
c:<int>, a + 3 + a[3]:<void> have incompatible types in c = a + 3 + a[3];
c must be a function in c()
...
$
```

The source code for this pattern is a complete static type checker for our C++ subset. By breaking the problem down into type computation, type promotion, and type checking, we've made things much easier to understand and implement.

Related Patterns

This pattern requires Pattern 20, *Computing Static Expression Types*, on page 184 and Pattern 21, *Automatic Type Promotion*, on page 193 before it can check for type compatibility. The next pattern alters Cymbol to have classes instead of **struct**s and checks polymorphic pointer assignments.

23 Enforcing Polymorphic Type Safety

Purpose

This pattern detects type incompatibilities in object pointer assignments in object-oriented languages like C++.

Discussion

Beyond the type checking done in Pattern 22, *Enforcing Static Type Safety*, on page 201, object-oriented languages have one more type hazard to worry about: *polymorphic* object pointer assignment. Polymorphism means that a pointer can refer to objects of multiple types. In contrast, C pointer assignments have to be between exact types. The key difference then between this pattern and the previous lies in the definition of type compatibility. Let's take a look at a C++ example that demonstrates what we need to handle:

```
Cat *pCat;
Bengal *pBengal; // assume Bengal subclasses Cat
pCat = pCat;     // target types, Cat, are the same, assignment is ok
pCat = pBengal;  // Bengal must be a subclass of Cat
```

Those assignments are OK, but pBengal=pCat is illegal because pCat could be any kind of cat, not just a bengal. pBengal=pTabby would also be illegal.

The semantic rule for polymorphic pointer assignment goes like this: for any assignment p=q, ensure that q's target type is the same as p's target type or that q's target type is a subclass of p's target type. The "target type" is the type of element pointed at by a pointer. This rule means that q's target type has to be a kind of p's target type.

We can check compatibility in one of two ways. Let's assume P *p; and Q *q. Then, either we look for Q at or below P in the class hierarchy or we look for P at or above Q. Pattern 19, *Symbol Table for Classes*, on page 167 builds class hierarchy trees with children pointing at their parents. So, let's ask Q if it has a P ancestor in the class hierarchy.

Polymorphism is meaningless without pointers, so we need to add them to the Cymbol language we've used throughout this chapter. (We've ignored pointers until now to keep things simple.) To demonstrate type checking in object pointer assignments, we need to extend Cymbol with these constructs:

- Classes with single inheritance (we'll remove **struct**s)

- Pointers to primitive and class types

- The & "address of" operator

- The * "pointer dereference" operator

- The -> "member access through object pointer" operator

To simplify our lives, we can normalize array references to the equivalent pointer arithmetic when building the AST (a[i] becomes *(a+i)). We'll do the same for member access through pointers (p->x becomes (*p).x). This way, the definition and type safety tree passes don't have to worry about the new syntax because the AST only has pointer arithmetic.

The next section extends the sample implementation from the previous pattern to handle classes and object pointer semantic rules.

Static vs. Dynamic Pointer Compatibility Checking

Static analysis tools and compilers are notoriously picky about pointer assignments. C++ in particular has to be very careful because anything goes at run-time. Bad pointer assignments can lead to incorrect field accesses and even memory violations. In dynamically typed languages like Python and Ruby, we don't even have to check for pointer compatibility at run-time. If we were to make a pointer assignment between incompatible types, the next member access on that object would generate an error.

Implementation

This section consists of two main chunks. The first section details how to implement polymorphic type checking. The second shows how to support pointers in Cymbol. Adding pointers gets a bit hairy, so you can skip it if you're only interested in the type checking part.

Checking for Polymorphism Between Object Pointers

Our implementation is an extension of Pattern 22, *Enforcing Static Type Safety*, on page 201 with symbol table support for classes from Pattern 19, *Symbol Table for Classes*, on page 167. The primary modification is a change in the definition of type compatibility in method canAssignTo(). The non-object-oriented version checks for exact type matches:

semantics/safety/SymbolTable.java
```
public boolean canAssignTo(Type valueType,Type destType,Type promotion) {
    // either types are same or value was successfully promoted
    return valueType==destType || promotion==destType;
}
```

whereas, for the object-oriented version, we need something looser. Because of this looser definition and because we need pointer support in Cymbol, it's easier to delegate functionality to the individual types:

semantics/oo/SymbolTable.java
```
public boolean canAssignTo(Type valueType,
                           Type destType,
                           Type promotion)
{   // handle both arithmetic types, objects, and object pointers.
    // either we can assign the value directly to the destination type or
    // it was promoted to the required destination type
    return valueType.canAssignTo(destType) || promotion==destType;
}
```

This means we need to add a new method to the Type interface for consistency across type objects in our symbol table:

semantics/oo/Type.java

```
public boolean canAssignTo(Type destType);
```

The built-in types like **int** require an exact type match in assignments:

semantics/oo/BuiltInTypeSymbol.java

```
public boolean canAssignTo(Type destType) { return this==destType; }
```

The same is true for objects such as Point or User. We can only assign Point objects to Point objects because we are copying an entire object (not just a pointer):

semantics/oo/ClassSymbol.java

```
public boolean canAssignTo(Type destType) { return this==destType; }
```

All of the fancy footwork for polymorphic type safety happens in Pointer-Type's canAssignTo() method. Class PointerType represents a pointer to a target type. For example, we can represent a pointer to class User with new PointerType(userClass), assuming userClass points to the ClassSymbol for User. This is analogous to ArrayType in Pattern 22, *Enforcing Static Type Safety*, on page 201.

For pointers to built-in types, the target types must be identical. Pointers to objects, on the other hand, only have to be related in the class hierarchy. The following method answers whether we can copy a pointer of one type to a destination type:

semantics/oo/PointerType.java

```
/** Can we assign this type to destination type?  destType must be
 *  pointer and to same type unless object ptr.  Then, we have to do a
 *  polymorphic check. [Ha! This method is a perfect example of
 *  static typing getting in the way. Look at all those type casts!]
 */
public boolean canAssignTo(Type destType) {
    // if not a pointer, return false
    if ( !(destType instanceof PointerType) ) return false;
    // What type is the target pointing at?
    Type destTargetType = ((PointerType)destType).targetType;
    Type srcTargetType = this.targetType;
    // if this and target are object pointers, check polymorphism
    if ( destTargetType instanceof ClassSymbol &&
         this.targetType instanceof ClassSymbol )
    {
        ClassSymbol thisClass   = (ClassSymbol)srcTargetType;
        ClassSymbol targetClass = (ClassSymbol)destTargetType;
        // Finally!  Here it is: the polymorphic type check :)
        return thisClass.isInstanceof(targetClass);
    }
```

```
    // not comparing object pointers; types we point at must be the same
    // For example: int *p; int *q; p = q;
    return srcTargetType == destTargetType;
}
```

The type check for polymorphism asks whether thisClass is the same as targetClass or is a subclass of targetClass via isInstanceof():

`semantics/oo/ClassSymbol.java`

```
/** Return true if 'ancestor' is this class or above in hierarchy */
public boolean isInstanceof(ClassSymbol ancestor) {
    ClassSymbol t = this;
    while ( t!=null ) {
        if ( t == ancestor ) return true;
        t = t.superClass;
    }
    return false;
}
```

OK, let's see what happens if we run the following Cymbol assignments through our test rig (which is identical to Test.java from the previous pattern):

`semantics/oo/t.cymbol`

```
class A { int x; };        // define class A
class B : A { int y; };    // define class B subclass of A
class C : A { int z; };    // define class C subclass of A
void f() {
  A a; A a2; B b; C c;     // define 4 object instances
  a = a2;          // a, a2 have same type A, so it's ok
  a = b;           // b's class is subclass of A but not ptr; NOT ok
  b = a;           // a's class is not below B so it's NOT ok
  b = c;           // b and c classes are siblings of A; not compatible
  A *pA; B *pB; C *pC;     // define 3 object pointers
  pA = pB;         // pB's points to B: B is a subclass of A so it's ok
  pB = pA;         // pA's points to class not below B so it's NOT ok
  pB = pC;         // pB and pC point to sibling classes of A; NOT ok
}
```

Only the first object assignment and first pointer assignment are valid. The polymorphic type checker emits errors for the rest:

```
$ java org.antlr.Tool Cymbol.g Def.g Types.g
$ javac *.java
$ java Test t.cymbol
a:<class A:{x}>, b:<class B:{y}> have incompatible types in a = b;
b:<class B:{y}>, a:<class A:{x}> have incompatible types in b = a;
b:<class B:{y}>, c:<class C:{z}> have incompatible types in b = c;
pB:<class B:{y}*>, pA:<class A:{x}*> have incompatible types in pB = pA;
pB:<class B:{y}*>, pC:<class C:{z}*> have incompatible types in pB = pC;
...
$
```

This completes the core of the material for this pattern. For completeness, though, you can read about adding pointers to Cymbol in the next section. Programming languages have moved away from explicit pointers (Java, C#, Ruby, and Python), but C and C++ aren't going away anytime soon. If you need to implement a language with pointers, take a look at the next section.

Adding Pointers to Cymbol

To support pointers, the first thing we need to do is add some syntax to our language. The following rule adds * as a valid prefix to a declaration's identifier:

```
semantics/oo/Cymbol.g
varDeclaration
    :   type ID ('=' expression)? ';'
            -> ^(VAR_DECL type ID expression?)
    |   type ID '[]' ('=' expression)? ';'
            -> ^(VAR_DECL ^('*' type) ID expression?)
    |   type '*' ID ('=' expression)? ';'
            -> ^(VAR_DECL ^('*' type) ID expression?)
    ;
```

It also normalizes array declarations to be the same as pointer declarations. Within expressions, we simulate array reference a[i] with the equivalent pointer arithmetic and dereference *(a+i). We also desugar member access operations such as p->x to (*p).x:

```
semantics/oo/Cymbol.g
postfixExpression
    :   (primary->primary)
        (
            (   '(' expressionList ')'
                -> ^(CALL["CALL"] $postfixExpression expressionList)
            |   r='[' expr ']' // convert a[i] to *(a+i)
                -> ^(DEREF[$r,"*"] ^(ADD["+"] $postfixExpression expr))
            |   '.' ID
                -> ^('.' $postfixExpression ID)
            |   r='->' ID // convert p->x to (*p).x
                -> ^(MEMBER[$r] ^(DEREF $postfixExpression) ID)
            )
        )*
    ;
```

After successfully building an AST, the symbol definition phase needs the rules to handle class definitions from Pattern 19, *Symbol Table for Classes*, on page 167.

It also replaces array support in rule **type** with pointer support:

semantics/oo/Def.g

```
type returns [Type type]
    :   ^('*' typeElement)  {$type = new PointerType($typeElement.type);}
    |   typeElement         {$type = $typeElement.type;}
    ;
```

In the symbol resolution and type computation phase, the **expr** rule invokes a helper method when it sees a pointer dereference:

semantics/oo/Types.g

```
    |   ^(ADDR a=expr)      {$type=new PointerType($a.type);}
    |   ^(DEREF a=expr)     {$type=symtab.ptrDeref($a.start);}
```

The helper method returns the target type of the dereferenced expression. For example, *pInt evaluates to **int** if pInt is a pointer to an **int**.

semantics/oo/SymbolTable.java

```java
public Type ptrDeref(CymbolAST expr) {
    if ( !(expr.evalType instanceof PointerType) ) {
        listener.error(text(expr)+" must be a pointer");
        return _void;
    }
    return ((PointerType)expr.evalType).targetType;
}
```

To support pointers in expressions, we need some small but pervasive changes to our type result tables. First, we need to introduce a new type index †PTR and increase the dimensions of our type tables by one. For example, here is the arithmetic result type table:

semantics/oo/SymbolTable.java

```java
/** Map t1 op t2 to result type (_void implies illegal) */
public static final Type[][] arithmeticResultType = new Type[][] {
    /*           struct boolean char   int     float,  void,  ptr */
    /*struct*/ {_void, _void,   _void, _void,  _void,  _void, _void},
    /*boolean*/{_void, _void,   _void, _void,  _void,  _void, _void},
    /*char*/   {_void, _void,   _char, _int,   _float, _void, _ptr},
    /*int*/    {_void, _void,   _int,  _int,   _float, _void, _ptr},
    /*float*/  {_void, _void,   _float,_float, _float, _void, _void},
    /*void*/   {_void, _void,   _void, _void,  _void,  _void, _void},
    /*ptr*/    {_void, _void,   _ptr,  _ptr,   _void,  _void, _void}
};
```

The table encodes the fact that we can add characters and integers to pointers on either side of an arithmetic operator. For example, arithmeticResultType[†INT][†PTR] is a pointer. But, we can't add two pointers together. arithmeticResultType[†PTR][†PTR] is invalid (**void**). We use _ptr to represent a generic pointer, but we need exact type results. The following addition to getResultType() returns the actual pointer type of the incoming pointer operand:

`semantics/oo/SymbolTable.java`

```
// check for pointer arithmetic; only one operand can be a ptr.
// if result and 'a' are ptrs, then result should be a's type
if ( result==_ptr && ta==tPTR ) result = a.evalType;
else if ( result==_ptr && tb==tPTR ) result = b.evalType;
```

There is one tricky entry in the promoteFromTo table for pointers. We need to encode the fact that characters become integers when added to pointers. In other words, we should interpret 'a'+p as (int)'a'+p. There is no way to promote a pointer to a character, so the table is not symmetric. The entry for adding an integer to a pointer is null, which means there is no need to promote the integer.

The source code shows a few more details, but you see the important elements here.

Related Patterns

This pattern is an object-oriented equivalent of Pattern 22, *Enforcing Static Type Safety*, on page 201. It incorporates Pattern 20, *Computing Static Expression Types*, on page 184 and Pattern 21, *Automatic Type Promotion*, on page 193.

Up Next

This pattern concludes our discussion of static type checking. As a learning tool, we broke down this problem into three pieces: type computation, type promotion, and type checking. The third and fourth patterns demonstrated type checking for non-object-oriented and object-oriented languages. Once you understand the entire picture, you would pick either Pattern 22, *Enforcing Static Type Safety*, on page 201 or this pattern to implement your own static type checker. The other patterns are components of the type checkers.

So far, we've learned how to write code to recognize sentences, construct AST intermediate representations, walk ASTs, populate symbol tables, manage nested scopes, construct class hierarchies, and enforce semantic type rules. In short, we've learned how to read in programs and check them for type safety. Now we need to figure out how to execute them. The next two chapters catalog the most common patterns for interpreting and translating programs.

Part III

Building Interpreters

Chapter 9

Building High-Level Interpreters

We've covered a lot of ground in the book so far and have reached an important milestone. We're ready to start actually building language applications. In the previous two parts of this book, we focused on patterns to verify the syntax of an input sentence and make sure that it follows a set of semantic rules. Now, it's time to start thinking about processing input sentences, not just validating them. In this part of the book, we're going to learn how to build language interpreters (programs that execute other programs).

To execute a program not written in machine code, we've got to interpret the program or translate it to the equivalent program in a language that already runs on that machine. We'll leave translation to Chapter 11, *Translating Computer Languages*, on page 279 and Chapter 12, *Generating DSLs with Templates*, on page 313. In the meantime, we're going to look at high-level and low-level interpreters in this chapter and the next. High-level interpreters directly execute source code instructions or the AST equivalent. (Low-level interpreters execute instructions called *bytecodes* that are close to CPU machine instructions.) Here are the two high-level interpreters we'll discuss:

- Pattern 24, *Syntax-Directed Interpreter*, on page 225: This interpreter consists of a parser that triggers interpreter action methods.

- Pattern 25, *Tree-Based Interpreter*, on page 230: This pattern triggers action methods by walking an AST created by the parser.

These high-level patterns are best suited to building DSLs rather than general-purpose programming languages. Usually, simplicity and low-cost implementation trump execution efficiency for DSLs.[1] Because it leads to simpler implementations, we'll also focus on dynamically typed languages for these patterns. Our goal is the minimal machinery needed to interpret a high-level language.

An interpreter simulates an idealized computer in software. Such "computers" have a processor, code memory, data memory, and (usually) a stack. The processor pulls instructions from the code memory, decodes them, and executes them. An instruction can read or write to the data memory or onto the stack. Function calls save return addresses so they can return to the instruction following the function call.

There are three things to consider when building an interpreter: how to store data, how and when to track symbols, and how to execute instructions. Let's investigate them in that order before diving into the patterns.

9.1 Designing High-Level Interpreter Memory Systems

High-level interpreters store values according to variable names, not memory addresses (like low-level interpreters and CPUs do). That means we've got to represent memory with a dictionary mapping names to values.

There are three kinds of memory spaces to worry about for most programming languages: global memory, function spaces (for parameters and locals), and data aggregate instances (**struct**s or objects). For simplicity, we can normalize all these spaces by treating them as dictionaries. Even fields are really just variables stored within an instance's memory space. To store a value into a space, we map a name to that value. A memory space is the run-time analog of a scope from static analysis.

Interpreters have one global memory space but multiple function spaces (assuming the language we're interpreting has functions). Each function call creates a new space to hold parameters and local variables. The interpreter keeps track of the function spaces by pushing them onto the stack. Upon returning from a function, the interpreter pops the top space off the stack. This way, parameters and local variables pop in and out of existence as we need them.

---

1. http://ftp.cwi.nl/CWIreports/SEN/SEN-E0517.pdf

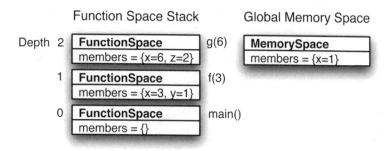

Figure 9.1: MEMORY SPACE STACK AFTER CALLING G()

Let's look at the global and function memory spaces used by the following C++ code snippet:

```
int x = 1;
void g(int x) { int z = 2; }
void f(int x) { int y = 1; g(2*x); }
int main() { f(3); }
```

In Figure 9.1, we see what the function space stack and global memory space of a C++ interpreter would look like after executing the assignment to z in g(). As g() returns, the interpreter would pop that function space. Then it'd pop the function space for the call to f() and finally the function space for main().

Just as we can have multiple function memory spaces, we can create multiple data aggregate instances. Those materialize in response to **new** expressions (or the equivalent in the language we're interpreting). We store references to those aggregates into a memory space just like any other variable. The following C++ code creates two **struct** instances and assigns them to local (pointer) variables.

```
struct A { int x; };
int main() {
    A *a = new A(); a->x = 1;
    A *b = new A(); b->x = 2;
}
```

In Figure 9.2, on the following page, we see the interpreter's memory spaces right before main() returns. main()'s function space has two variables, a and b, each pointing to a separate **struct** memory space. To

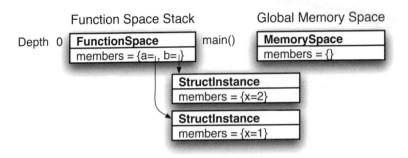

Figure 9.2: TWO STRUCT INSTANCES SAVED AS LOCAL VARIABLES A AND B

implement assignment a->x=1;, the interpreter invokes something like a.put("x",1); in its implementation language.

To handle class instances instead of **struct**s, the easiest thing to do is to pack all fields (inherited or direct members) into a single instance space. Inheritance is really just a glorified include when it comes to fields. So, even objects are just another memory space.

Now we've got to consider which assignments are valid. Depending on the language, assignment to an unknown variable could be an error (C++) or could create a local variable (Python). Python can even create fields at will by assigning values to fields. Regardless of the interpreted language's semantics, memory spaces have to know what kind of things can go into them. The easiest way to do this is to track the program entity associated with a memory space. For example, function spaces point at their function definition symbols, and instances point at their class definition symbols. In the next section, we'll figure out what kind of symbol tables we need for interpreters.

9.2 Tracking Symbols in High-Level Interpreters

Given a variable reference x in a program, we need to figure out which memory space it lives in so we can load or store its value. The interpreter figures this out by resolving x and asking for its surrounding scope. That scope tells the interpreter in what kind of scope the variable belongs: global, function, or data aggregate instance. Once the interpreter knows the kind of memory space, it can pick the proper dictionary in physical memory.

If the symbol table says x is a global variable, the interpreter loads it from the global space. If resolves to a local variable or parameter, the interpreter loads it from the function space on the top of the function space stack.

If x is a field of a class, we know that it's really this.x (or whatever this is called in the interpreted language). The interpreter should load this from the function space on the top of the function space stack and then load x from the space this points to.

Because symbol table management happens at run-time in an interpreter, it's easy to confuse resolving a variable with loading its value. Just keep in mind that resolving a variable means figuring out which program entity it refers to. We can do this without even running the program for statically typed languages. Loading a variable, on the other hand, is purely a run-time operation. We resolve a variable to figure out the space in which its value lives. For a single program entity, such as a local variable, there can be multiple values (in different function spaces) at run-time.

Resolving variables at run-time is expensive, so many languages ask the programmer to indicate each variable's scope. For example, in Ruby we say $x to mean x is a global variable, and we say @x to mean that x is a field of an object. In Python, we say self.x to mean x is a field.

Because dynamically typed languages don't declare variables and their types prior to usage, there's no point in populating a symbol table with VariableSymbol objects. That doesn't mean, though, that we can get away without symbol table management at run-time. Error checking is one reason. We don't want to access undefined parameters or fields. This means that, at the very least, we need some symbol table objects to track formal parameter lists and field lists.

An interpreter might need to treat parameters and locals differently. For example, in the following Python function, the interpreter must distinguish between parameter x and local variable y:

```python
def f(x):
    x = 1 # set parameter value to 1 (don't create local variable)
    y = 2 # create a local variable called y and set to 2
```

Without the formal parameter list in the function definition, Python couldn't distinguish between locals and parameters.

Statically typed languages like C++ and Java really need scope trees, so Pattern 25, *Tree-Based Interpreter*, on page 230 shows you how to build a full scope tree before execution (even though it doesn't technically need it).

OK, it's time to figure out how to execute instructions in an interpreter now that we know what interpreter memory systems look like.

9.3 Processing Instructions

The basic idea behind executing instructions is called the *fetch-decode-execute cycle*. First, we load an instruction from code memory. Then, we decode the instruction to find the operation and operands. Finally, we execute the operation. Rinse and repeat. Ultimately the interpreter runs out of instructions in the main program, or it executes a halt instruction.

The nature of the processor depends on what the code looks like in code memory. At the one extreme lies Pattern 24, *Syntax-Directed Interpreter*, on the facing page where we directly execute the text of the source code. At the other extreme, just above machine code, lies the bytecode interpreters in Chapter 10, *Building Bytecode Interpreters*, on page 239. Pattern 25, *Tree-Based Interpreter*, on page 230 is somewhere in between. The more highly we process the program before execution, the faster it will go at run-time.

The processor for Pattern 24, *Syntax-Directed Interpreter*, on the next page is a parser augmented with actions that decode and execute instructions. The processor for Pattern 25, *Tree-Based Interpreter*, on page 230 triggers actions as it walks the tree with Pattern 13, *External Tree Visitor*, on page 116. Regardless of the pattern, interpreting a program is all about executing a code snippet for each input instruction.

Here's a summary of the patterns' suitability:

Pattern	When to Apply
Pattern 24, *Syntax-Directed Interpreter*, on the facing page	This pattern works best for small languages that are really just lists of instructions or declarations. It's not super-efficient but has the fewest components to build.

Pattern	**When to Apply**
Pattern 25, *Tree-Based Interpreter*, on page 230	Because this pattern performs a preprocessing pass to build an AST and scope tree, it supports forward references. Before execution, we can perform optimizations, squirrel away information from analysis, or do rewrites on the AST like x to this.x. This pattern is typically faster than a source-level interpreter because it doesn't waste time reparsing input. We can skip an entire subtree by moving a pointer instead of parsing over it.

24 Syntax-Directed Interpreter

☐

Purpose

This pattern directly executes source code without building an intermediate representation and without translating it to another language.

The sample implementation for this pattern focuses on building a syntax-directed interpreter for an SQL subset.

Discussion

A syntax-directed interpreter mimics what we do when we trace source code manually. As we step through the code, we parse, validate, and execute instructions. Everything happens in the parser because a syntax-directed interpreter doesn't create an AST or translate the source code to bytecodes or machine code. The interpreter directly feeds off of syntax to execute statements.

The good news is that there are very few "moving parts" in a syntax-directed interpreter. There are really only two key components:

- *The source code parser*: The parser recognizes input construct and immediately triggers actions. In the sample implementation for this pattern, that means triggering methods like select() and createTable().
- *The interpreter*: The interpreter maintains state and houses instruction implementation methods. Depending on the language,

the interpreter will have code memory (the input stream) and a global memory space (to hold name-value pairs for variables).

The bad news is that syntax-directed interpreters are only suitable to a narrow range of languages. They work best on small DSLs instead of general-purpose programming languages. More specifically, interpreting **if** statements, loops, functions, and classes in syntax-directed interpreters is extremely awkward. (There is a sample syntax-directed implementation[2] of the Pie language from the next pattern on the ANTLR wiki.) This awkwardness comes from the fact that the interpreter would sometimes have to parse statements without triggering interpreter actions. For example, when an interpreter sees a function definition, it shouldn't execute the statements in the function body. It should only execute the body when another part of the program calls that function.

Use this pattern when your input language looks like a sequence of instructions or simple declarative statements. Examples include graphics languages, network protocols, text-processing languages, job control languages, and simple shell scripting languages. This pattern is not suitable for rule or constraint-based languages such as Prolog or Object Constraint Language (OCL). Those applications typically need an internal representation of the rules or constraints. (This pattern does not create a data structure from the input before interpretation.)

Before looking at a sample implementation, let's see how the parser drives the interpreter. To interpret an input construct, the parser triggers a method that implements the appropriate functionality. This means that the grammar (or hand-built parser) looks like a bunch of "match this, call that" pairs. So, when we see an assignment, we want to call an assign() or store() method in the interpreter. In an ANTLR grammar-based implementation, we might have rules like this:

```
assignment : ID '=' expr {interp.assign($ID, $expr.value);} ;
expr returns [Object value] : ... ; // compute and return value
```

There's an implementation method for every statement and expression operation. For example, here's the algorithm to perform an assignment:

```
void assign(String id, Object value) { // execute "id = value"
    MemorySpace targetSpace = «space-containing-id»;
    if «not-found-in-any-space» then targetSpace = currentSpace;
    targetSpace[id] = value;
}
```

---

2. http://www.antlr.org/wiki/display/ANTLR3/Pie

After decoding the assignment statement and triggering an action, the parser continues to the next statement. This is just like a physical processor moving onto the next machine instruction. In the next section, we'll fill in some details by implementing a subset of SQL suitable for implementation with this pattern.

Implementation

SQL in its full glory is too complicated for this pattern, but we can make a nice syntax-directed interpreter demo using an SQL subset. SQL is a DSL designed to define schemas, insert data, and perform queries for a relational database. To keep things simple, let's avoid the complexity of a real database and build our own in-memory database. We can represent tables as lists of rows and can represent rows as lists of column values. This SQL subset could also form the basis of a nice interface to HBase.[3,4] (HBase's goal is to host massive tables in a cloud computing environment.)

Our SQL subset can define tables with dynamically typed columns, query those tables, store values in global variables, and print values. For example, here's a sample script:

interp/syntax/t.q

```
create table users (primary key name, passwd);
insert into users set name='parrt', passwd='foobar';
insert into users set name='tombu', passwd='spork';
p = select passwd, name from users; // reverse column order
print p;
```

The main program in QInterp opens the file and passes it to the interpreter for execution. Here's the output we get:

```
$ java QInterp t.q
foobar, parrt
spork, tombu
```

Here's another sample script that demonstrates how to filter the rows in a table:

interp/syntax/t4.q

```
create table users (primary key name, passwd, quota);
insert into users set name='parrt', passwd='foobar', quota=99;
insert into users set name='tombu', passwd='spork', quota=200;
insert into users set name='sri', passwd='numnum', quota=200;
```

---

3. http://hadoop.apache.org/hbase
4. Thanks to Paul Ambrose for this idea.

```
tombuQuota = select quota from users where name='tombu';
print tombuQuota;
names = select name from users where quota=tombuQuota;
print names; // print all names with same quota as tombu
```

And here's the output:

```
$ java QInterp t4.q
200
tombu
sri
$
```

The **where** clause only allows the equality operator. If we need complex conditionals, this pattern won't work. Conditionals have to execute as we scan through a table rather than as we parse the **select** statement itself. The next pattern would be much more suitable.

The implementation of our persistence layer is just Java code (classes Table, Row, ResultSet) that manipulates dictionaries and lists. So, let's focus on the core of the interpreter: the SQL subset grammar and the actions it triggers. Each table has a name and a list of columns, where the first column is the primary key:

interp/syntax/Q.g

```
table
    :   'create' 'table' tbl=ID
        '(' 'primary' 'key' key=ID (',' columns+=ID)+ ')' ';'
        {interp.createTable($tbl.text, $key.text, $columns);}
    ;
```

After recognizing the pattern, the ANTLR-generated parser triggers createTable() in Interpreter to create the new Table and define the columns:

interp/syntax/Interpreter.java

```
public void createTable(String name,
                        String primaryKey,
                        List<Token> columns)
{
    Table table = new Table(name, primaryKey);
    for (Token t : columns) table.addColumn(t.getText());
    tables.put(name, table);
}
```

The Interpreter class tracks the set of tables and space for a global memory to hold variables:

interp/syntax/Interpreter.java

```
Map<String, Object> globals = new HashMap<String, Object>();
Map<String, Table> tables = new HashMap<String, Table>();
```

Storing values in global memory is straightforward. After matching the assignment, the grammar invokes an implementation method in the interpreter:

`interp/syntax/Q.g`

```
assign : ID '=' expr ';'  {interp.store($ID.text, $expr.value);} ;
```

The implementation method maps the variable name to that value in a dictionary:

`interp/syntax/Interpreter.java`

```
public void store(String name, Object o) { globals.put(name, o); }
```

To look up a variable's value, we reverse the process and look up the variable name in the dictionary.

To store values in a table rather than in the global memory space, we use the **insert** statement. After matching the syntax, rule **insert** triggers insertInto():

`interp/syntax/Q.g`

```
insert
    : 'insert' 'into' ID 'set' setFields[interp.tables.get($ID.text)] ';'
      {interp.insertInto($ID.text, $setFields.row);}
    ;
```

Before matching the field assignments, the rule creates a Table and passes it to rule **setFields**:

`interp/syntax/Q.g`

```
setFields[Table t] returns [Row row]
@init { $row = new Row(t.columns); } // set return value
    :   set[$row] (',' set[$row])*
    ;
set[Row row] // pass in Row we're filling in
    :   ID '=' expr {row.set($ID.text, $expr.value);}
    ;
```

After matching all the assignments, **setFields** returns the Row it created. To get column values, **setFields** invokes **expr**:

`interp/syntax/Q.g`

```
// Match a simple value or do a query
expr returns [Object value] // access as $expr.value in other rules
    :   ID      {$value = interp.load($ID.text);}
    |   INT     {$value = $INT.int;}
    |   STRING  {$value = $STRING.text;}
    |   query   {$value = $query.value;}
    ;
```

Rule **expr** not only matches the appropriate syntax but also returns the computed value. The last alternative lets us store the ResultSet computed by a **select**:

```
tombuQuota = select quota from users where name='tombu';
```

At this point, you've seen all the key pieces of a syntax-directed interpreter. This type of interpreter is the simplest possible because it does not construct any internal data structures from the input. But, of course, this limits the kind of languages it can handle. In the next pattern, we're going to build an interpreter for a much more complicated language. To get more power, we'll build an AST first and then walk it repeatedly to interpret input programs.

Related Patterns

This pattern is analogous to Pattern 29, *Syntax-Directed Translator*, on page 296, which emits output according to input syntax. Actions embedded within Pattern 4, *LL(k) Recursive-Descent Parser*, on page 43 drive the interpreter.

☐ | 25 | Tree-Based Interpreter |

Purpose

This pattern executes programs by constructing an AST from the source code and walking the tree.

This tree-based interpreter pattern builds a complete scope tree before executing a program. That means it can support both statically typed languages like Java and dynamically typed languages like Python. (It can resolve all symbols statically before execution.)

Discussion

The previous pattern directly executed source code, without processing it in any way. At the opposite extreme, a compiler translates source code to machine code, which we can then run natively on the processor. Per the compiler application pipeline from Chapter 1, *Language Applications Cracked Open*, on page 3, a compiler builds an intermediate representation and ultimately generates optimized machine code from that IR.

A tree-based interpreter is like a compiler front end with an interpreter grafted onto the end instead of a code generator. Conceptually, this pattern isn't very different from Pattern 24, *Syntax-Directed Interpreter*, on page 225. The biggest difference is that we don't drive the interpreter with the parser. Instead, we build an AST with the parser and then drive the interpreter with a tree visitor.

This structural change to the pipeline leads to a few advantages over a syntax-directed interpreter:

- We can separate symbol definition from symbol resolution, partitioning the tasks between parsing and execution. This allows forward references.

- Tree-based interpreters are more flexible because we can do substitutions while building the AST if necessary. For a statically typed language like Java, we could substitute the subtree for x with a subtree for this.x. We could also rewrite the tree in a separate tree pass before execution to perform optimizations and so on.

Building an interpreter for a language like Prolog or LISP is a lot different from building one for Python or Java. To narrow the focus of this pattern, we need to pick a particular language—one that is similar to the language(s) you're likely to build. Since this high-level interpreter works best for dynamically typed programming languages and DSLs, we'll invent a Python-like dynamically typed language called Pie.

Defining a Sample High-Level Language

A Pie program consists of a series of function definitions, **struct** definitions, and statements. Function definitions specify the name and argument list as well as a sequence of instructions followed by a period on a line by itself:

```
x = 1       # define global variable x
def f(y):   # define f in the global space
    x = 2   # set global variable x
    y = 3   # set parameter y
    z = 4   # create local variable z
.           # end of statement list
f(5)        # call f with parameter y = 5
```

The comments on the assignment statements specify the variable creation semantics. If we don't see a previous definition in the function scope or the global scope, we create a local variable. Referencing a variable that doesn't exist is an error.

Pie has **return**, **print**, **if**, **while**, and call statements. Expressions can have identifiers and the following literals: characters, integers, and strings. The operators are ==, <, +, -, *, new (create **struct** instance), and . (member access).

Pie defines **struct**s in the global or function scopes using C-like syntax but without the type specifiers. The following program illustrates the struct definition and member access syntax:

```
struct Point {x, y}  # define a struct symbol in global scope
p = new Point        # create a new Point instance; store in global var
p.x = 1              # set the fields of p
p.y = 2
```

To resolve expression p.x, we resolve p and then look up x within that memory space. Pie makes sure that x and y exist as fields in p's **struct** definition before allowing the assignment.

Before jumping into a sample implementation of Pie, let's take a look at managing symbol tables in a tree-based interpreter and executing code with a tree walker.

Managing Symbol Table

This pattern doesn't define function and **struct** symbols while it executes the input program. It does all that while parsing and building the AST. During execution, it can resolve symbols using a conventional scope tree built during the parse. Because we're resolving symbols after having defined them, this pattern allows forward references. We can call a function defined later in the file, for example.

Separating symbol table construction from execution significantly simplifies the interpreter. The parser deals with symbol scopes, and the interpreter deals with memory spaces. Memory spaces don't do double duty as scopes. During execution, though, we still need scope information to resolve symbols.

To carry scope information forward from the parser to the interpreter, we can annotate the AST nodes. Let's look at how a function call in a Pie program carries through both phases. A call to f() results in a (CALL f) subtree. After creating the subtree, the parser sets the **CALL** node's scope field to the current scope (as we did in Pattern 19, *Symbol Table for Classes*, on page 167). Then, during execution, the call() action method can call resolve("f") relative to that scope.

Executing Code with a Tree Visitor

The interpreter uses Pattern 13, *External Tree Visitor*, on page 116 to trigger action methods as it walks the AST created by the parser. The visitor dispatcher method triggers actions like assign(), ifstat(), and call() upon seeing subtrees with =, if, and **CALL** root tokens. The dispatcher is a giant **switch** statement, as you'll see in the next section.

The action methods take a single AST parameter and so must decode instructions by walking the children. (In a syntax-directed interpreter, the parser decodes instructions and passes the relevant operands to the interpreter methods.) Extracting information from subtrees manually is tedious but straightforward. We also have to be sure that we send the visitor down the various subtree children. Otherwise, the interpreter won't interpret the entire program.

With all the generalities out of the way, let's implement our first programming language interpreter.

Implementation

The first thing we need to do is build a grammar in Pie.g that parses Pie code, constructs a scope tree, and constructs an AST (Pattern 9, *Homogeneous AST*, on page 94). Then, we'll write methods in Interpreter that implement the various Pie instructions and operations. Interpreter also has the exec() dispatcher method for our visitor.

The nodes of the AST are of type PieAST and extend ANTLR's CommonTree with a scope field. InterPie has the code that tells ANTLR to build PieAST nodes instead of CommonTree nodes.

The scope tree created by our parser consists of a variety of scope objects per Pattern 18, *Symbol Table for Data Aggregates*, on page 161. The scopes holds VariableSymbol (for fields and parameters), Function-Symbol, and StructSymbol objects. Here's the complete symbol table class hierarchy for this pattern:

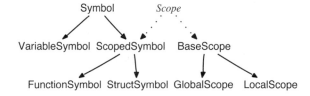

Technically, we don't need a full symbol table to execute Pie code. A full symbol table and scope tree makes this implementation more general, though. Some of you will want to build interpreters for statically typed languages.

Other than the implementation methods and visitor dispatcher, our Interpreter object houses a pointer to the AST root (our code memory), the global memory, the function memory space stack, and a pointer to the global scope:

<code>interp/tree/Interpreter.java</code>

```
GlobalScope globalScope;    // global scope is filled by the parser
MemorySpace globals = new MemorySpace("globals");        // global memory
MemorySpace currentSpace = globals;
Stack<FunctionSpace> stack = new Stack<FunctionSpace>();// call stack
PieAST root;                   // the AST represents our code memory
TokenRewriteStream tokens;
PieLexer lex;                  // lexer/parser are part of the processor
PieParser parser;
```

Because we've already seen parsing (Chapter 2, *Basic Parsing Patterns*, on page 21), AST construction (Chapter 4, *Building Intermediate Form Trees*, on page 73), and scope tree construction before (Chapter 7, *Managing Symbol Tables for Data Aggregates*, on page 155), we can focus on fusing a visitor onto our implementation methods. The most important method is the visitor dispatcher, exec(). The goal of the dispatcher is to invoke a method to handle each kind of subtree found in the tree. We can implement that with a **switch** that looks like this:

```
/** visitor dispatch according to node token type */
public Object exec(PieAST t) {
    switch ( t.getType() ) {
        case PieParser.BLOCK : block(t); break;
        case PieParser.ASSIGN : assign(t); break;
        case PieParser.RETURN : ret(t); break;
        case PieParser.PRINT : print(t); break;
        case PieParser.IF : ifstat(t); break;
        case PieParser.CALL : return call(t);
        case PieParser.NEW : return instance(t);
        case PieParser.ADD : return add(t);
        case PieParser.INT : return Integer.parseInt(t.getText());
        case PieParser.DOT : return load(t);
        case PieParser.ID :  return load(t);
        ...
        default : «error» // catch unhandled node types
    }
}
```

"Handling" a subtree means executing the appropriate interpreter action and walking the subtree nodes. The combined visitor-action methods take a single parameter: the root of the subtree it should handle.

It's up to the method to extract operands from the subtree's children. For example, here is how to handle assignment subtrees:

`interp/tree/Interpreter.java`

```java
public void assign(PieAST t) {
    PieAST lhs = (PieAST)t.getChild(0);    // get operands
    PieAST expr = (PieAST)t.getChild(1);
    Object value = exec(expr);             // walk/evaluate expr
    if ( lhs.getType()==PieParser.DOT ) {
        fieldassign(lhs, value); // field ^('=' ^('.' a x) expr)
        return;
    }
    // var assign ^('=' a expr)
    MemorySpace space = getSpaceWithSymbol(lhs.getText());
    if ( space==null ) space = currentSpace; // create in current space
    space.put(lhs.getText(), value);       // store
}
```

The left child of the = root will be either a **ID** node or a member access expression with a . root node. In either case, we need to evaluate the expression on the right side of the assignment. We grab the second child (the expression) and evaluate it by recursively calling exec().

The semantic rules for creating local variables are the same as in Python. If a variable on the left of an assignment isn't in the current function space or the global space, we create a new variable. Here's how to figure out whether a variable already exists:

`interp/tree/Interpreter.java`

```java
/** Return scope holding id's value; current func space or global. */
public MemorySpace getSpaceWithSymbol(String id) {
    if (stack.size()>0 && stack.peek().get(id)!=null) { // in top stack?
        return stack.peek();
    }
    if ( globals.get(id)!=null ) return globals;        // in globals?
    return null;                                        // nowhere
}
```

Assigning to a **struct** field is like assigning to a variable in a StructSpace instead of FunctionSpace or global MemorySpace. The main difference is that we want to ensure the field is defined instead of creating a new field. Here is the core of fieldload() that stores to «*expr*».fieldname:

```java
Object a = load(«expr»);
StructInstance struct = (StructInstance)a;
if ( struct.def.resolveMember(fieldname) == null ) {
    listener.error("can't assign; "+struct.name+" has no "+fieldname+
                " field", f.token);
    return;
}
struct.put(fieldname, value);
```

Finally, let's turn our attention to functions. To call a Pie function, we make sure the function exists and then create a FunctionSpace to hold parameter values:

interp/tree/Interpreter.java

```
String fname = t.getChild(0).getText();
FunctionSymbol fs = (FunctionSymbol)t.scope.resolve(fname);
if ( fs==null ) {
    listener.error("no such function "+fname, t.token);
    return null;
}
FunctionSpace fspace = new FunctionSpace(fs);
MemorySpace saveSpace = currentSpace;
currentSpace = fspace;
```

Before storing parameters into that space, we have to make sure that there is no mismatch in the number of parameters. The number of actual parameters passed to the function has to be the same as in the formal parameter list:

interp/tree/Interpreter.java

```
int argCount = t.getChildCount()-1;
// check for argument compatibility
if ( fs.formalArgs==null && argCount>0 || // args compatible?
     fs.formalArgs!=null && fs.formalArgs.size()!=argCount ) {
    listener.error("function "+fs.name+" argument list mismatch");
    return null;
}
```

Then, we assign the actual parameters to the formal parameter names in the order given by the formal parameters:

interp/tree/Interpreter.java

```
int i = 0; // define args according to order in formalArgs
for (Symbol argS : fs.formalArgs.values()) {
    VariableSymbol arg = (VariableSymbol)argS;
    PieAST ithArg = (PieAST)t.getChild(i+1);
    Object argValue = exec(ithArg);
    fspace.put(arg.name, argValue);
    i++;
}
```

At that point, we're ready to execute the body of the target function with exec(). The FunctionSymbol knows the AST for the function's body (field blockAST). To execute it, though, we've got an issue.

We have to get the **return** statement in the called function to pop back out of multiple method calls in our implementation. The **return** statement should make the interpreter return to the statement following the calling statement. Clearly, though, we can't map **return** in the interpreted language to **return** in our implementation language:

```
void ret() { return; } // oops; improper return mechanism
```

We need to unroll the ret() and exec() implementation methods all the way back to the call() method. That's exactly what exceptions do. So, all we've got to do is wrap the execution of the function body in a **try-catch**:

interp/tree/Interpreter.java

```
Object result = null;
stack.push(fspace);        // PUSH new arg, local scope
try { exec(fs.blockAST); } // do the call
catch (ReturnValue rv) { result = rv.value; } // trap return value
stack.pop();               // POP arg, locals
currentSpace = saveSpace;
return result;
```

Method ret() throws a ReturnValue exception (or whatever you want to call it). If there is a return value, we can store it in the exception object. This mechanism isn't slow if we share the same exception object. Only creating exceptions is expensive; throwing them is no big deal. So, no matter how deep our implementation's method call stack is, ret() will always get us back to the statement following the function body execution.

Because we define all functions and **structs** during parsing, function calls and **new** operations during execution can see any definition in the program. For example, the following Pie code works with this pattern but not in the syntax-directed interpreter because of forward references:

interp/tree/forward.pie

```
print f(4)            # references definition on next line
def f(x) return 2*x
print new User        # references definition on next line
struct User { name, password }
```

The interpreter sees the definitions with no problem:

```
$ java InterPie forward.pie
8
{name=null, password=null}
$
```

Here's a program that tests the interpreter's error handling:

`interp/tree/structerrors.pie`

```
struct User { name, password }
u = new User
u.name = "parrt"      # make u.name a string
u.name.y = "parrt"    # u.name is a string not a struct
u.x = 3               # x isn't a field of User; can't write to it
print u.x             # check for unknown field in expr as well
```

The interpreter correctly identifies the three errors:

```
$ java InterPie structerrors.pie
line 4: u.name is not a struct in u.name.y
line 5: can't assign; User instance has no x field
line 6: User instance has no x field
null
$
```

Related Patterns

This pattern implements an interpreter for our dynamically typed Pie language just like Pattern 24, *Syntax-Directed Interpreter*, on page 225. It uses the following patterns: Pattern 4, *LL(k) Recursive-Descent Parser*, on page 43, Pattern 9, *Homogeneous AST*, on page 94, Pattern 13, *External Tree Visitor*, on page 116, and Pattern 18, *Symbol Table for Data Aggregates*, on page 161.

Up Next

This pattern concludes our chapter on high-level interpreters. These interpreters are best suited to implementing DSLs rather than general-purpose programming languages. They are not too hard to build and are very flexible. (We can add new instructions without much trouble.) But, they are not particularly efficient at run-time. To squeeze memory resources down and to accelerate execution speed, we need to process the input source code more. In the next chapter on bytecode interpreters, we'll do exactly that. The upcoming patterns are useful for making efficient DSL and general-purpose language interpreters.

## Chapter 10

Building Bytecode Interpreters

In the previous chapter, we explored interpreters that operate on high-level programs with little to no preprocessing before execution. Those interpreters are great for implementing DSLs because they are the fastest path to getting a language up and running. Their only drawback is run-time efficiency. If we really care about efficiency for a particular DSL or need to implement a more general programming language, those interpreters aren't appropriate.

In this chapter, we'll explore another category of interpreters that is much more efficient. Unfortunately, the efficiency comes at the cost of a more complicated implementation. In essence, we need a tool that translates the high-level source code down into low-level instructions called *bytecode instructions* (instructions whose operation code fits in an 8-bit byte). Then, we can execute those bytecodes on an efficient interpreter called a *virtual machine*[1] (VM). (We're conjuring up an imaginary machine.) Most of the currently popular languages are VM-based (Java, JavaScript, C#, Python, Ruby 1.9).

The interpreter patterns in this chapter are real in the sense that they resemble the core of most industrial-strength language implementations. In practice, the industrial-strength implementations are a lot faster because they're implemented in C or hand-tuned machine code, not Java. Many of them even translate bytecode instructions to native machine code on the fly. They also would have many more instructions to deal with the complete set of arithmetic operators, arrays, classes instead of **struct**s, switches, and so on. The sample implementations in

---

1. These machines are to be distinguished from the virtual machines that run one operating system inside another.

this chapter don't include those instructions for simplicity reasons, but we'd implement them in much the same way.

If we're translating source code to low-level bytecodes, you might ask why we don't compile all the way down to machine code and skip the interpreter altogether. Raw machine code would be even more efficient. Bytecode interpreters have a number of useful characteristics including portability. (Machine code is specific to a CPU, whereas bytecodes run on any computer with a compatible interpreter.) But, the biggest reason we avoid generating machine code is that it's pretty hard.

CPU instructions have to be very simple so that we can implement them easily and efficiently in hardware. The result is often an instruction set that is quirky, irregular, and far removed from high-level source code. Bytecode interpreters, on the other hand, are specifically designed to be easy to *target* (generate code for). At the same time, instructions have to be low-level enough that we can interpret them quickly.

In this chapter, we're going to explore the instruction sets and implementations for the two most common bytecode interpreter patterns, starting with useful assembler pattern:

- Pattern 26, *Bytecode Assembler*, on page 252. To avoid having to program our interpreters in binary, this pattern provides a general bytecode assembler. It translates (assembles) human-readable bytecode assembly code down to bytecode machine code.

- Pattern 27, *Stack-Based Bytecode Interpreter*, on page 259. This pattern simulates a *stack machine*, a machine that holds all temporary values such as operation results on an operand stack. Stack-based interpreters go back a long, long way. One of the most influential was the UCSD p-code[2] interpreter (partly because of its influence on James Gosling's Java interpreter).

- Pattern 28, *Register-Based Bytecode Interpreter*, on page 267. This pattern simulates a *register machine* very much like the underlying hardware. Rather than pushing and popping operands from a stack, it uses simulated general-purpose registers. (A *register* is a memory cell within a processor that the processor can access much faster than going off-chip to the main memory.)

---

2. http://en.wikipedia.org/wiki/UCSD_Pascal

Rather than programming a bytecode interpreter by hand, we prefer to program in a high-level language. That means we need a bytecode compiler that can translate it to bytecodes. We'll focus on the interpreters themselves here, though. The next two chapters provide the translation and generation background you'd need to build a bytecode compiler. There's also a sample compiler on the ANTLR wiki that generates an intermediate representation very similar to bytecode.[3]

Before dissecting the guts of a bytecode interpreter, let's figure out how to program these critters.

10.1 Programming Bytecode Interpreters

Programming a bytecode interpreter is very much like programming a real processor. The biggest difference is that bytecode instruction sets are much simpler and slightly higher-level. For example, we don't have to worry about running out of registers in a register-based interpreter. (We can assume there are an infinite number of registers.)

Like the assembly language for a physical processor, each instruction only does a tiny amount of work. For example, it takes four instructions to say print 1+2 in the assembly language syntax of Pattern 28, *Register-Based Bytecode Interpreter*, on page 267:

```
iload r1, 1      ; load int 1 into register one: r1 = 1
iload r2, 2      ; r2 = 2
iadd r1, r2, r3  ; r3 = r1 + r2
print r3         ; print value in r3
```

These instructions are similar to other register-based interpreters such as Lua's[4] and the Dalvik VM's.[5] Operands and operation results go into registers.

Stack code, on the other hand, works like the old HP calculators that used Reverse Polish Notation[6] (RPN). We push operands onto a stack and then execute the operation:

```
iconst 1         ; push int 1 onto operand stack
iconst 2         ; push int 2 onto operand stack
iadd             ; pop and add top 2 elements on stack, push result
print            ; pop and print top value on stack
```

---

3. http://www.antlr.org/wiki/display/ANTLR3/LLVM
4. http://www.tecgraf.puc-rio.br/~lhf/ftp/doc/jucs05.pdf
5. http://source.android.com
6. http://h41111.www4.hp.com/calculators/uk/en/articles/rpn.html

The biggest difference between the two is that stack code doesn't have to figure out which register to use for which value; instructions have implicit operands (the top of the stack).

Notice that the arithmetic operation instructions are all typed. That is, the instruction encodes the type of the operands. For example, iadd is "integer add," but we can define fadd ("floating-point add") or even sadd ("string add"). The idea is that we want to do as little thinking as possible at run-time. Figuring out whether to do an integer or floating-point add at run-time costs time. For statically typed languages like Java, we can figure out the appropriate type using the patterns in Chapter 8, *Enforcing Static Typing Rules*, on page 181. We can't figure out types in general for dynamically typed languages like Python, so we'd use generic bytecodes like add instead of iadd.

Bytecode interpreters do not execute these examples in assembly language (text) form as we've written them. The interpreter actually needs those instructions in machine code. Pattern 26, *Bytecode Assembler*, on page 252 reads assembly programs and fills a byte array with bytecodes and operands. For example, here's the byte array memory formats for an instruction with no operands, one operand, and two operands:

+0		+0	+1	+2	+3	+4		+0	+1	+2	+3	+4	+5	+6	+7	+8
op		op	a_3	a_2	a_1	a_0		op	a_3	a_2	a_1	a_0	b_3	b_2	b_1	b_0

Operands a and b are always 4-byte integers and stored from high byte (a_3) to low byte (a_0) sequentially in memory. Here is a code memory dump (in decimal) for the stack code snippet for print 1+2:

```
0000:   19   0   0   0   1  19   0   0
0008:    0   2   1  28
```

Values 19, 1, and 28 are the bytecodes for instructions iconst, iadd, and print, respectively. Pattern 26, *Bytecode Assembler*, on page 252 also provides a*disassembler*, which converts machine code back to assembly code. This is what the disassembled stack code looks like:

```
0000:   ICONST   1   ; bytes = 19 0 0 0 1
0005:   ICONST   2   ; bytes = 19 0 0 0 2
0010:   IADD         ; bytes = 1
0011:   PRINT        ; bytes = 28
```

When debugging bytecode programs or even the bytecode interpreter itself, an *instruction trace* is extremely useful. It shows the relevant state of the interpreter as it encounters instructions. Here is the instruction trace for our stack code example:

```
0000:   ICONST   1      stack=[ ]      calls=[ main ]
0005:   ICONST   2      stack=[ 1 ]    calls=[ main ]
0010:   IADD            stack=[ 1 2 ]  calls=[ main ]
0011:   PRINT           stack=[ 3 ]    calls=[ main ]
```

The stack shows the state of the machine before the execution of the instruction on that line. You can see the stack grow (to the right) and shrink according to the instructions. (We'll see what the call stack is for when we discuss function calls in a moment.) The two interpreter patterns in this chapter provide three command-line options to access these features: -dump, -dis, and -trace.

With these examples in mind, let's get a little bit more formal. The next section describes the general assembly language syntax that we'll use for our interpreters.

10.2 Defining an Assembly Language Syntax

A bytecode assembly language program defines globals as well as a sequence of functions and instructions:

```
.globals «number-of-global-variable-slots»
«function-definitions»
.def main: args=0, locals=«num-locals-or-registers»: ; begin exec here
    ...
    halt
```

For each function, we define the name, how many parameters it has, and how much local space it needs:

```
.def «function-name»: args=«num-args», locals=«num-locals-or-registers»
    ...
    ret
```

Execution begins in function main() or at code address 0 if you don't specify one.

The instructions themselves have a bytecode and up to three parameters:

$$op \; operand_1, \; operand_2, \; \ldots, \; operand_n$$

Rather than hard-coding the instruction names (like ret and store), the implementation provided below in Pattern 26, *Bytecode Assembler*, on page 252, lets us specify them with an array of instruction descriptors.

Instruction Set Design Affects Interpreter Speed

Even within the same kind of interpreter, there's considerable freedom in terms of what instructions we define. The first DSL I implemented was a language called Karel for controlling industrial robots (using Pattern 27, *Stack-Based Bytecode Interpreter*, on page 259). After defining a basic instruction set to support the high-level robot control instructions, I focused on a few specialized instructions to make the interpreter faster.

Oddly enough, *adding* instructions increased its speed dramatically. For example, I created a special iconst0 instruction to get 0 onto the stack using a single byte in code memory (instead of the general-purpose integer load, iconst *n*). The general instruction required 3 bytes (bytecode plus a 2-byte integer) in code memory vs. 1 byte for iconst0. Avoiding those memory fetches and operand decodes saved quite a bit. I also squashed the four instructions necessary to increment a variable into a single inc instruction. Adding specialized instructions for common operations is the easiest way to speed up an interpreter.

That way, we can use the assembler for both interpreter patterns in this chapter.

To label code memory addresses, use an identifier followed by a colon. Instructions can refer to labels defined previously or below in the assembly file. For example, in the following code, start and done are code labels used by branch instructions:

```
start:                  ; start of the loop
    ...                 ; check loop termination condition
    brt done            ; br out if condition met (true)
    ...
    br start            ; branch back to top of loop
done:                   ; end of the loop
```

The only real difference between a register and a stack machine is in the way we program them. We either load operands into registers or push them onto the stack; the difference is as simple as that. Syntactically, register code is a minor superset of stack code because of its register operands. Their architecture and implementations are almost identical as well. The next section describes general bytecode architecture, leaving register and stack machine specifics to the individual patterns.

10.3 Bytecode Machine Architecture

A bytecode interpreter simulates a computer with the following components:

- *Code memory*: This byte array holds a program's bytecode instructions (bytecodes plus operands). Addresses are integers.
- *ip register*: The instruction pointer is a special-purpose "register" that points into code memory at the next instruction to execute.
- *Global memory*: Global memory holds a fixed number of slots for variables. The memory slots can point at Integer, Float, String, and **struct** instances. Unlike the high-level interpreters from the previous chapter, we access variables by integer address rather than name.
- *CPU*: To execute instructions, the interpreter has a simulated CPU that amounts to a loop around a giant "**switch** on bytecode" statement. This is called the instruction *dispatcher*.
- *Constant pool*: Anything that we can't store as a 4-byte integer operand goes into the constant pool. This includes strings, floating-point numbers, and function symbols. Instructions like sconst and fconst use an index into the constant pool instead of the actual operand.
- *Function call stack*: The interpreter has a stack to hold function call return addresses as well as parameters and local variables.
- *fp register*: A special-purpose register called the frame pointer that points to the top of the function call stack. StackFrame represents the information we need to invoke functions.

In addition to those elements, Pattern 27, *Stack-Based Bytecode Interpreter*, on page 259 has the following:

- *Operand stack*: Rather than loading values into registers, the interpreter pushes temporary values onto the operand stack. All instruction operands are either in code memory or on the stack.
- *sp register*: A special-purpose register called the stack pointer that points to the top of the operand stack.

Instead of an operand stack, Pattern 28, *Register-Based Bytecode Interpreter*, on page 267 register machine has the following:

- *An infinite and regular register set* per function call. Functions can access any element in the register array, whereas a stack can only access elements at the end. Our sample register machine implementation reserves register 0 to hold function return values.

It's worth zooming in on the processor and the constant pool. Then we can look at how function calls work.

Bytecode Processors

The processor is the heart of an interpreter and has a simple job: it loops around a fetch-decode-execute mechanism. The processor fetches a bytecode and then jumps to a code fragment that executes that instruction:

```
void cpu() {
    short bytecode = code[ip];
    while ( «bytecode-not-halt» && ip < code.length ) {
        ip++; //jump to next instruction or first byte of operand
        switch (bytecode) {
            case «bytecode1» : «exec-bytecode1»; break;
            case «bytecode2» : «exec-bytecode2»; break;
            ...
            case «bytecodeN» : «exec-bytecodeN»; break;
        }
        bytecode = code[ip];
    }
}
```

The CPU stops when it hits a halt instruction or runs out of instructions to execute at the end of the code memory.

The cases in the **switch** statement execute the code fragment necessary to simulate the instructions. For example, here is how we execute the br instruction (branch to a new code memory address):

```
case BR :       // branch to instruction's address operand
    int addr = «convert-4-bytes-at-code[ip]-to-int»;
    ip = addr; // jump
    break;
```

If the instruction has an operand (which is always right next to the bytecode), the code fragment pulls the operand from code memory and bumps the instruction pointer by four bytes. As another example, here is the code to execute the stack-based iconst instruction (push an integer constant onto the operand stack):

```
case ICONST :
    int word = «convert-4-bytes-at-code[ip]-to-int»;
    ip += 4;  // jump over integer constant operand in code memory
    «push-word-onto-operand-stack»
    break;
```

Some instructions take data not code address operands. These instructions can access globals, parameters, locals, and **struct** instances. We'll worry about parameters and locals in the specific patterns. Now, let's see how instructions manipulate global memory and data aggregates.

The gstore instruction (for both interpreters) stores a value into global memory. To implement that, we can treat the global memory space as an array of objects:

```
globals[«address»] = «value»;
```

The gload instruction does the opposite. It loads a value from global memory into a register or pushes it onto the operand stack.

The fields of a **struct** look just like a small memory space. The operands of the fload and fstore instructions are field indexes into the structure. Given a value, a structure, and a field index, the fstore instruction executes as follows:

```
«struct».fields[«field-index»] = «value»;
```

We can get data values either from memory or from an instruction operand. Some of these operands, though, won't fit in the 4-byte slot following a bytecode. We've got to stick them in the constant pool.

Storing Large Constants in the Constant Pool

All instruction operands must be integers or convertible to an integer. (Characters convert to an integer.) Strings obviously don't fit in a 4-byte integer, so we've got to store them outside of code memory. Bytecode interpreters store strings and other noninteger constants in a *constant pool*. Instead of the actual object, the instruction operand is an index into the constant pool. The constant pool is just an array of objects and is commonly used by bytecode interpreters (like the Java VM). Besides strings, there are two other items we've got to store in the constant pool: floating-point numbers and function descriptors.

The float type in Java is 32 bits and could fit in code memory no problem. But, let's store floating-point operands in the constant pool like the Java VM does. In Figure 10.1, on the next page, we can see the relationship between (stack) bytecode instruction operands and the constant pool for the following code snippet. The assembler converts the sconst and fconst operands to indexes into the constant pool.

```
sconst "hi"
fconst 3.4
iconst 10
cconst 'c'
```

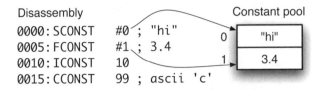

Figure 10.1: BYTECODE OPERAND AND CONSTANT POOL RELATIONSHIP

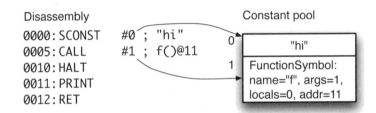

Figure 10.2: FUNCTION SYMBOLS IN CONSTANT POOL

The last kind of object you'll see in the constant pool is a FunctionSymbol. The call instruction needs to know how many parameters and local variables each function needs. It looks at the constant pool entry for the function to get this information. In Figure 10.2, we can see how the assembler converts the call operand to an index into the constant pool for the following program:

```
    sconst "hi" ; start by getting parameter onto operand stack
    call f()
    halt
.def f: args=1, locals=0
    load 0      ; get 1st parameter
    print       ; print
    ret         ; return no value
```

Function calls involve more than the constant pool. They also use the call stack (and, for the stack-based interpreter, the operand stack), as we'll see in the next section.

Calling Functions

The mechanism for calling a function and returning is the same for both Pattern 27, *Stack-Based Bytecode Interpreter*, on page 259 and Pattern 28, *Register-Based Bytecode Interpreter*, on page 267. The only difference lies in how they handle parameters, locals, and return values. We'll leave the details of how those temporary values work to the individual interpreter patterns. In this section, we'll focus on the general mechanism for calling and returning from a function. Let's start with a simple program that has two functions:

```
.def main: args=0, locals=0 ; void main()
    call f()
    halt
.def f: args=0, locals=0    ; void f()
    call g()
    ret
.def g: args=0, locals=0    ; void g()
    ret
```

The main program calls f(), which calls g(). Right before g() returns, the interpreter has pushed three StackFrame objects onto the call stack. A *stack frame* is an object that tracks information about a function call. For both interpreters, stack frames store parameters, local variables, and the return address. In Figure 10.3, on the next page, we can see the call stack with the fields of the stack frames filled in. (The locals array is called registers in a register machine.) The frames point at the appropriate function symbol held in the constant pool. The first stack frame is from the implicit call to main() from the interpreter. The other two frames are for the explicit calls to f() and g().

The easiest way to see what's going on is to look at the instruction trace because it shows how the stacks grow and shrink for each instruction:

```
0000:   CALL    #1; f()@6    stack=[]  calls=[ main ]
0006:   CALL    #2; g()@12   stack=[]  calls=[ main f ]
0012:   RET                  stack=[]  calls=[ main f g ]
0011:   RET                  stack=[]  calls=[ main f ]
```

The stacks grow to the right and indicate the state before each instruction executes. After each call instruction, the call stack grows by one stack frame. The call stack shrinks by one at each ret instruction.

At this point, we know what bytecode programs look like and how bytecode interpreters represent them in simulated code memory and in a constant pool. We also looked at interpreter architecture to see how interpreters execute instructions. This material, along with the patterns

```
Disassembly                          Constant pool                    Call stack
0000: CALL   #1 ; f()@6        0   FunctionSymbol:           0   StackFrame:
0005: HALT                         name="main", args=0,         sym =
0006: CALL   #2 ; g()@12           locals=0, addr=0             ret-address =
0011: RET                      1   FunctionSymbol:              locals = []
0012: RET                          name="f", args=0,
                                   locals=0, addr=6         1   StackFrame:
                                                                sym =
                               2   FunctionSymbol:              ret-address = 5
                                   name="g", args=0,            locals = []
                                   locals=0, addr=12
                                                            2   StackFrame:
                                                                sym =
                                                                ret-address = 11
                                                                locals = []
```

Figure 10.3: FUNCTION CALL STACK RIGHT BEFORE RET IN G()

that follow, is enough to help you build a bytecode interpreter for a DSL. Unfortunately, a lot more is going on in a general-purpose programming language interpreter than what we've discussed here. (These bytecode interpreters rely heavily on the Java VM.) The next section gives you a taste of what's involved in building a more general and more efficient interpreter.

10.4 Where to Go from Here

In this chapter, we had to completely ignore garbage collection, executing code from more than one source file (linking), classes, libraries, and debuggers. But, we'd need all of that to build an interpreter for a general-purpose programming language. The best way to figure out how all that works is to dig into the source for an existing interpreter. Interpreter source code is available for just about every common language, both dynamically typed and statically typed. You can also read the literature on the Smalltalk and Self interpreters as well as garbage collection and dynamic method dispatch. A good paper to read on register-based bytecode machines is *The Implementation of Lua 5.0* [IdFC05].

One of the things you'll discover quickly when reading source code or building your own interpreter is that making an interpreter go really

Comparing Interpreter Speed

Out of curiosity, I compared the speed of the two bytecode interpreters in this chapter. For a simple "count to 100 million" loop, I found that hand-optimized register code was about twice as fast as stack code (5.9 seconds vs. 12). The stack machine is still a substantial 4.5 times faster than Pattern 25, *Tree-Based Interpreter*, on page 230, which clocks in at a pokey 54 seconds.

fast is not that easy. Every CPU clock cycle and memory access counts. For that reason, Java is not the best implementation language since we have no control over the underlying hardware (but I didn't want to switch to C++ on you in the middle of the book). In fact, the core of most fast interpreters is some hand-tuned assembly code. Knowledge of computer architecture, such as cache memory and CPU pipelines, is essential.

In January 2009, I spoke with Dan Bornstein, the guy who designed the Dalvik[7] VM (a register-based VM that runs Java programs on Google's Android mobile platform, though with a different bytecode). He described the amazing gymnastics he and the VM team went through to squeeze every last drop of efficiency out of the phone's ARM,[8] CPU, and flash memory. (Flash memory is much slower than dynamic memory but doesn't get amnesia when you lose power.) Aside from being slow, there isn't much flash memory on the phone device. The Dalvik VM tries to share data structures and compress them whenever possible.

On average, the Dalvik VM uses a bit more code memory than the Java VM's stack-based instruction set for a given method. But, as Bornstein explains, the trade-off is totally worth it. The Dalvik VM executes many fewer instructions to achieve the same result. (It can reuse registers to avoid unnecessary operand stack pushes and pops.) Because of the overhead to execute each instruction, fewer instructions means much less overhead and higher performance.

---

7. http://source.android.com
8. http://www.arm.com

The Dalvik VM implementation details are beyond the scope of this intermediate-level book, but you can learn more by looking at the Dalvik VM source code. (You can also learn some of the underlying principles by doing a web search for *threaded interpreter*.)

Let's finish up this introductory material with a summary of when to use our bytecode patterns:

Pattern	When to Apply
Pattern 26, *Bytecode Assembler*	Both bytecode interpreters need this unless we want to program in raw binary machine code.
Pattern 27, *Stack-Based Bytecode Interpreter*, on page 259	A stack machine is more or less the traditional bytecode interpreter. Some people prefer a stack over registers purely for style reasons. It's suitable for efficiently executing DSLs and general purpose programming languages.
Pattern 28, *Register-Based Bytecode Interpreter*, on page 267	Register machines can often execute high-level programs faster than stack machines. Generating register code is as easy as generating stack code, but the generated code could be bigger and slower. To attain their full potential, either the compiler or the interpreter has to massage code blocks to reuse registers and do other optimizations.

Get your spelunking gear on. It's time to explore bytecode interpreter patterns.

☐ ## 26 Bytecode Assembler

Purpose

This pattern translates a text-based human-readable assembly language program into binary bytecode instructions.

The assembly language instruction set accepted by this pattern is reprogrammable (it isn't fixed) and handles both stack-based and register-based instructions.

Discussion

Bytecode interpreters feed off low-level byte arrays full of bytecodes (operation codes that fit into a byte) and integer operands. Generating raw bytecodes from a bytecode compiler is an extra burden on an already complex compiler. It's easier to generate text-based assembly code and then have an assembler convert that to machine code. In other words, rather than generating bytes 14, 0, 0, 0, 0, and 21, it's easier to generate the following equivalent (stack machine) assembly code that prints "hi":

```
sconst "hi"      ; push a string constant onto the stack
print            ; print the object on the top of the stack
```

From a text-based assembly program, an assembler yields the following four key elements:

- *Global data space size*: How many variable slots to reserve in global memory.
- *Code memory*: This byte array contains the instruction stream derived from the assembly program. It contains bytecodes and any instruction operands.
- *Main program address*: The code memory address at which the interpreter should start executing the program. This is the address associated with the main() function, or address zero if it's not specified.
- *Constant pool*: This table keeps noninteger operands out of code memory. It tracks strings, floating-point numbers, and function descriptors. Instruction operands can refer to constant pool elements via an integer index (see Section 10.3, *Storing Large Constants in the Constant Pool*, on page 247).

We're going to start our discussion by looking at the basic architecture of an assembler and how to generate machine code from assembly code. Then, we'll look at how to fill the constant pool with operands that don't fit in code memory. Finally, we'll look at assembly code symbol table management. At that point, we'll be ready to tackle a sample implementation.

Generating Bytecodes into Code Memory

The basic idea behind an assembler is to trigger appropriate action methods upon seeing the various input constructs. (Later, we'll recognize this as Pattern 29, *Syntax-Directed Translator*, on page 296.)

Here are some of the methods in the assembler's interface:

```
protected void gen(Token instrToken) {;}
protected void gen(Token instrToken, Token operandToken) {;}
...
protected void defineFunction(Token idToken, int nargs, int nlocals) {;}
protected void defineLabel(Token idToken) {;}
```

We clearly need a parser to read in the text assembly code, but that parser shouldn't directly implement the assembler functionality. It should contain the minimal actions necessary to call the code generation and symbol table management methods. We can isolate the method implementations in a subclass. (This is a generically useful pattern whereby we separate functionality from language syntax.) For example, here's a grammar rule that handles instructions with two operands:

```
instr2 : ID operand ',' operand {gen(«instr-name»,«opnd1»,«opnd2»);}
```

The **operand** rule would match the various kind of operands such as labels, registers, functions, integers, and so on. The action invokes the gen() method with information obtained while parsing the instruction.

As the assembler reads instructions, it writes bytecodes and operands to a code array. To keep its place, it moves along an ip (instruction pointer). ip is always the next write address. For instructions with no arguments, the assembler writes a single byte to the code array and bumps ip by one. Instructions with one argument are 5 bytes long, 1 for the bytecode and 4 bytes for the operand. We write the bytecode and the operand, bumping ip by 5 bytes as we go. All bytecode operands are 4-byte integers, so we've got to do something fancy with nonintegers, as we'll see next.

Filling the Constant Pool

As we saw in Section 10.3, *Storing Large Constants in the Constant Pool*, on page 247, any operand we can't store or convert to an integer goes into the constant pool. The operand is then an index into the constant pool. We can store characters as integers, but we have to store strings, floats, and function symbols in the constant pool. (We'll look at function symbols in the next section.) Here is the algorithm for writing bytecode operands:

```
switch ( «kind-of-operand» ) {
    case «int-or-char»    : v = «int-value»;
    case «float-or-string» : v = «get-constant-pool-index»;
    case «func-ref»       : v = «get-constant-pool-index»;
    case «label»          : v = «label-address»;
    case «register»       : v = «register-number»;
}
«write-v-to-code-memory»
```

To compute a constant pool index, this code returns the index of an existing pool entry or adds the object to the pool (and returns the new index):

```
int «get-constant-pool-index»(Object o) {
    if ( «constant-pool-contains-o» ) return «its-index»;
    else { «add-to-pool»; return «index-of-o»; }
}
```

Every reference to the same floating-point number or string results in the same constant pool index. In that sense, the constant pool is like a flat scope (Pattern 16, *Symbol Table for Monolithic Scope*, on page 141) for operand values. That scope also contains function symbols for use as operands of the function call instruction.

Tracking and Referencing Functions

Bytecode interpreters don't know anything about symbols. For speed reasons, they only deal with code addresses, data addresses, and constant pool indexes. Bytecode assembly language, on the other hand, knows about two kinds of symbols: functions and code labels. Both live in their own private Pattern 16, *Symbol Table for Monolithic Scope*, on page 141. We'll look at functions here and then check out code labels in the next section.

Function information from the assembly code must survive the assembly process. Bytecode interpreters need function parameter and local variable information at run-time. We can tuck this information into the constant pool along with the strings and floats. That means adding a FunctionSymbol using the «*get-constant-pool-index*» algorithm from the previous section. The assembler stores the constant pool index as the operand for the call instruction. At execution time, the interpreter finds the function's code start address by looking in the constant pool using that index. Here's the algorithm for defining a function:

```
void defineFunction(Token idToken, int args, int locals) {
    fs = «new-FunctionSymbol-based-upon-args»;
    if ( «function-referred-to-before-definition» )
        «replace-element-in-constant-pool-with-fs-at-same-index»;
    else «save-fs-into-constant-pool»;
}
```

If the assembly program refers to a function before it's defined, the algorithm adds a dummy FunctionSymbol and fills in the details later when it sees the definition.

Assembly language code labels work almost the same way, as we'll see next.

Handling Labels and Forward References

To jump around an assembly language program, branch instructions use code label operands. A code label is just a symbol that marks a location in code memory and saves the programmer from having to manually compute addresses. During execution, though, the interpreter expects branch operands to be integers, not symbols.

In a sense, the assembler needs to "erase" labels during translation to bytecodes by converting label operands to code addresses. After assembling the program, the assembler can toss out the scope of labels. If a branch instruction refers to a label defined earlier in the program, the assembler can just look it up in the label scope (Pattern 16, *Symbol Table for Monolithic Scope*, on page 141).

But, forward references are a bit trickier to handle. If a label is not yet defined, we have to remember the branch instruction operand address. Later, when we see the label definition, we can update that operand to have the correct value (that's called *backpatching*). Let's see how this works by looking at two forward references in the following assembly program:

```
        br end ; tracks operand code addr 1 in forward ref list
        br end ; adds addr 6 to forward ref list of "end"
end:           ; label address is 10
        halt
```

At the first br instruction, we create a LabelSymbol and add it to the label scope. The operand address is the second byte in code memory (address 1). We set flag isForwardRef to true and isDefined to false in the symbol. We do the same thing at the second br except that we add address 6 to the list of operands to resolve later.

At the label definition, we resolve forward references by walking the list of forward references for that symbol to patch br operands. The disassembly shows the patched forward code labels:

```
0000:   BR      10  ; patched operand points at "end"
0005:   BR      10  ; patched operand points at "end"
0010:   HALT
```

After reading the entire program, the assembler makes sure that all forward references have an associated definition.

In summary, an assembler consists of a parser that triggers code generation and symbol table management actions. All of the work happens in a subclass of the parser that implements methods such as gen() and defineFunction(). In the next section, we'll look at a sample implementation to tease out the remaining details.

Implementation

To complete our discussion of bytecode assemblers, let's build an assembler that we can use for the two bytecode interpreter patterns that follow. We need to build an assembly language grammar in Assembler.g, create a flexible instruction definition mechanism, and implement the code generation and symbol table management functions in Bytecode-Assembler.

Let's start with the goal: filling in the code memory and constant pool, which we can represent as fields in our main class:

`interp/asm/BytecodeAssembler.java`

```java
public class BytecodeAssembler extends AssemblerParser {
    public static final int INITIAL_CODE_SIZE = 1024;
    protected Map<String,Integer> instructionOpcodeMapping =
        new HashMap<String,Integer>();
    protected Map<String, LabelSymbol> labels = // label scope
        new HashMap<String, LabelSymbol>();
    /** All float and string literals have unique int index in constant
     *  pool. We put FunctionSymbols in here too. */
    protected List<Object> constPool = new ArrayList<Object>();
    protected int ip = 0; // Instruction pointer; used to fill code[]
    protected byte[] code = new byte[INITIAL_CODE_SIZE]; // code memory
    protected int dataSize; // set via .globals
    protected FunctionSymbol mainFunction;
```

To use the assembler, we create a lexer and parser and then call the start rule (**program**) as we've done throughout the book:

```java
AssemblerLexer assemblerLexer =
    new AssemblerLexer(new ANTLRInputStream(input));
CommonTokenStream tokens = new CommonTokenStream(assemblerLexer);
BytecodeAssembler asm = new BytecodeAssembler(tokens, «instructions»);
asm.program(); // start parsing at program rule
```

The only difference here is that we create a subclass of AssemblerParser (from Assembler.g) called BytecodeAssembler that houses our implementation functions.

One of the key rules in the grammar is **instr**, which recognizes instructions and calls the code generation methods:

```
instr
    :   ID NEWLINE                          {gen($ID);}
    |   ID operand NEWLINE                  {gen($ID,$operand.start);}
    |   ID a=operand ',' b=operand NEWLINE {gen($ID,$a.start,$b.start);}
    |   ID a=operand ',' b=operand ',' c=operand NEWLINE
        {gen($ID,$a.start,$b.start,$c.start);}
    ;
```

It calls the appropriate version of gen() according to the number of operands. Expressions such as $operand.start evaluate to the starting token matched by rule **operand**. Here's the code to generate an instruction that has no operands:

```
protected void gen(Token instrToken) {
    String instrName = instrToken.getText();
    Integer opcodeI = instructionOpcodeMapping.get(instrName);
    if ( opcodeI==null ) {
        System.err.println("line "+instrToken.getLine()+
                        ": Unknown instruction: "+instrName);
        return;
    }
    int opcode = opcodeI.intValue();
    ensureCapacity(ip+1);
    code[ip++] = (byte)(opcode&0xFF);
}
```

The assembler learns about the instruction set from field instructionOpcodeMapping. That dictionary maps instruction names to integer bytecodes. If you look in the BytecodeDefinition classes in the interpreter patterns, you'll see the instruction definitions. To get this generic assembler to compile, we can define a fake set of instruction descriptors:

```
public static Instruction[] instructions = new Instruction[] {
    null, // <INVALID>
    new Instruction("iadd",REG,REG,REG), // index is the opcode
};
```

This Instruction array is what we pass into the assembler constructor:

```
BytecodeAssembler asm = new BytecodeAssembler(tokens, «instructions»);
```

For instruction operands, the assembler writes 32-bit values to the code memory using genOperand() in BytecodeAssembler. To write 32-bit integers into a byte array, the assembler breaks them up into bytes using writeInt(). It writes them highest to lowest byte, sequentially in memory.

There are two assembly language instructions that don't result in code memory elements. First is the global memory definition instruction .globals, which we can recognize with the following rule:

`interp/asm/Assembler.g`

```
globals : NEWLINE* '.globals' INT NEWLINE {defineDataSize($INT.int);} ;
```

Second is the function declaration instruction:

`interp/asm/Assembler.g`

```
functionDeclaration
    : '.def' name=ID ':' 'args' '=' a=INT ',' 'locals' '=' n=INT NEWLINE
      {defineFunction($name, $a.int, $n.int);}
    ;
```

Without an actual instruction set definition, this assembler can't really do anything. So, we'll leave building and testing it to the interpreter patterns that use it.

Related Patterns

Pattern 27, *Stack-Based Bytecode Interpreter* and Pattern 28, *Register-Based Bytecode Interpreter*, on page 267 use this assembler to read in assembly programs.

---

27 Stack-Based Bytecode Interpreter

Purpose

This pattern executes bytecode instructions that store temporary values on an operand stack.

Discussion

A stack-based bytecode interpreter simulates a hardware processor with no general-purpose registers. That means that bytecode instructions must use an operand stack to hold temporary values. Temporary values include arithmetic operands, parameters, and return values. Because the introductory material for this chapter explained general bytecode interpreter architecture, we can focus on the details specific to stack machines.

Let's look at the operand stack first, since it's the key identifying feature. Any time we want to load a value from memory or compute a result, we push the result onto the operand stack. For efficiency, we'll use a simple object array with a special-purpose register called *sp* to indicate the top of stack. To push a value, we increment *sp* and store the value:

```
operands[++sp] = «value»;
```

For example, here's how to push a value from global memory:

```
operands[++sp] = globals[«address»];
```

To pop a value, we do the opposite by decrementing *sp*:

```
Object value = operands[sp--]; // pop, sp-- decrements sp after index
```

In Figure 10.4, on the facing page, and Figure 10.5, on page 262, we can see a sample instruction set for a stack machine. (The sample code in the source directory implements this instruction set.) Just about all of those instructions expect values on the operand stack. The instruction set is pretty minimal but good enough for demonstration purposes. In reality, we'd need at least a few more instructions to handle the other arithmetic operators. Function calls also make heavy use of the operand stack for parameters and local variables so we need to investigate them in detail.

Passing Function Parameters

The call instruction expects parameters to be on the operand stack, which is where we compute all expression values. When call pushes a stack frame, the frame constructor creates space for the parameters and local variables. Both parameters and locals go into a single locals object array field, parameters first. call knows how much space to create because of the FunctionSymbol in the constant pool. Before transferring control to the function's starting address, call moves the parameters from the operand stack into the stack frame:

```
void call(int functionConstPoolIndex) {
    FunctionSymbol fs = constPool[functionConstPoolIndex];
    StackFrame f = new StackFrame(fs, «return-address»);
    calls[++fp] = f;
    for (int a=«num-args»-1; a>=0; a--) f.locals[a]=operands[sp--];
    ip = fs.address; // jump to the start address
}
```

Instruction	Description
iadd, isub, imul	Arithmetic operators for integers. Pop two operands, perform operation, and push result back on stack.
fadd, fsub, fmul	Arithmetic operators for floating-point.
ilt, ieq, flt, feq	Equality operators for integers and floating-point. Pop two operands, perform operation, and push result back on stack.
itof	Convert top of stack integer to floating-point.
cconst n, iconst n	Push character or integer constant operand onto the operand stack. operands[++sp]=n.
sconst s, fconst f	Push constant string s or floating-point number f from the constant pool onto the operand stack. operands[++sp]=constPool[«*index-of-s-or-f*»].

Figure 10.4: STACK-BASED ARITHMETIC BYTECODE INSTRUCTIONS

Let's see how this works when we call a function with two parameters and one local variable:

```
.def main: args=0, locals=0
; print f(10,20)
    iconst 10               ; push first argument
    iconst 20               ; push second argument
    call f()
    print                   ; print return value
    halt
.def f: args=2, locals=1    ; int f(int x, int y)
; x is at locals[] index 0, y at 1, and z at 2
; int z = x + y
    load 0                  ; push first argument x
    load 1                  ; push second argument y
    iadd
    store 2                 ; store into local z
; return z
    load 2
    ret
```

In Figure 10.6, on page 263, we can see the stack frame zoomed in for the call to f() from main(). The call needs three slots to hold parameters and locals. Parameters come first and locals come next, so the local variable's index is 2.

The trace shows that, right before the call to f(), the operand stack has two parameters:

```
0010:   CALL    #0 ; f()@17   stack=[ 10 20 ]   calls=[ main ]
0017:   LOAD    0             stack=[ ]         calls=[ main f ]
```

Instruction	Description
call $f()$	Call function f (via f's constant pool entry). Push new stack frame onto call stack, move parameters from operand stack to stack frame, and branch to function start address.
ret	Return from function call. Any return value is on the operand stack. Pop the top stack frame off and return to return address stored in that stack frame.
br a, brt a, brf a	Branch to a always, if operands[sp] is true, or is false.
gload a, gstore a	operands[++sp]=globals[a], globals[a]=operands[sp--].
load i, store i	operands[++sp]=calls[fp].locals[i] where fp is the frame pointer and i is the local value index, calls[fp].locals[i]=operands[sp--].
fload i, fstore i	Pop **struct** address s off the operand stack then do operands[++sp]=s.fields[i] where i is the field index from 0, s.fields[i]=operands[sp--].
print	Pop from the operand stack and print to standard output.
struct n	Create a **struct** with n fields slots and push it onto the operand stack.
null	Push a null pointer onto the operand stack.
pop	Throw away the top of the operand stack.
halt	Halt program execution.

Figure 10.5: STACK-BASED GENERAL BYTECODE INSTRUCTIONS

After the call, the parameters are in the stack frame's locals space, not the operand stack. The function can manipulate locals and parameters with load and store. load, for example, pulls a value from the locals field and pushes it onto the operand stack:

```
operands[++sp] = calls[fp].locals[«address-operand»];
```

When the function is done, it executes a ret instruction to return. ret doesn't have to clean up the stack because call removes parameters at the start of the function. It only has to pop a stack frame off the call stack and jump to the return address found in that frame:

```
StackFrame fr = calls[fp--];     // pop stack frame
ip = fr.returnAddress;           // branch to ret addr
```

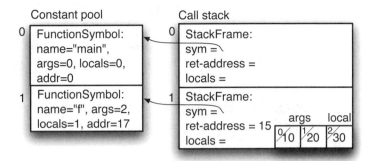

Figure 10.6: STACK FRAME FOR CALL TO F() WITH TWO ARGUMENTS

To return a value, a function pushes a value onto the operand stack and then executes the ret instruction.

Returning Function Values

After executing a function call, the calling code expects any return value to be on the operand stack. Here's a trace until after the call to f():

```
0033:   LOAD     2          stack=[ ]          calls=[ main f ]
0038:   RET                 stack=[ 30 ]       calls=[ main f ]
0015:   PRINT               stack=[ 30 ]       calls=[ main ]
```

The ret instructions pops the stack frame for f() off the call stack and jumps to the return address (15) in main().

If a function returns a value that the calling code does not use, the calling code must pop that value off the operand stack anyway. For example, the following program throws away the value returned from f().

```
.def main: args=0, locals=0
    call f()            ; assume f() has return value
    pop                 ; drop top of stack
    halt
```

Now that we know how to use the operand stack, it's time to look at the implementation details for a stack-based interpreter.

Implementation

The bulk of our bytecode interpreter lives in Interpreter. Other than that, we'll need a few support classes: StackFrame, BytecodeDefinition, and StructSpace (holds the fields of a **struct**). We'll use Pattern 26, *Bytecode Assembler*, on page 252 to assemble programs before execution. (BytecodeDefinition defines the instruction set.) The assembler pattern also provides a suitable FunctionSymbol that we'll need for our constant pool.

The Interpreter contains the processor (in cpu()) that we discussed in the introductory material and the fields that represent our simulated memory, stacks, and special-purpose registers:

```
interp/stack/Interpreter.java
int ip;               // instruction pointer register
byte[] code;          // byte-addressable code memory.
int codeSize;
Object[] globals;     // global variable space
protected Object[] constPool;
/** Operand stack, grows upwards */
Object[] operands = new Object[DEFAULT_OPERAND_STACK_SIZE];
int sp = -1;          // stack pointer register
/** Stack of stack frames, grows upwards */
StackFrame[] calls = new StackFrame[DEFAULT_CALL_STACK_SIZE];
int fp = -1;          // frame pointer register
FunctionSymbol mainFunction;
```

The main() method creates an Interpreter object, loads and assembles the bytecode program, and then executes starting at the main function:

```
interp/stack/Interpreter.java
Interpreter interpreter = new Interpreter();
load(interpreter, input);
interpreter.trace = trace;
interpreter.exec();
if ( disassemble ) interpreter.disassemble();
if ( dump) interpreter.coredump();
```

Loading and assembling the input program is a matter of creating an assembler and calling the **program** rule. After it returns, we can ask the assembler for the code memory and any other goodies we need:

```
interp/stack/Interpreter.java
AssemblerLexer assemblerLexer =
    new AssemblerLexer(new ANTLRInputStream(input));
CommonTokenStream tokens = new CommonTokenStream(assemblerLexer);
BytecodeAssembler assembler =
    new BytecodeAssembler(tokens, BytecodeDefinition.instructions);
assembler.program();
interp.code = assembler.getMachineCode();
interp.codeSize = assembler.getCodeMemorySize();
interp.constPool = assembler.getConstantPool();
```

```
interp.mainFunction = assembler.getMainFunction();
interp.globals = new Object[assembler.getDataSize()];
interp.disasm = new DisAssembler(interp.code,
                                 interp.codeSize,
                                 interp.constPool);
```

To begin execution, the interpreter calls the bytecode program's main method and invokes cpu():

interp/stack/Interpreter.java

```java
public void exec() throws Exception {
    // SIMULATE "call main()"; set up stack as if we'd called main()
    if ( mainFunction==null ) {
        mainFunction = new FunctionSymbol("main", 0, 0, 0);
    }
    StackFrame f = new StackFrame(mainFunction, ip);
    calls[++fp] = f;
    ip = mainFunction.address;
    cpu();
}
```

OK, let's start looking at some instructions. (Interestingly, the fragments look very much like the code we'd write in a hardware description language such as Verilog.)[9] Here's the implementation of the integer add instruction (a **case** of the **switch** in cpu()):

interp/stack/Interpreter.java

```java
case BytecodeDefinition.INSTR_IADD :
    a = (Integer)operands[sp-1]; // 1st opnd 1 below top
    b = (Integer)operands[sp];   // 2nd opnd at top of stack
    sp -= 2;                     // pop both operands
    operands[++sp] = a + b;      // push result
    break;
```

The floating-point version is the same except that we treat the top two operands on the stack as floats:

interp/stack/Interpreter.java

```java
case BytecodeDefinition.INSTR_FADD :
    e = (Float)operands[sp-1];
    f = (Float)operands[sp];
    sp -= 2;
    operands[++sp] = e + f;
    break;
```

The call instruction's operand is an index into the constant pool for the target function. It calls support method getIntOperand() to pull a

---

9. http://en.wikipedia.org/wiki/Verilog

4-byte integer out of the code memory at location *ip* and then delegates functionality to the call() method we saw earlier in this pattern:

interp/stack/Interpreter.java

```
case BytecodeDefinition.INSTR_CALL :
    int funcIndexInConstPool = getIntOperand();
    call(funcIndexInConstPool);
    break;
```

call pushes a stack frame that holds the return address space for parameters and locals (in a single field, locals):

interp/stack/StackFrame.java

```
public class StackFrame {
    FunctionSymbol sym; // associated with which function?
    int returnAddress;  // the instruction following the call
    Object[] locals;    // holds parameters and local variables
    public StackFrame(FunctionSymbol sym, int returnAddress) {
        this.sym = sym;
        this.returnAddress = returnAddress;
        locals = new Object[sym.nargs+sym.nlocals];
    }
}
```

OK, that should give you a taste of the relevant implementation details. Let's get this to build. All we've got to do is run ANTLR on the assembler grammar file and compile the Java code:

```
$ java org.antlr.Tool Assembler.g
$ javac *.java
$
```

Let's try this on an sample program that stores a value into two global variables and prints one of them:

interp/stack/t.pcode

```
; int x,y
.globals 2

.def main: args=0, locals=0
; x = 9
        iconst 9
        gstore 0
; y = x
        gload 0
        gstore 1
; print y
        gload 1
        print
        halt
```

To run t.pcode into Interpreter and dump out all the relevant memory spaces, we can use option -dump:

```
$ java Interpreter -dump t.pcode
9
Constant pool:
0000: FunctionSymbol{name='main', args=0, locals=0, address=0}

Data memory:
0000: 9 <Integer>
0001: 9 <Integer>

Code memory:
0000:  18   0   0   0   9  25   0   0
0008:   0   0  22   0   0   0   0  25
0016:   0   0   0   1  22   0   0   0
0024:   1  27  31
$
```

Looking at the code memory, only 7 out of the 26 bytes are bytecodes—the rest are operands. The first step in making this pattern more efficient would be to create a denser instruction set (loading and decoding those operands repeatedly gets expensive). For example, we could define instructions that used 2-byte operands instead of 4-byte operands (or even 1-byte operands). Most of the time, addresses and constants fit in one or two bytes.

The biggest speed impediment for a stack-based interpreter, though, is the extra work involved in constantly flogging the operand stack. In the next pattern, we'll look at a bytecode interpreter that avoids a lot of unnecessary traffic to and from memory by using registers.

Related Patterns

This pattern reuses Pattern 26, *Bytecode Assembler*, on page 252 and is extremely similar to Pattern 28, *Register-Based Bytecode Interpreter*.

---

28   Register-Based Bytecode Interpreter

☐

Purpose

This pattern executes bytecode instructions that store function parameters, local variables, and temporary values in simulated registers.

Instruction	Description
iadd r_i, r_j, r_k	Arithmetic operators for integers. $r_k = r_i$ op r_j
isub r_i, r_j, r_k	
imul r_i, r_j, r_k	
fadd r_i, r_j, r_k	Arithmetic operators for floating-point numbers.
fsub r_i, r_j, r_k	$r_k = r_i$ op r_j
fmul r_i, r_j, r_k	
ilt r_i, r_j, r_k	Equality operators for integers and floating-point: less-
ieq r_i, r_j, r_k	than and equal. Save boolean result in r_k. $r_k = r_i$ op r_j
flt r_i, r_j, r_k	
feq r_i, r_j, r_k	
itof r_i, r_j	Convert integer in r_i to floating-point and save in r_j.
cconst r_i, c	Load character into r_i. $r_i = c$.
iconst r_i, n	Load integer into r_i. $r_i = n$.
sconst r_i, s	Load string into r_i. r_i = constPool[«*index-of-s*»].
fconst r_i, f	Load floating-point value into r_i. r_i = constPool[«*index-of-f*»].

Figure 10.7: REGISTER-BASED ARITHMETIC BYTECODE INSTRUCTIONS

Discussion

A register-based bytecode interpreter is identical to a stack-based inter-preter except for the instruction set and where it keeps local variables, parameters, return values, and any temporary values. The instructions use registers instead of an operand stack. Our simulated machine gives each stack frame an "infinite" set of registers.

Let's reserve the first element of the register array to hold return values. (This is just one possible strategy.) The parameters and locals are then at index 1 and greater:

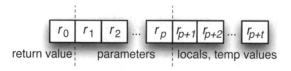

That image shows the registers for a function definition with p parameters and t locals and temporaries ($n = 1 + p + t$):

```
.def foo: args=p, locals=t
```

As you can see in the sample instruction set for this pattern (Figure 10.7, on the facing page, and see Figure 10.8, on page 271), all the instructions manipulate registers. (The sample code in the source directory implements this instruction set.) To get the ball rolling, we'll look at how basic instructions and data aggregate instructions use registers. Then, we'll explore function calls in detail. It's important to understand exactly how the call and ret instructions shuffle registers around between stack frames on the call stack. Otherwise, you'll find it hard to read the sample implementation.

Implementing Basic Instructions

To access a register, an instruction has to know where the current registers are. The current registers are in the stack frame on the top of the call stack, calls[fp]. So, we can define a shortcut to the current registers like this:

```
Object r[] = calls[fp].registers; // shorthand for "current registers"
```

Then, instructions like iconst (integer load) can save values into the r shortcut array (this code snippet lives in our fetch execute loop cpu()):

```
case BytecodeDefinition.INSTR_ICONST : // E.g., iconst r1, 99
    i = «get-register-number-operand»;
    v = «get-integer-operand»;
    r[i] = v;
    break;
```

Once we pull the register number and integer value operands from the code memory, the iconst instruction stores the value into the appropriate register.

The iadd integer add mechanism is pretty similar. Once we know the three register numbers, we can access their values, cast them to integers, perform the operation, and store the result in a register:

```
case BytecodeDefinition.INSTR_IADD : // E.g., iadd r1, r2, r3
    i = «get-register-number-operand»;
    j = «get-register-number-operand»;
    k = «get-register-number-operand»;
    r[k] = r[i] + r[j];
    break;
```

OK, now that we know how to access registers, let's look at accessing the fields of a data aggregate.

Creating and Accessing Data Aggregates

To create a data aggregate, the struct instruction needs a target register and how many fields to create:

```
case BytecodeDefinition.INSTR_STRUCT :
    i = «get-register-number-operand»;
    int nfields = «get-integer-operand»;
    r[i] = new StructSpace(nfields); // save struct in r[i]
    break;
```

A StructSpace object has a fields array that we can access with the fload and fstore instructions. Both instructions take two register operands and one integer operand. The first register is the target of the load or the value to write. The second register is the base address of the data aggregate. The integer is the field index. For example, here is the mechanism for loading a field:

```
case BytecodeDefinition.INSTR_FLOAD :    // E.g., fload r1, r2, 0
    i = «get-register-number-operand»;    // r[i] is target register
    j = «get-register-number-operand»;    // r[j] is the struct
    fieldIndex = «get-integer-operand»;   // which field?
    r[i] = r[j].fields[fieldIndex];
    break;
```

All the instructions we've seen so far only deal with the registers in a single stack frame. To perform a function call, though, we have to copy registers between frames (since all nonglobal variables and all temporary values live in registers).

Passing Data During Function Calls

The mechanism for passing parameters to functions and returning values is a bit tricky. Let's see how it works by looking at the relationship between a sample program and its call stack. Take a look at the flow of control in the following program. It goes from main() to f() to g().

```
.def main: args=0, locals=1 ; void main() { print f(10); }
    iconst r1, 10             ; put 10 into r1
    call f(), r1              ; call f, argument is in r1
    print r0                  ; print return value
    halt

.def f: args=1, locals=3     ; int f(int x) { return g(2*x, 30); }
    iconst r2,2               ; get int 2 into 1st non-arg register
    imul r1,r2,r3             ; mult arg by 2
    iconst r4,30              ; get int 30 into a reg
    call g(), r3              ; leave result in r0; args=[r3,r4]
    ret                       ; return value in r0
.def g: args=2, locals=0     ; int g(int x, int y) { return x+y; }
    iadd r1, r2, r0           ; return x+y
    ret                       ; return value in r0
```

Instruction	Description
call f(), r_i	Call function f (via f's constant pool entry). For n parameters, registers $r_i..r_{i+n-1}$ contain the parameter values. Use r_0 if there are no parameters. Push new stack frame onto call stack, and move parameters from previous stack frame to this stack frame. Branch to function start address.
ret	Return from function call. Any return value is in r_0. Pop the top stack frame off, and return to the return address stored in that stack frame.
br a	Branch to a always, if r_i is true, or r_i is false.
brt r_i, a	
brf r_i, a	
gload r_i, a	r_i=globals[a] and globals[a]=r_i.
gstore r_i, a	
fload r_i, r_j, n	$r_i=r_j[n]$ and $r_j[n]=r_i$.
fstore r_i, r_j, n	
move r_i, r_j	$r_j=r_i$.
print r_i	Print r_i to standard output.
struct r_i, n	r_i=new **struct** with n field slots.
null r_i	r_i=null.
halt	Halt program execution.

Figure 10.8: REGISTER-BASED GENERAL BYTECODE INSTRUCTIONS

In Figure 10.9, on the following page, we can see the state of the call stack at the ret instruction in g(). If we ignore the registers, it looks like the general stack frame shown in the introductory material (see Figure 10.3, on page 250). The first stack frame on the call stack is for the simulated call to main() from the interpreter. The next stack frame is for the call to f(). The top of the call stack is the stack frame for the call to g().

The dashed arrows indicate register copying. The downward arrows indicate parameter passing, and the upward arrows indicate values returning to the invoking function. The call to f() has one parameter, which is stored in r[1] (courtesy of main()'s first iconst instruction). The call to f() copies r[1] in main()'s stack frame to r[1] in f()'s stack frame. The r[1] in main()'s stack frame is a temporary value (since it has no parameters), whereas r[1] is a parameter in f()'s stack frame.

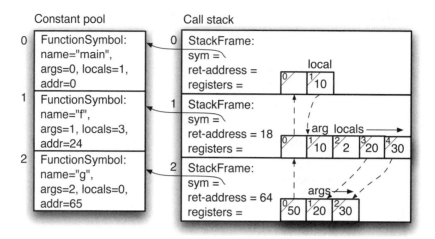

Figure 10.9: REGISTER TRANSFERS AND STATE OF CALL STACK AT RET IN G()

The execution trace illustrates how the registers for the various stack frames change over time (the | character separates r[0] from the parameters and the parameters from the locals in the register array):

```
0000: ICONST  r1, 10       main.registers=[?||?]       calls=[main]
0009: CALL     #1:f(), r1   main.registers=[?||10]      calls=[main]
0024: ICONST  r2, 2         f.registers=[?|10|? ? ?]    calls=[main f]
0033: IMUL    r1, r2, r3    f.registers=[?|10|2 ? ?]    calls=[main f]
0046: ICONST  r4, 30        f.registers=[?|10|2 20 ?]   calls=[main f]
0055: CALL     #2:g(), r3   f.registers=[?|10|2 20 30]  calls=[main f]
0065: IADD    r1, r2, r0    g.registers=[?|20 30]       calls=[main f g]
0078: RET                   g.registers=[50|20 30]      calls=[main f g]
0064: RET                   f.registers=[50|10|2 20 30] calls=[main f]
0018: PRINT   r0            main.registers=[50||10]     calls=[main]
```

As g() hits the ret at code address 78, it moves its r[0], 50, to f()'s r[0]. When the call to f() returns, it moves r[0] to main()'s r[0]. The print instruction in main() can then print out its r[0].

The operands of the call instruction are a little weird, so it's worth exploring them in more detail. Once we've done that, we'll be ready to look at our sample implementation.

Decoding the call Instruction Operands

The call instruction knows how many parameters to pass because its first operand refers to a FunctionSymbol sitting in the constant pool. The second operand is a register number and tells the instruction where the parameters are. That register number indicates which register holds the first parameter. Any other parameters live in the next contiguous registers. An operand of r0 indicates there are no parameters.

Since f() has one parameter, the call in main() knows to copy just r[1] to the parameter register in the stack frame it creates. g() takes two parameters that live that r[1] and r[2] in its stack frame. f() computes the first parameter to g() in r[3] and the second in r[4]. That's why, in Figure 10.9, on the facing page, we see interframe dashed lines from r[3] to r[1] and from r[4] to r[2]. The following algorithm fills in the rest of the details for the call instruction:

```
void call(int functionConstPoolIndex, int baseRegisterIndex) {
    FunctionSymbol fs = constPool[functionConstPoolIndex];
    StackFrame f = new StackFrame(fs, «return-address»);
    StackFrame callingFrame = calls[fp];
    calls[++fp] = f; // push new stack frame
    // copy arguments from calling stack frame to new stack frame
    for (int a=0; a<«num-args»; a++) {
        f.registers[a+1] = callingFrame.registers[baseRegisterIndex+a];
    }
    ip = fs.address; // jump to the start address
}
```

The details of the ret instruction are much simpler. ret just copies r[0] of the current frame to r[0] in the calling frame and pops off the current stack frame:

```
case BytecodeDefinition.INSTR_RET :
    StackFrame f = calls[fp--]; // pop stack frame
    calls[fp].registers[0] = f.registers[0]; // copy r0
    ip = f.returnAddress;       // jump back to calling instruction
    break;
```

At this point, we've hit the highlights of how to implement register machine instructions. In the next section, we'll take a quick peek at a sample implementation.

Implementation

Register machines are nearly identical to stack machines. In fact, the implementation for this pattern differs from Pattern 27, *Stack-Based*

Bytecode Interpreter, on page 259 in only two spots. First, the locals field in StackFrame is now called registers:

interp/reg/StackFrame.java

```
// Allocate space for registers; 1 extra for r0 reserved reg
registers = new Object[sym.nargs+sym.nlocals+1];
```

Second, the **switch** statement inside cpu() has implementations for the register-based instructions rather than stack-based instructions:

interp/reg/Interpreter.java

```
protected void cpu() {
    int i=0, j=0, k=0, addr=0, fieldIndex=0;
    short opcode = code[ip];
    while (opcode!= BytecodeDefinition.INSTR_HALT && ip < codeSize) {
        if ( trace ) trace();
        ip++; //jump to next instruction or first byte of operand
        Object r[] = calls[fp].registers; // shortcut to current registers
        switch (opcode) {
            case BytecodeDefinition.INSTR_IADD :
                i = getRegOperand();
                j = getRegOperand();
                k = getRegOperand();
                r[k] = ((Integer)r[i])+((Integer)r[j]);
                break;
            // ...
```

Although the instruction sets for the stack-based and register-based machines look very different, we're able to reuse Pattern 26, *Bytecode Assembler*, on page 252 verbatim for both. For example, here's a sample register-based assembly program the assembler readily translates to bytecodes:

interp/reg/t.rcode

```
; int x,y
.globals 2

.def main: args=0, locals=3
; x = 9
        iconst r1, 9
        gstore r1, 0
; y = x
        gload r2, 0
        gstore r2, 1
; print y
        gload r3, 1
        print r3
        halt
```

To build and execute that file, we run ANTLR on the assembler grammar file, compile all the Java code, and run t.rcode into Interpreter:

```
$ java org.antlr.Tool Assembler.g
$ javac *.java
$ java Interpreter t.rcode
9
$
```

This implementation isn't the fastest in town (when compared to Sun's Java VM in pure interpreter mode, -Xint). My design goals for this book were simplicity and readability rather than bytecode execution speed and memory efficiency. That said, it wouldn't be that hard to get this interpreter to perform within a factor of two or three of Sun's interpreter. Basically, we just need to introduce a few dense instructions for common operations. For example, pushing zero on the stack is extremely common; we can represent that with a single-byte iload0 instruction instead of the general iload instruction that takes 5 bytes (including the 4-byte operand).

Related Patterns

This pattern uses Pattern 26, *Bytecode Assembler*, on page 252 to read in bytecode assembly language programs. The source code for this pattern is remarkably similar to that of Pattern 27, *Stack-Based Bytecode Interpreter*, on page 259.

Up Next

Building an interpreter is one way to implement a language, but we can also build a translator from the new language to an existing language. In the next chapter, we're going to look at code generation, the final stage of a source-to-source translator.

Part IV

Translating and Generating Languages

Chapter 11

Translating Computer Languages

So far, we've focused on reading in programs and other structured text in this book. Previously, we built input models (usually ASTs) of the input and then analyzed or even executed that input by scanning the model. In this next part of the book, we're going to reverse the process and build text-to-text translators and generators that emit structured text. Translators let us implement new DSLs and programming languages quickly by translating them to existing languages. For example, the first C++ implementation (cfront) translated C++ to C. Translators are also heavily used for migrating legacy code and data formats.

A translator is a program that maps input constructs to output constructs. Sometimes we can do this purely with syntax. For example, translating a scalar multiply like a x b in a mathematics DSL to a*b in Java doesn't require semantic information. If that DSL has matrices (2D arrays), though, we need to alter the translation based on type information. For example, to translate matrix multiply A x B, we need to generate a nested **for** loop in Java. Things can get really tricky when we need lots of semantic information spread across an entire project. For example, doing a static field move from one class to another forces a refactoring engine to find all uses of it.

Translators vary in difficulty depending on a number of factors including the relative order of input and output constructs, the presence of forward references, whether we need to preserve comments and formatting, sheer input file size, and so on.[1] But, regardless of the translation strategy, we need to keep an important design principle in mind.

---

1. http://www.antlr.org/wiki/pages/viewpage.action?pageId=1773

Translation involves fully understanding each input phrase, picking an appropriate output construct, and filling it with elements from the input model. Trying to cleverly replace input symbols with output symbols rarely works well. You end up with what we call a *literal translation* in a natural language.[2] For example, *faire un canard* in French means literally "to make a duck." The real translation, though, is "to hit a wrong note."

In a computer translator, to "understand" a phrase means to syntactically and semantically analyze it. We usually have to create an input model like an AST because we can't always do semantic analysis properly as we parse. As we did in Chapter 8, *Enforcing Static Typing Rules*, on page 181, we have to create symbol tables and compute expression types from the input model. According to the needs of the task at hand, we compute everything we need to know about the input and then make a decision about mapping an input phrase to an output phrase.

Translation is a huge topic, and we can devote only one chapter to it, so we're going to focus on overall strategies and a few of the most common patterns:

- Pattern 29, *Syntax-Directed Translator*, on page 296: This translator consists of a parser (or grammar) with embedded actions that immediately generate output. The key distinguishing feature is that syntax-directed translators don't build an internal representation. They have to do everything in one pass.

- Pattern 30, *Rule-Based Translator*, on page 302: Rule-based translators use the DSL of a particular rule engine to specify a set of "this goes to that" translation rules. Combined with a grammar describing the input syntax, a rule engine can automatically perform translations.

- *Model-driven translation*: There are lots of variations within the model-driven translator strategy, but they all have one thing in common: an internal representation of the input. From the input model, a translator can emit output directly, build up strings, build up templates (documents with "holes" in them where we can stick values), or build up specialized output objects (Pattern 31,

---

2. I'll never forget trying to learn French by reading comic books. It took me forever to figure out why the cartoons had "Bread! Bread!" stamped all over them during action scenes. It turns out that *"Pain! Pain!"* sounds like "Bang! Bang!" and is the way to say it in French.

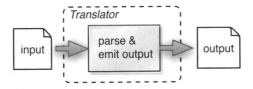

Figure 11.1: Syntax-directed translator

Target-Specific Generator Classes, on page 308). Depending on the complexity of the translation, the translator might need multiple passes over the input model before the generation phase.

Because most industrial translators use the model-driven approach, we'll spend most of our time talking about mapping input to output models. Then, as part of the patterns, we're going to implement a make build tool, a wiki to HTML translator, and a simple SQL CREATE TABLE statement generator. Let's get the ball rolling by looking at the simplest possible translator design.

11.1 Syntax-Directed Translation

A syntax-directed translator reads input and immediately emits output as it goes. In Figure 11.1, we see the one-stage application pipeline. Even though it has few moving parts, we can use this for a surprising number of DSLs.

Syntax-directed translators consist of a grammar (or equivalent hand-built parser) and output actions. For example, here is a rule that translates a scalar multiply, such as a x b, to Java:

```
mult : a=ID 'x' b=ID {System.out.println($a.text+"*"+$b.text);} ;
```

Because syntax-directed translators make only one pass through the input, they can't deal with forward references. For example, we needed multiple passes in Pattern 19, *Symbol Table for Classes*, on page 167 to handle forward references to methods and fields. They also can't perform very sophisticated translations because their application pipeline is only one stage deep. It has no opportunity to analyze an input model, which is typically required for complex translations.

Syntax-directed translators also break down when the order of input and output constructs differs significantly. For example, imagine a translation that negates a list of integers and spits them out in reverse order. A syntax-directed translator would negate the first number and immediately spit it out. Without buffering up the negated integers, we can't deal with radically different input and output orders.

Building a syntax-directed translator means writing a lot of informal code by hand. To understand what such a translator implements, we've got to imagine the emergent behavior of all those actions. We'll explore the details in Pattern 29, *Syntax-Directed Translator*, on page 296. Let's move on to DSLs designed to make translation easier and less *ad hoc*.

11.2 Rule-Based Translation

To build a translator, we have to define an input-to-output mapping (a set of "this goes to that" rules) no matter what translator architecture we use. Instead of coding them with a general-purpose programming language, we can use a translation DSL. There are a number of excellent rule-based systems available such as ASF+SDF,[3] Stratego/XT,[4] and TXL.[5] The ANTLR project also has a simple rule engine called ANTLRMorph.[6]

To use these engines, we feed them an input language grammar and a set of translation rules, as shown in Figure 11.2, on the facing page. From the grammar, the engine builds a parse tree from the input and then applies the rules to get the output. As we saw in Section 5.4, *Decoupling Tree Traversal from Pattern Matching*, on page 110, a rule-based approach has a number of advantages. We get to focus on the input constructs (subtrees) we care about, and we don't have to specify tree-walking details.

To demonstrate the rule-based approach with a simple translation DSL, let's look at an awk script that extracts class names by looking for the **class** keyword:

```
/^public\ class/ {print $3} # In "public class foo", foo is 3rd element
/^class/         {print $2} # In "class foo", foo is 2nd element
```

---

3. http://www.meta-environment.org
4. http://strategoxt.org
5. http://www.txl.ca
6. http://www.antlr.org/wiki/display/Morph/Home

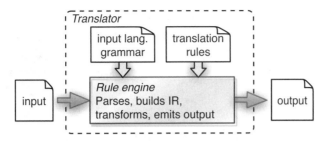

Figure 11.2: RULE-BASED TRANSLATOR

awk scripts are a series of patterns (regular expressions in /.../) and actions (in {...}). awk walks an input file line by line, executing actions associated with patterns that match the current line.

Notice that we don't have to specify an entire Java grammar to make this work. Of course, this is a simple transformation. In general, we need complete syntactic and semantic analysis like any other translation approach. Still, it's amazing what we can build with just a few pattern-action rules. For example, we're going to build a wiki-to-HTML translator in Pattern 30, *Rule-Based Translator*, on page 302.

All of these tools allow multiple translation and information-gathering passes using different sets of rules. For example, it's extremely common to have a symbol definition pass and then a symbol resolution pass. We might also need a type computation pass. All of this has to happen before we can apply the translation rules.

Rule-based systems are particularly good at legacy code conversions because we want the translated code to be natural. For example, If we see a nested loop implementation for a matrix multiply in Java, we want to recognize that pattern and convert it to a simple A x B in a mathematics DSL (not another nested loop). Rule-based systems let us just lay out all the input-output transformations we want. We can add new ones easily as we think of them.

I took advantage of this fact when writing this book. The publisher has an excellent proprietary DSL for writing books, but to reduce the strain on my hands, I designed a really terse DSL and built a translator from my language to their internal format. As I write this book, I think of new timesaving commands and add them to my list of translation rules.

This all sounds great. These rule engines let us say *what* to do, not *how* to do it. They are powerful, implementation-language independent, expressive, formal, and beautiful. It might surprise you, then, that these pure rule-based translation systems don't enjoy widespread usage in industry.

From what I can tell, developers have a number of objections. These systems tend to be complex beasts. With a large number of translation rules, translations can be slow (though we might not care). Some also find the rule engines' functional programming style too different from the imperative programming style they're used to. The rule engines themselves are black boxes, which can make it hard to understand what's gone wrong in a translation. Some of these systems were also designed to be the center of the universe, making them tricky to integrate into applications.

If you need sophisticated pattern matching that integrates well with Java, take a look at Tom[7] (Tom also supports C, Python, C++, and C#) and the Scala[8] programming language (which looks like Java + ML).

Next we're going to look at the translator architecture used most often in industry. It's a hybrid approach that glues together components from different formal tools. As you'd expect, as we reduce the level of abstraction, we've got more work to do. In compensation, we get to work with simpler tools and use familiar programming languages. We also get greater control over efficiency.

11.3 Model-Driven Translation

In a model-driven translator, everything centers around an input model created by the parser. In its simplest form, a model-driven translator creates an AST input model and then walks it to generate output with print statements.[9] The only difference between this and a syntax-directed translator is that we generate text while walking a tree instead of while parsing a token stream.

The advantage of creating an AST first is that we can do semantic analysis before generating output. Most of the time, we'll need to annotate

---

7. http://tom.loria.fr
8. http://www.scala-lang.org/
9. The figures in this section use the more general term *intermediate representation* (IR), instead of AST.

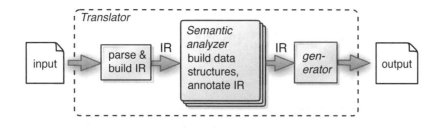

Figure 11.3: MODEL-DRIVEN TRANSLATOR

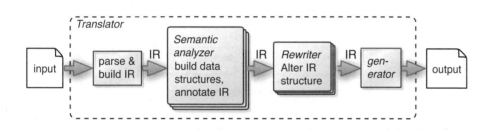

Figure 11.4: MODEL-DRIVEN TRANSLATOR WITH TREE REWRITING

the AST with symbol and type information before generating output. In Figure 11.3, we can see the overall architecture. From a software engineering point of view, it's also nice to keep output-language specific actions out of the parser. Sequestering them in a separate tree walker lets us reuse the parser for other tasks.

Once we've got an AST, we can also restructure it as part of the translation, as shown in Figure 11.4. The role of tree rewriting in translator design is a pretty big topic and too much to go into here. Unless you have a lot of experience building translators, I'd avoid rewriting the tree unless you're doing some simple optimizations like we did in Pattern 15, *Tree Pattern Matcher*, on page 123. The majority of (noncompiler) translators skip tree writing and go directly to output generation.

From the AST input model, we're going to learn how to derive an appropriate output model instead of immediately generating output. Simple print statements fall flat when the input and output phrase orders don't line up. We really need to buffer up the translated phrases and arrange them later in the proper order. As we walk the input model, we'll match subtrees and create output objects to represent translated

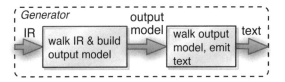

Figure 11.5: GENERATOR FOR MODEL-DRIVEN TRANSLATORS

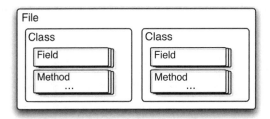

Figure 11.6: NESTED OUTPUT MODEL FOR JAVA FILE

phrases (as summarized by Figure 11.5). These output objects can be mindless strings, templates, or custom-built objects. The key is organizing them into a proper output model.

The structure of an output model is always a nested arrangement of output objects. For example, in Figure 11.6, we see a hypothetical output model for a specific Java program. The overall File object embeds Class objects, which embed Field and Method objects, and so on. For large Java programs, this data structure can be deeply nested.

Personally, I like to think of these nested structures as trees. In Figure 11.7, on the facing page, we see the equivalent tree structure, which should look familiar. It's a syntax (parse) tree. As we learned in Chapter 2, *Basic Parsing Patterns*, on page 21, a syntax tree represents the underlying syntactic structure of a phrase. My point is that using a hierarchy of output objects to represent the output makes sense because it's equivalent to a syntax tree.

In this section, we're going to learn about the different kinds of output objects and why we need to create those objects in the first place. After that, we'll dig into the mechanics of constructing output model hierarchies.

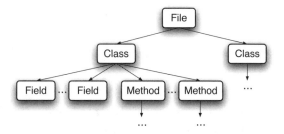

Figure 11.7: HIERARCHY VIEW OF NESTED OUTPUT MODEL FOR JAVA FILE

Creating Target-Specific Generator Classes

Because we're programmers, we tend to write classes to solve problems. For example, to generate SQL CREATE TABLE statements, it seems like a good idea to design a Table class (see Pattern 31, *Target-Specific Generator Classes*, on page 308). We can then render it to text by calling its toString( ) method. This approach works and feels very comfortable.

The problem is that it's often a huge pain to create such output data structures manually. It's easier just to emit the output directly while walking the input model. For example, let's say we want to generate the Java bytecodes for a "hello world" main( ) method. To create a bytecode output model for main( ), we can use the Byte Code Engineering Library (BCEL). Here is the sample code from the BCEL manual[10] to create the method definition object:

```
MethodGen mg =
    new MethodGen(ACC_STATIC | ACC_PUBLIC, // access flags
                Type.VOID,                 // return type
                new Type[] {               // argument types
                new ArrayType(Type.STRING, 1) },
                new String[] { "argv" }, // arg names
                "main", "HelloWorld",    // method, class
                «an InstructionList», «a ConstantPoolGen»);
```

That seems like a lot of work just to define a method. All of these constructor calls really add up quickly to a very large code generator. Rather than using these target-specific generator classes, it's easier to use a few print statements to generate a method definition in a byte-

---

10. http://jakarta.apache.org/bcel/manual.html

code DSL. For example, using the Jasmin[11] bytecode assembler, here's what main() looks like:

```
.method public static main([Ljava/lang/String;)V
    ...
.end method
```

This is much more clear. Of course, we have to learn a tiny bit of syntax, but that's easier than learning the vagaries of a library such as BCEL. The only strange bits are the [Ljava/lang/String; and V strings, which are Java type encodings[12] representing an array of String objects and **void**, respectively.

Aside from being a hassle, it's usually not worth the development and run-time cost to create a data structure when the input model itself is close enough to be workable. If we have an AST subtree, for example, that represents the main() method, there's no point in writing a class like MethodGen. Here's a sample AST (Pattern 11, *Irregular Heterogeneous AST*, on page 99) node for a method definition:

```
class MethodNode extends StatNode {
    String name;
    Type returnType;
    List<String> modifiers; // public, static, final, ...
    List<ArgNode> args;
    BlockNode body;
    ...
}
```

From that, we can directly generate the Jasmin code, letting Jasmin do all of the work to emit the .class file:

```
void gen(MethodNode m) {                    // method node visitor
    System.out.print(".method ");
    «print m.modifiers»
    System.out.print(m.name+"(");
    for (ArgNode a : m.args) gen(a); // visit the arguments
    System.out.print(")");
    «println m.returnType»
    gen(m.body);                            // visit the method body
    System.out.println(".end method");
}
```

This principle also applies when we are generating high-level source code, not bytecodes. For example, rather than building up objects that

---

11. http://jasmin.sourceforge.net
12. http://java.sun.com/docs/books/jvms/second_edition/html/ClassFile.doc.html#1169

represent Java program phrases such as WhileStatement and AssignStatement, we can just spit out Java code by walking the AST. Here is how we could generate code for Java assignments using Pattern 13, *External Tree Visitor*, on page 116:

```
class AssignNode extends ExprNode { String id; ExprNode valueExpr; }
...
void gen(AssignNode n) {
    System.out.println(n.id+"="); // emit left-hand-side and '='
    gen(n.valueExpr);             // walk right-hand-side expression
    System.out.println(";");      // emit final ';'
}
```

OK, so we can save some work by generating text on the fly while walking a suitable input model instead of creating an output model. The bad news is that print statements don't always work.

Print Statements Are Easy but Inflexible

Visitors that directly emit text with print statements work fine as long as the order of input and output constructs is very similar. The order in which we visit input model nodes has to match the order in which we need to generate output.

This turns out to be pretty restrictive. Take Java to C translation, for example. Because C doesn't allow forward references, we need to generate a list of function declarations at the top of the output C file:

```
extern int f(float y);       // f declaration
extern void g();             // g declaration
int f(float y) { g(); }      // f definition; forward reference to g()
void g() { ... }             // g definition
```

Without the **extern** declaration of g(), a C compiler would complain about the call to g() inside f(). So, for each function, we need to emit both a declaration and a definition. Our first attempt might look like this:

```
void gen(MethodNode m) {
    «compute and emit extern C declaration»
    «translate Java body and emit C function»
}
```

Unfortunately, this won't work. The output would interleave the declarations and definitions:

```
extern int f(float y);       // f declaration
int f(float y) { g(); }      // f definition; forward reference to g()
extern void g();             // g declaration; TOO LATE!
void g() { ... }             // g definition
```

Oops. We need all the declarations first. Somehow, we have to separate when we translate phrases from when we spit them out.

Decoupling Input Model Traversal from Output Order

There are two ways to solve input-output ordering mismatches. First, we can walk the tree twice, once for declarations and again for definitions using two visitor methods:

```
void genDecl(MethodNode m) {«compute and emit extern C declaration»}
void genDef(MethodNode m)  {«translate Java body and emit C function»}
```

This works but is inefficient because we have to walk the (potentially very large) tree twice. This is an *output-driven* approach because it "pulls" information from the input model according to the output order.

The second choice is to walk the input model a single time, collecting the declarations and definitions in lists instead of directly emitting text:

```
void gen(MethodNode m) {
    «compute and add extern C declaration to a list»
    «translate Java body and add C function to a list»
}
```

Once we've got those two lists, we can emit the proper C file by printing the lists one after the other. This *input-driven* approach lets us decouple the input and output order, albeit at the cost of buffering up the various output pieces. It's totally worth it, though. One of the most important lessons I've learned over the years is that *we should compute information and translate phrases when it's convenient and efficient to do so, not when the output order demands it.*

Let's see what the input-driven approach looks like. Instead of printing on the fly, we'll create strings. Here's a visitor method that returns a string representing an assignment:

```
String gen(AssignNode n) {
    String e = gen(n.valueExpr);  // walk right-hand-side expression
    return n.id + "=" + e + ";";
}
```

Or, instead of writing the AST visitor manually, we could use Pattern 14, *Tree Grammar*, on page 119:

```
assign returns [String s]
    :  ^('=' ID e=expression) {$s = $ID.text + "=" + $e.s + ";";}
    ;
expression returns [String s] : ... ;
```

Chess Analogy for Input- vs. Output-Driven Generation

Setting up a chessboard involves putting the chess pieces in specific locations on the board. We can think of the jumble of chess pieces as the input model (an unsorted list of pieces). The output is a 2x8 matrix, assuming we're setting up only one player's side. The output-driven approach marches through the output matrix position by position. At each spot, it scans through the input model looking for the right piece. In contrast, the input-driven approach simply places pieces in the right spot as it encounters them:

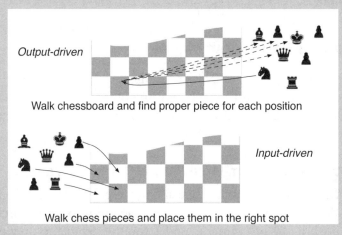

Output-driven

Walk chessboard and find proper piece for each position

Input-driven

Walk chess pieces and place them in the right spot

The dashed lines signify the output-driven generator searching for the right piece.

The point is that we've created the same text as we did in the previous section. We just aren't emitting it as we compute it. Whoever calls method gen() or rule **assign** can decide what to do with the translated text.

Let's review what we've learned so far. We know that the translation process is about creating an input model, enriching it with semantic information, and then creating an appropriate output model. Target-specific generator classes are familiar and well-structured, but building them is a lot of work, and they're often a hassle to use. Visitors that generate text directly are much more convenient. Unfortunately, print statements lock the order of the output elements to the input model traversal order. Besides, computing output strings in a general-purpose programming language ain't exactly pretty.

All is not lost, though. We can use templates, which are the best of both worlds. A template is a text document with "holes" that we can fill in. Templates are specialized generator objects that support a DSL designed for generating structured text. We'll explore templates in great detail in the next chapter.

In the meantime, let's finish off our discussion of the translation process. We need to learn some of the engineering details involved in creating output models.

11.4 Constructing a Nested Output Model

To build a translator, we need to look at the mechanics of matching an input construct and creating the right output object. Then, we have to figure out how to organize all those translated pieces into a nested hierarchy.

Creating Output Objects from Input Phrase Components

Translating an individual input phrase means creating the appropriate output model object and injecting it with elements from the input phrase. Here's what the assignment node example from the previous section looks like using an AST visitor and a target-specific generator object:

```
Statement gen(AssignNode n) {
    Expression e = gen(n.valueExpr); // walk right-hand-side expression
    return new AssignmentStatement(n.id, e);
}
```

Notice that we're not specifying the actual output literals. That would hard-code the translation. It would also make our translator hard to read because we'd be mixing the syntax of two languages (that of the implementation language and that of the output language). When using such explicit generator classes, the "pipe" between input and output model is usually the constructor arguments.

Mapping an assignment subtree to an assignment output object is reasonably clear, so let's try something a little harder: translating scalar and matrix multiplication. The syntax is the same for both, but semantically, they are very different. So, our translation method has to test the type of these subexpressions in order to create the proper output object.

```
// Match scalar a x b and matrix A x B multiplies for a math DSL
// Assume nodes contain result types. match ^('x' expression expression)
Expression gen(MultiplyNode n) {
    Expression a = gen(n.left);
    Expression b = gen(n.right);
    if ( «subexpressions have matrix types» )
        return new MatrixMultiply(a, b);
    else
        return new ScalarMultiply(a, b);
}
```

The *«subexpressions have matrix types»* conditional would test the subexpression types stored in the AST nodes like we did in Pattern 22, *Enforcing Static Type Safety*, on page 201.

To move things around locally within a phrase, all we have to do is change some parameters. For example, we can change the order of scalar multiplication operands by swapping the order of constructor parameters: ScalarMultiply(b, a). To send a translated phrase to a radically different spot in the output, though, we need to figure out how to organize the overall output model.

Organizing Translated Phrases into a Nested Model

To create an output model, we have to build up a nested data structure composed of output objects. (For the purposes of this discussion, we'll continue using specialized generator objects.) Let's start with the easiest case where the input and output element orders match up.

Let's say we've got a Java method AST input model and want to create a C# output model. Using a visitor, we could have all the methods return an output object. An invoking visitor method would incorporate the return value into its own output object. For example, given a MethodNode, the following visitor method returns a Method object representing a C# method.

```
Method gen(MethodNode m) { return Method(m.id, gen(m.bodyBlock)); }
```

This visitor method injects the name and translated body returned from gen(m.bodyBlock) into the Method instance. The following visitor method handles the body translation:

```
Block gen(BlockNode b) {
    List<Statement> stats = new ArrayList<Statement>();
    for (StatementNode s : b.stats) stats.add( gen(s) );
    return new Block(stats);
}
```

Whetting Your Appetite for Templates

As a teaser for the next chapter, here's how we'd use a template and an ANTLR tree grammar to map input patterns to output constructs:

```
assign:
    ^('=' ID e=expression) -> assign(id={$ID.text}, e={$e.st}) ;
```

The rule matches an input assignment tree and creates an instance of the template called **assign**. The **assign** template definition might look like this:

```
assign(id, e) ::= "<id> = <e>;"
```

The names inside angle brackets are the "holes" we can fill in. Templates are like generator classes except that we only use a single class called StringTemplate.

For mapping a x b to the appropriate output constructs, we could use the following tree grammar rule with template constructors and a predicate:

```
// Match scalar a x b and matrix A x B multiplies in a math DSL
// Assume each node knows its result type. Each
// rule also implicitly returns a template output model object.
mult:   ^('x' a=expression b=expression)
        -> {«subexpressions have matrix types»}?
           matrixMult(a={$a.st}, b={$b.st})
        -> scalarMult(a={$a.st}, b={$b.st})
    ;
```

It queues up the translated statements and injects them into the Block return value. Among the statement subtree visitor methods, we'd have something like the following to translate assignments:

```
AssignStatement gen(AssignNode a) {
    return new AssignStatement(a.id, gen(a.expr));
}
```

Now let's deal with the situation where the output element order differs from the input order. As we saw in Section 11.3, *Decoupling Input Model Traversal from Output Order*, on page 290, translating Java to C code requires that we generate a declaration for each function definition. Most important, those declarations must appear before all the function definitions. To translate a Java class to C, we need to generate the following strict sequence.

```
CFile cfile = new CFile();
void gen(ClassNode c) {
    cfile.struct = new Struct(c.name);
    «foreach member m in c.members»
        gen(m);
}
void gen(FieldNode f) {
    Variable v = «C var def from f»;
    cfile.struct.fields.add(v);
}
void gen(MethodNode m) {
    cfile.declarations.add(«C function declaration»);
    cfile.definitions.add(«C function from Java method»);
}
```

Figure 11.8: ASSEMBLING A C FILE MODEL USING JAVA AST VISITOR

```
#include <stdio.h>
«struct»        // has all fields extracted from Java class
«declarations»  // function declarations from Java methods
«definitions»   // function definitions from Java methods
```

The output model is shown graphically in Figure 11.8, which also shows how visitor methods would fill the model. One of the key elements of the code fragment is the "global" cfile variable. In general, translators need to track a few locations in the output model. These locations are typically things such as the current file object, the current class object, or the current method object. It's like remembering where the refrigerator and spice cabinets are in your kitchen. They tell you where to put things and effectively organize your kitchen.

The visitor method for ClassNodes indirectly triggers the other two visitor methods for field and method nodes. Those methods need to inject data into the model starting at the root (the outermost output object). The visitor methods don't bother returning output objects because they can directly inject elements. (In my experience, you'll have some visitor methods that return output objects and some that don't.)

When the visitor finishes walking the input model, we can generate code by calling toString() on the root, cfile. That, in turn, renders its embedded objects with toString(), and so on, recursing down the output object hierarchy. And with that toString() call, we finish the story of how we translate text using the model-driven approach.

At this point, you're familiar with the three translation strategies. You've also learned a lot about the model-driven approach. We learned that print statements aren't always powerful enough but that they are much easier to use than writing specific output classes. In the next chapter, we'll see that templates are often a good compromise between the two. They let us construct the nested output models we need without having to define a new class for every output construct. Before we get there, though, let's formally define the patterns we've talk about in this chapter:

Pattern	When to Apply
Pattern 29, *Syntax-Directed Translator*	This pattern is the simplest mechanism because it uses print statements to generate output rather than creating an output model. Use this pattern if you can get away with it. In other words, if you don't need information appearing later in the input, syntax-directed translation works. These translators also cannot generate output in a radically different order from the input.
Pattern 30, *Rule-Based Translator*, on page 302	Rule-based systems are elegant but often difficult to learn. They are also black boxes, which can make it difficult to debug translators. At the very least, it makes some programmers uncomfortable. In the hands of programmers with very strong theoretical backgrounds, these systems often prove extremely powerful.
Pattern 31, *Target-Specific Generator Classes*, on page 308	This pattern represents the final output model for a model-driven translator. Each output language construct corresponds to a specific class. The fields of an output object track any embedded output objects.

29 Syntax-Directed Translator

Purpose

This pattern generates text using a grammar, or equivalent hand-built parser, embedded with actions.

Discussion

Syntax-directed translators are little more than grammars salted with actions (code snippets). They don't build internal models and then walk them to generate output.

Putting actions directly in a grammar sometimes makes the grammar difficult to read. It also locks the grammar into a single bit of translator functionality. It's often a good idea to disentangle actions from the grammar by following what we did in Pattern 26, *Bytecode Assembler*, on page 252 (another example of a syntax-directed translator). The assembler grammar defined placeholder methods that describe the translator functionality:

```
protected void gen(Token instrToken) {;}
protected void gen(Token instrToken, Token operandToken) {;}
protected void defineFunction(Token idToken, int nargs, int nlocals) {;}
...
```

Then, the actions in the grammar invoked these methods to trigger translation:

```
instr
    :   ID NEWLINE               {gen($ID);}
    |   ID operand NEWLINE       {gen($ID,$operand.start);}
    ...
    ;
```

To implement the translation, we created a subclass that defined the concrete methods:

```
/** Subclass the AssemblerParser to actually implement the necessary
 *  symbol table management and code generation functions. */
public class BytecodeAssembler extends AssemblerParser {...}
```

If we wanted to make it easier to change the behavior of the translator on the fly, we could pass in a strategy object. We'd move the placeholder methods into an interface such as AssemblerBehavior. The actions would then look like this: behavior.gen($ID) instead of just gen($ID). We'd pass behavior in from the object using the assembler. In the next section, we'll follow this approach for our sample implementation.

Implementation

Let's now implement a make-like build dependency DSL that translates input like the following to an equivalent Java program:

```
«target-file» : «dependencies»
      «action(s) that create target-file»
```

For example, here are some rules from the sample makefile included in the source directory:

```
t.o : t.c
        gcc -c -o t.o t.c
go: t.o u.o
        gcc -o go t.o u.o
        echo done
```

Our goal is to generate makefile.java from file makefile. The entire process looks like this:

```
$ javac *.java          # build translator tool
$ java Maker makefile   # translate makefile to makefile.java
$ javac makefile.java
$
```

Once we've got an executable version of makefile, we can ask it to build the targets. By asking it to make target go, it has to first build the t.o and u.o dependencies. Then it can create the go file:

```
$ java makefile go       # build target "go"
build(t.o): gcc -c -o t.o t.c
build(u.o): gcc -c -o u.o u.c
build(go): gcc -o go t.o u.o
build(go): echo done
done
$
```

If we run the same target again, it gives no output because go now exists and is newer than its dependencies:

```
$ java makefile go               # nothing to do now
$ java makefile clean            # wipe out all files
build(clean): rm t.o u.o go
$ java makefile clean            # oops, files are already cleaned up
build(clean): rm t.o u.o go
rm: t.o: No such file or directory
rm: u.o: No such file or directory
rm: go: No such file or directory
$ java makefile go               # build again
build(t.o): gcc -c -o t.o t.c
...
$
```

As you can see, makefile collects and emits any standard output and standard error from the actions (processes) it executes.

Building Support Code and Defining the Translation

There are two key components to implementing this DSL: the translator itself and the run-time support. Before we can figure out how to build the translator component, we need to create the run-time support and manually translate a make file to Java code.

Let's create an object to represent a make target, with all of its dependencies and actions:

`trans/make/Target.java`

```
public class Target {
    String name;
    List<String> actions = new ArrayList<String>();
    List<String> dependencies = new ArrayList<String>();
```

Then we need a dictionary that maps target names to Target objects and a build() method to build a particular target. Let's stick all of this in MakeSupport. The details of walking the dependency list and checking file system timestamps aren't important here. We can assume the support code just works.

Now, let's figure out the translation. We can get away with a syntax-directed translator because we can generate appropriate Java code as we read the build instructions. Let's start by mapping a sample target to Java code. Given the t.o target rule, we need to generate something like this:

```
target = new Target("t.o");
target.addDependency("t.c");
target.addAction("gcc -c -o t.o t.c");
targets.put("t.o", target);
```

We also need to wrap that in a method within a class like this:

```
import java.io.IOException;
class «makefile-name» extends MakeSupport {
    public «makefile-name»() throws IOException {
        Target target = null;
        «code-for-targets»
    }
}
```

The name of the class is the same as the input file, such as makefile. Also in that class, we need to make a main() that creates an instance of the generated object. Then, we can ask it to build a target specified on the command line:

```
makefile m = new makefile();   // create Target dictionary
int r = m.build(args[0]);      // build the target
System.exit(r);                // exit with code from target build
```

So, that's what the translation looks like. Now we have to build a grammar that automates it by triggering code generation actions.

Building the Translator

With some foresight, we can spec out the list of actions to trigger and put them into an interface:

`trans/make/MakeGenerator.java`

```java
public interface MakeGenerator {
    public void start();
    public void finish();
    public void target(String t);
    public void dependency(String d);
    public void action(String a);
    public void endTarget(String t);
}
```

This means we have to pass a MakeGenerator object into the ANTLR-generated parser:

`trans/make/Make.g`

```
@members {
MakeGenerator gen;
public MakeParser(TokenStream input, MakeGenerator gen) {
    super(input);
    this.gen = gen;
}
}
```

Let's write a grammar for our make-like DSL. A make file looks like a series of rules:

`trans/make/Make.g`

```
rules
    :   {gen.start();} rule+ {gen.finish();}
    ;
```

To generate the header and trailer of the Java class, we trigger start() and finish() methods.

Each rule has a target file name, an optional list of file dependencies, and at least one action:

`trans/make/Make.g`

```
rule
    :   target=ITEM ':'     {gen.target($target.text);}
        (i=ITEM {gen.dependency($i.text);})* '\n'
        (ACTION {gen.action($ACTION.text);})+
                            {gen.endTarget($target.text);}
    |   '\n' // ignore blank lines
    ;
```

Once we match the target name, we trigger target(). Then, we trigger dependency() for each file dependency and action() for each action we find. The endTarget() trigger gives us the hook to generate the put() to the targets dictionary.

The code generation implementations are messy (without templates) but straightforward. For example, here is what we generate upon the start() trigger:

`trans/make/JavaGenerator.java`

```
public void start() {
    out.println(
        "import java.io.IOException;\n" +
        "class "+makefile+" extends MakeSupport {\n" +
        "    public "+makefile+"() throws IOException {\n" +
        "        Target target = null;\n");
}
```

The majority of the methods are much smaller. Here's how we respond to target():

`trans/make/JavaGenerator.java`

```
public void target(String t) {
    t = t.trim();
    out.println("\ttarget = new Target(\""+t+"\");");
}
```

The translator main() program lives in Maker. It creates the ANTLR-generated parser and lexer as usual but passes in a JavaGenerator:

`trans/make/Maker.java`

```
JavaGenerator gen = new JavaGenerator(makefileName);
MakeParser p = new MakeParser(tokens, gen);
try { p.rules(); } // parse, triggering code generation actions
```

Other than support code, that's all there is to it. Our parser directly generates Java code that implements a make DSL. We compile it and run it like any other Java program.

Related Patterns

This pattern is sort of a degenerate version of a model-driven translator. We can think of the tokens as the input model and the generated text as the output model.

Building an Interpreted Version

Some of you might be wondering how we could interpret rather than translate a makefile. The idea would be to create a dictionary full of Target objects as an internal model. We'd need grammar actions to create Target objects and set dependencies and actions:

```
rule:   target=ITEM ':'
        {Target t = new Target($target.text);}
        (i=ITEM {t.addDependency($i.text);})* '\n'
        (ACTION {t.addAction($ACTION.text);})+
        {targets.put(t.name, t);}
    |   '\n' // ignore blank lines
    ;
```

☐ **30** **Rule-Based Translator**

Purpose

A rule-based translator expresses a translation with a set of "x becomes y" rules, written in the DSL of a pattern-matching engine.

Discussion

To use a rule-based system, we have to feed it two things: a grammar that describes input sentences and a set of translation rules. The reason we need the grammar is to get a Pattern 8, *Parse Tree*, on page 90. The parse tree concretely defines what the various phrases and subphrases are. That's how they can avoid applying transformations inside comments in the input stream, for example. Although it looks like we're doing text-to-text transformations, the underlying engine is actually doing tree rewrites.

For complicated translators, we need to build a lot of ancillary data structures beyond trees such as symbol tables and control-flow graphs (that tell us which statements can get to other statements). We can do all of that and then have the engine execute our transformation rules based upon these data structures.

In practice, I use rule-based translators when I don't have or don't need a full grammar. Most of the time I'm extracting or translating just some

Syntax	Description
«*first-line-of-file*»	The first line of text in the file is the title of the page.
*«*text*»*	Bold «*text*».
«*text*»	Italics «*text*».
@«*url*»@	Link to «*url*».
@«*url*»|«*text*»@	Link to «*url*» and make the link text be «*text*».
### «*title*»	<h1> header.
## «*title*»	<h2> header.
# «*title*»	<h3> header.
* «*item*»	A <ul> bullet list item. The * must start at the left edge.
[«*rows*»]	A table full of rows, separated by -- on a line by itself. Separate columns with |.

Figure 11.9: A SIMPLE WIKI SYNTAX

of the input phrases. To work without a full grammar describing the entire input, the elements have to be easy to identify lexically (with special characters) or with a simple grammatical structure. For example, the ANTLR website has an example fuzzy Java parser that extracts class, method, variable definitions, and method call sites.[13]

Since we've already looked at tree transformations, let's see what we can do with a set of lexical rules.

Implementation

Let's translate the syntax of a simple wiki to HTML. This is actually sort of tricky, which you might not expect. Translating *foo* to <b>foo</b> doesn't seem that hard. But, bullet lists and tables take some thought.

Defining a Wiki Syntax

Let's start by defining some wiki syntax in Figure 11.9; then we'll look at a sample translation. File t.wiki in the source directory exercises the various wiki features. With a little help from a CSS file, our translator generates HTML that renders like the image in Figure 11.10, on the next page.

---

13. http://www.antlr.org/download/examples-v3.tar.gz

Agenda

Ad eundum quo nemo ante iit. Age. Fac ut gaudeam. Altissima **quaeque** flumina minimo sono labi

Ipsissima verba Ipsissima verba Ipsissima verba Ipsissima verba Ipsissima verba Ipsissima verba Ipsissima verba Ipsissima verba

Alibi

Inventas vitam iuvat excoluisse per artes. Inventas vitam iuvat excoluisse per artes. Inventas vitam iuvat excoluisse per artes translator with a series of lexical rules. Link to antlr site

Alias

- E pluribus unum
- Emeritus
- Ergo

Vinum bellum iucunumque est, sed animo corporeque caret. Vinum bellum iucunumque est, sed animo corporeque caret. Vinum bellum iucunumque est, sed animo corporeque caret

Ipso facto	Ipso facto	Ipso facto. Ipso facto. Ipso facto.	
Ipso facto. **Ipso** facto	*newlines* are ok	Verbatim Verbatim Verbatim	
Veni, vidi, vici	Verso Versus	nested table	Ipso facto. Ipso facto
		Ventis secundis, tene cursum	Vide ut supra
foo	bar	blort	

Vinum bellum iucunumque est, sed animo corporeque caret.

Figure 11.10: HTML TRANSLATED FROM T.WIKI

Our translator treats the first line of text as the title of the page. Within the file, we need to put a blank line before paragraphs, bullet lists, sections, and tables. Here's a sample bullet list:

```
* E pluribus unum
* Emeritus
* Ergo
```

A blank line terminates the list. Tables live inside square brackets. The -- row separator has to be on a line by itself to make it more obvious. | is the column separator. Here's a sample table:

```
[
row 1 col 1 | row 1 col 2
--
row 2 col 1 | row 2 col 2
]
```

You can take a look at the t.wiki file to see a nested table and examples of italics elements, and so on. Any text other than the wiki syntax should pass through unchanged. That's one of the benefits of this method. We don't have to specify the syntax of the entire file, just the parts we care about.

This isn't the most sophisticated wiki in the world, but it's complicated enough to give the rule-based approach a workout. This example is highly ANTLR-specific, but any rule-based solution will have to deal with the DSL and details of a particular tool.

Defining the Translation Rules and Main Program

Our implementation consists of only two files: a grammar full of lexical rules and a main program that sets things up. Here's the core of the main program:

```
trans/wiki/WikiToHTML.java
```
```java
header(out);
Wiki lex = new Wiki(new ANTLRReaderStream(fr), out);
try {
    Token t = lex.nextToken();
    while ( t.getType() != Token.EOF ) t=lex.nextToken();
}
finally { fr.close(); }
trailer(out);
```

Since this is still a lexer, we need to loop around a call to nextToken(). This forces the lexer to consume all the input. Before and after this loop, we call header() and trailer() to spit out the HTML file header and trailer. The grammar will be an ANTLR lexer grammar with option filter turned on. This tells ANTLR to try the rules in order. So, if an input chunk matches more than one rule, it will match to the first rule. As a catchall, we've got an **ELSE** rule at the end that copies the input character to the output:

```
trans/wiki/Wiki.g
```
```
ELSE:    c=. {out.print((char)$c);} ; // match any char and emit
```

There's a number of interesting things going on in this grammar:

- We're using semantic predicates to turn rules on and off depending on the line number or character position within a line. Syntax {*«expr»*}? is a semantic predicate that provides extra information about the viability of a rule. Since ANTLR uses semantic predicates only if syntax alone is insufficient, we need to use a special version of a semantic predicate: {*«expr»*}?=>. The extra => forces ANTLR to always test the predicate when choosing viable rules.
- We need to keep some state information like "we're in a bullet list."
- We use recursion (in a lexer) to allow nested tables. Rule **TABLE** calls **ROW**, which calls **COL**, which matches a bunch of **TABLE_CONTENT**. Rule **TABLE_CONTENT** matches everything up until the end of a column. Within that text, it looks for nested tables and bold or italics items.

Our first rule matches the title by matching a single line of text as long as it occurs on the first line of the file:

trans/wiki/Wiki.g

```
TITLE
    :   {getLine()==1}?=> TAIL
        {out.println("<title>"+$TAIL.text+"</title>");}
    ;
```

Rule **TAIL** is a helper (**fragment**) rule that matches any character other than a newline:

trans/wiki/Wiki.g

```
fragment
TAIL : ~'\n'+ ;
```

ANTLR tries only the nonfragment rules when looking for a match. Normal (nonfragment) rules have to call fragment rules explicitly. **TAIL** is in a separate rule because it's convenient to say $TAIL.text in **TITLE**.

Since both the bold and bullet list items start with *, we have to distinguish them. According to our syntax, bullet list items have to start at the left edge. So, rule **BOLD** is only applicable when it's not on the left edge:

trans/wiki/Wiki.g

```
BOLD:   {getCharPositionInLine()>0}?=>
        '*'                             {out.print("<b>");}
        (c=~'*' {out.print((char)$c);})+
        '*'                             {out.print("</b>");}
    ;
```

This rule matches * followed by any non-* characters followed by a terminating * character. As it matches characters, it spits them to the output stream.

Many of our wiki constructs have to appear after a blank line (bullet lists, sections, tables, and regular paragraphs):

trans/wiki/Wiki.g

```
BLANK_LINE
    :   '\n\n'                  {out.println("\n"); closeList(); }
        (   UL
        |   SECTION
        |   TABLE
        |   /* paragraph */  {out.println("<p>");}
        )
    ;
```

The call to closeList() makes sure that any prior lists have their terminating `</ul>` tag. We can easily generate the starting `<ul>` tag when we match the first bullet list item after a blank line. Rule **BLANK_LINE** invokes **UL** after matching \n\n. Here's **UL**:

```
fragment
UL: '* ' {out.print("<ul>\n<li>"); context.push("ul");} ;
```

The rules track context using a context stack. We only need to worry about bullet list context, but we could add numbered lists and so on. When the stack is empty, we're not in a special context. A blank line after a bullet list item terminates the list. At that blank line, then, we need to check for unterminated lists, which is the reason for the call to closeList() in **BLANK_LINE**. That method pops the top context and ends that element by emitting the proper HTML tag:

```
Stack<String> context = new Stack<String>();
void closeList() {
    if ( context.size()==0 ) return;
    String list = context.pop();
    out.println("</"+list+">");
}
```

The bullet items beyond the first one can emit `<li>` tags without worrying about context:

```
LI: {getCharPositionInLine()==0}?=>'* '  {out.print("<li>");} ;
```

Now let's figure out how nested tables work. We need recursive rules, which ANTLR fortunately supports even among lexical rules. The overall table structure looks like this:

```
fragment
TABLE
    :   '['                       {out.print("<table border=1>\n");}
        ROW ('\n--\n' ROW)* '\n'
        ']'                       {out.print("\n</table>");}
    ;
```

Eventually, **TABLE** invokes **TABLE_CONTENT**, which can include another (nested) table.

trans/wiki/Wiki.g

```
fragment
TABLE_CONTENT
    :    TABLE
    |    BOLD
    |    ITALICS
    |    {!upcomingEndOfCol()}?=> c=. {out.print((char)$c);}
    ;
```

The last alternative matches anything not matched by the other alternatives. The predicate !upcomingEndOfCol() ensures that we match
characters only until we see the end of a column or table coming.
upcomingEndOfCol() manually checks up to three characters ahead to
make sure we don't consume too much in **TABLE_CONTENT**:

trans/wiki/Wiki.g

```
boolean upcomingEndOfCol() {
    return input.LA(1)=='/' ||
           (input.LA(1)=='\n'&&
            (input.LA(2)=='-'&&input.LA(3)=='-')||input.LA(2)==']');
}
```

This sample implementation illustrates what a rule-based system looks
like, but it's nowhere near as sophisticated as the rule engines we mentioned in the introductory material for this chapter. That said, this lexical filter mechanism is easier to learn and still very useful.

Related Patterns

This pattern lets us specify only those patterns we care about, just like
we did with trees in Pattern 15, *Tree Pattern Matcher*, on page 123. Most
rule-based translation engines internally use Pattern 8, *Parse Tree*, on
page 90. The sample implementation for this pattern uses an *LL(k)* version of Pattern 2, *LL(1) Recursive-Descent Lexer*, on page 33.

☐

31   Target-Specific Generator Classes

Purpose

*This pattern describes a class library whose sole purpose is to represent
and generate output constructs in a particular language.*

Discussion

Rather than use print statements to generate programs or data, generator classes let us insulate application code from the exact syntax of an output language. In that sense, they are similar to templates. The difference is, we're defining a special class for each output element, whereas, with templates, we use a single StringTemplate class. In both cases, the objects hold the data necessary to generate the associated output constructs. The only (minor) advantage to using specialized generator classes is that we can name the data fields.

Each generator class has a method, usually toString(), that renders the object to text in the right format. The typical generator class look something like this:

```
class «OutputConstruct» {
    «field1»
    «field2»
    ...
    «fieldN»
    public «OutputConstruct»(«field args») { «set fields» }
    public String toString() { «compute string from fields» }
}
```

Let's think about generating HTML. We could build a library with classes such as Document, Head, Title, Table, ListItem, and so on. Title instances would hold a title string, for example. Its toString() method would emit <title>«a-title»</title>.

It's reasonable to make generator classes handle slight differences in the output language, such as different versions of HTML. But, it's best not to think of these generator classes as generating radically different output according to some parameter. These classes are part of the output model. Their job is simply to emit text in the right format, not perform a translation.

Implementation

To demonstrate generator classes, let's build Table and Column classes to represent SQL table creation statements. An SQL table needs to know the table name and the list of columns:

```
public class Table {
    String name; // SQL table name
    List<Column> columns = new ArrayList<Column>();
    public String toString() {
        StringBuffer buf = new StringBuffer();
        buf.append("CREATE TABLE "+ name+" (\n");
```

```
        int i = 0;
        for (Column c : columns) {
            if ( i>0 ) buf.append(",\n");
            buf.append("    "); // indent a bit
            buf.append(c);
            i++;
        }
        buf.append(");\n");
        return buf.toString();
    }
}
```

For each column, we need to know its name, its type, and the list of attributes like NOT NULL and UNIQUE:

```
public class Column {
    String name;                    // SQL column name
    String type;                    // SQL column type
    List<String> attrs;             // SQL column attributes
    public String toString() {
        StringBuffer attrBuf = new StringBuffer();
        int i = 0;
        for (String a : attrs) {
            if ( i>0 ) attrBuf.append(", ");
            attrBuf.append(a);
            i++;
        }
        return name+" "+type+" "+attrBuf.toString();
    }
}
```

To use these classes, we create a Table and then Column instances for each column and fill in their fields. To generate text, we'd print the result of calling toString() on the Table instance.

Instead of creating strings in toString(), we could use templates. In that case, though, we might as well avoid the special generator classes and just use templates all by themselves.

Related Patterns

These generator classes are sort of like hard-coded templates.

Up Next

This chapter gives you the big picture on computer language trans-lation. In the next chapter, we're going to drill down further into the model-driven approach. We'll learn how to use templates to generate a number of DSLs and programming languages. The examples feed off of a variety of input models to create template-based output models.

Before we move on, let me highlight the two important lessons from this chapter. First, to properly translate an input phrase, we can't just cleverly replace input symbols with output symbols. We have to fully understand the input syntactically and semantically and then pick the proper output construct. Second, when using the model-driven approach, we need to decouple input model traversal order from the order dictated by the output language. This input-driven approach lets us compute information and translate phrases when it's convenient and efficient to do so.

## Chapter 12

Generating DSLs with Templates

Unlike the other chapters in this book, this chapter doesn't have any patterns. Instead, we're going to learn by example. We're at the point where we need to look at some bigger problems and start applying the patterns we've learned. In this chapter, we're going to build a number of template-driven generators to demonstrate the model-driven strategy from the previous chapter. In the previous chapter, we'll see how language patterns apply to some interesting problems. The implementations are up to you, but I'll get you started by laying out the basic application architectures.

We're going to use a template engine called StringTemplate[1] (ST) throughout this chapter. There are lots of other template engines (such as Velocity, XText, Ruby's RGEN, and Microsoft T4), but only ST strictly enforces *model-view separation*.[2] In a nutshell, that means we keep all the logic in code and all the output text in the templates. By doing so, we can reuse templates with different generators and generate different languages from a single model.

Though we'll use ST in these examples to generate output, this chapter is really about using template engines in general to generate structured text. Remember, when learning to fly, there's no getting around picking an airplane. Later, you can transfer these techniques to another template engine.

---

1. http://www.stringtemplate.org
2. http://www.cs.usfca.edu/~parrt/papers/mvc.templates.pdf

Here are the examples we're going to build with ST:

- *Webpage link visualizer*: From a list of links between pages, this example generates DOT graphics files for Graphviz.[3] We'll create a simple input model and then walk that model to create a nested tree of templates. It demonstrates the basic principle of walking an input model to create templates.

- *AST visualizer*: This example walks ASTs to generate DOT descriptions. It demonstrates that we can reuse templates with a completely different input model (an AST this time). While walking the AST, though, it doesn't match any subtrees. It just generates DOT code to show ASTs visually.

- *C code generator*: We'll generate Cymbol code from a Cymbol AST using Pattern 14, *Tree Grammar*, on page 119. The example matches subtrees and maps them to appropriate templates. It's the kind of generator we really need to perform a translation. We'll encode "this goes to that" transformation rules in a general-purpose programming language.

- *SQL schema generator*: Using Java's reflection API as an input model, this example generates SQL CREATE TABLE statements. The SQL describes a schema suitable to store simple Java objects. We'll get familiar with a key ST principle: applying a template to a list of data elements (ST doesn't have a foreach loop).

- *Combined SQL and Java code generator*: This final example puts a lot of things together and explains how to build a retargetable code generator. The sample code can generate both the SQL schema from the previous example and the associated Java serialization methods. The generator uses the same input model but different templates to create different output hierarchies.

Before diving into the examples, we should build a trivial code generator to get familiar with the ST engine.

12.1 Getting Started with StringTemplate

ST templates are chunks of text and expressions enclosed in angle brackets: *<expression>*. (You can also tell it to use *$expression$*.) ST ignores everything outside the expressions, treating it as just text to spit out. ST is a lightweight library (not a tool or server) with two key

---

3. http://www.graphviz.org

classes: StringTemplate and StringTemplateGroup. We can create StringTemplate objects using a string literal in code or load them from a template group file using StringTemplateGroup.

The basic idea behind constructing output is that we create a template and inject it with *attributes* (any Java object). The expressions within a template feed on these attributes to compute text values. We create nested template hierarchies by injecting templates as attributes into other templates.

To try out ST, the first thing we have to do is make sure that Java can see the ST library. For your convenience, the main code directory includes an uber-JAR called antlr-3.2.jar that contains ST as well as all the ANTLR stuff. Otherwise, you can download ST[4] and its dependent library ANTLR v2.7.7.[5] (It's currently written in an older version of ANTLR than the v3 we're using in the rest of the book.) It's a good idea to add these JARs to your CLASSPATH environment variable.

Here's a simple example that generates an assignment statement (see the code/trans/intro directory):

```
import org.antlr.stringtemplate.*;
import org.antlr.stringtemplate.language.*;
...
String assign = "<left> = <right>;";
StringTemplate st = new StringTemplate(assign,
                                AngleBracketTemplateLexer.class);
st.setAttribute("left", "x");   // attribute left is a string
st.setAttribute("right", 99);   // attribute right is an integer
String output = st.toString();  // render template to text
System.out.println(output);
```

Creating a template is as simple as passing a string to the StringTemplate constructor. In this case, we're also making sure that ST uses angle brackets for expression delimiters. Once we've got a template, we can inject left and right attributes and ask ST to evaluate the template by calling toString().

To try this example, jump into the right directory, compile Test.java, and run Test:

```
$ cd root-code-dir/trans/intro
$ ls
Test.java  antlr-2.7.7.jar  stringtemplate-3.2.jar
```

---

4. http://www.stringtemplate.org/download.html
5. http://www.antlr2.org/download//antlr-2.7.7.jar

```
$ javac -cp ".:antlr-2.7.7.jar:stringtemplate-3.2.jar" Test.java
$ java -cp ".:antlr-2.7.7.jar:stringtemplate-3.2.jar" Test
x = 99;
$
```

If you have the JARs in your CLASSPATH, you don't need the -cp option.

Now that we've got some idea of what a template looks like and how to execute it, let's take a look at ST's four fundamental operations:

- *Attribute references such as <user>*: ST evaluates this expression by looking up user in the attribute dictionary for this template and calling its toString() method. If the attribute has multiple values (an array, List, Map, and so on), ST calls toString() on each value.

- *Template references*: Referencing another template acts like an #include or macro expansion. It embeds the referenced template within the surrounding template, adding another level to the template hierarchy. When generating Java code, we might factor out a bunch of **import** statements into a separate template called **imports**. In the main Java file template, for example, we could include the imports with expression <imports()>.

- *Conditional includes*: ST can conditionally include subtemplates based upon the presence or absence of an attribute. For example, the following conditional emits one of two strings depending on whether attribute retValue exists (it's non-null in the attribute dictionary):

  `<if(retValue)>return <retValue>;<else>return;<endif>`

  The one special case is that ST tests the value of Boolean objects, not their presence or absence.

- *Template application*: Instead of a **foreach** loop, ST applies (maps) templates to multivalued attributes. For example, <strings:def()> applies template **def** to the list of elements in attribute strings. The colon is the "apply" operator. ST automatically creates an instance of **def** for each element in attribute strings, passes in strings[i], and renders the template to text.

  Sometimes it's easier to in-line a template. If we have a list of function names, for example, we can generate a call to each one of them with the following expression:

  `<names:{n | <n>();}> // parameter n iterates through names`

  If names contains f and g, the expression evaluates to f();g();.

As we'll see in the examples, building an overall template means building a template tree. The overall template contains subtemplates that themselves contain subsubtemplates, and so on. Let's say we wanted to generate a C code file. We'd build the overall template from a list of function templates. We'd build the function templates from statement templates. We'd build those statement templates from expression templates.

A template hierarchy is the dual of a parse tree. We want to create an "unparse tree," you might say. A parse tree has rules as internal nodes and tokens as leaves. A nested template tree has templates for internal nodes and attributes as leaves. Once we've got the tree, we can convert it to text with a recursive walk. Calling toString() on the root template triggers a call to toString() on each child template, and so on, until it reaches the attribute leaves.

ST has some interesting features and characteristics that distinguish it in many ways from other template engines. Let's take a quick look at them.

12.2 Characterizing StringTemplate

ST is a *dynamically typed*, *pure functional* language with *dynamic scoping* and *lazy evaluation*. Those fancy terms highlight some important characteristics, so let's define them:

- *Dynamically typed*: ST uses toString() to convert attributes to string values. Since all Java objects answer this method, ST works with any Java object. Also, if you ask for property b of attribute a (with a.b), it's up to you to make sure attribute a has that property at run-time. Python and Ruby programmers should feel very much at home.

- *Pure functional*: All expressions are side-effect free. There's no direct way for ST to alter data values or data structures that we pass in. (Well, you could code a toString() method to erase the hard drive, but there's no way ST can prevent that.) The end result is that ST is free to evaluate template expressions in any order it wants.

- *Dynamic scoping*: In most programming languages, if function f() calls g(), g() cannot see the local variables of f(). Most languages are *statically* scoped. For a DSL such as ST, though, dynamic scoping makes more sense. Imagine an overall **file** template that contains a number of embedded **method** templates. Dynamic scoping means that **method** can reference **file**'s attributes, such as the filename attribute.

- *Lazy evaluation*: Lazy evaluation means two things. First, ST only evaluates the expressions that it has to. This is just like the familiar **if** statement where the **then** clause executes only if the condition is true. Second, lazy evaluation allows us to defer execution until all attributes and embedded templates are available. This is like building up a string in Python before execution using eval. We can reference any variable we want in the strings without fear Python will prematurely evaluate them. All we have to do is make sure that they're defined before we call eval(). Here's a sample Python session:

```
>>> e = 'x'+'*'+'10' # ref x before it's defined
>>> x=3 # must define x before evaluating expression "x*10"
>>> print eval(e)
30
```

Lazy evaluation in templates means we can construct our template tree and inject attributes in any order we want without fear of premature evaluation. We just have to make sure we set all attribute values before calling toString() on the root template. Some of the templates in Section 12.7, *Building Retargetable Translators*, on page 337 rely on lazy evaluation.

All right, now that we know a little bit about ST, we'll focus on building examples for the rest of the chapter.

12.3 Generating Templates from a Simple Input Model

There are many cases where we have an internal data structure, such as a tree or network graph, that we'd like to visualize for documentation or debugging purposes. This is a perfect opportunity to flex our code generation muscles. We can generate graphical descriptions using the DOT DSL of Graphviz, an open source graph visualization tool.

As an example application, let's visualize the link interconnections between web pages. It'll teach us the basics of creating output templates from an input model. From a list of Link objects, we'll generate a series of *from->to* edge definitions in a DOT file surrounded by some bookkeeping definitions.

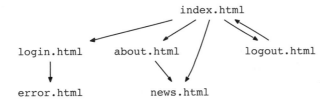

Figure 12.1: WEB VIZ

```
digraph testgraph {
    node [shape=plaintext, fontsize=12, fontname="Courier", height=.1];
    ranksep=.3;
    edge [arrowsize=.5]
    "index.html" -> "login.html"
    "index.html" -> "about.html"
    ...
}
```

You can ignore the node, ranksep, and edge definitions if you want. They only affect how big the elements of the graph are. The key to this example is how we generate output, not exactly what we're generating.

For convenience, let's create a LinkViz class whose toString() method uses ST to generate a proper DOT file. Then we can add a series of page links and print out the DOT:

`trans/web/GenDOT.java`

```
LinkViz viz = new LinkViz();
viz.addLink("index.html", "login.html");
viz.addLink("index.html", "about.html");
viz.addLink("login.html", "error.html");
viz.addLink("about.html", "news.html");
viz.addLink("index.html", "news.html");
viz.addLink("logout.html", "index.html");
viz.addLink("index.html", "logout.html");
System.out.println(viz.toString());
```

In Figure 12.1, we see the graph we get after running the generated DOT output through Graphviz.

LinkViz is just a list of Link objects:

`trans/web/LinkViz.java`

```
List<Link> links = new ArrayList<Link>();
public static class Link {
    String from;
    String to;
    public Link(String from, String to) {this.from = from; this.to = to;}
}
```

LinkViz's toString() method walks these links to create **edge** templates and embeds them within the overall **file** template:

`trans/web/LinkViz.java`

```
public String toString() {
    StringTemplate fileST = templates.getInstanceOf("file");
    fileST.setAttribute("gname", "testgraph");
    for (Link x : links) {
        StringTemplate edgeST = templates.getInstanceOf("edge");
        edgeST.setAttribute("from", x.from);
        edgeST.setAttribute("to",   x.to);
        fileST.setAttribute("edges", edgeST);
    }
    return fileST.toString(); // render (eval) template to text
}
```

To inject an attribute value, we use setAttribute() with a name-value pair. Calling setAttribute() more than once with the same attribute name, such as edges, builds up a list—it doesn't replace the previous value (that method should really be called addAttribute()). Before we can execute toString(), we have to load our template library from a group file. Our constructor can handle this for us:

`trans/web/LinkViz.java`

```
public LinkViz() throws IOException {
    FileReader fr = new FileReader("DOT.stg");
    templates = new StringTemplateGroup(fr);
    fr.close();
}
```

Moving on to the templates now, let's look at the overall **file** template:

`trans/web/DOT.stg`

```
file(gname,edges) ::= <<
digraph <gname> {
  node [shape=plaintext, fontsize=12, fontname="Courier", height=.1];
  ranksep=.3;
  edge [arrowsize=.5]
  <edges; separator="\n">
}
>>
```

It accepts two attributes: a graph name and a list of **edge** templates. The first ST expression, <gname>, references the gname attribute. It evaluates to the attribute we sent in via setAttribute( ). The <edges; separator="\n"> expression spits out the results from calling toString( ) on each element of edges. The separator option says to put a newline in between the edges so we get each one on its own line.

The **edge** template also has two attribute parameters that we inject from LinkViz's toString( ):

trans/web/DOT.stg

```
edge(from,to) ::= <<"<from>" -> "<to>">>
```

This code generator, then, is just a small input model, a bit of code to walk that data structure, and two templates. We create templates and inject attributes as we walk (the input-driven approach). We don't evaluate or emit anything until we've created the entire template tree.

You might be wondering why we go through the trouble of using templates for this simple generation problem. We could fairly easily generate the appropriate output with print statements or by building up a string buffer. Print statements aren't the best solution because we might want to include the DOT output in another data structure. Piecing together a string buffer isn't the most flexible solution either, as we saw in the previous chapter. It totally cements the output fragments into our input model's Java code.

In the next section, we'll see that we can reuse templates for a totally different application using a different input model.

12.4 Reusing Templates with a Different Input Model

We've done a lot with ASTs in this book, and it's nice to see them visually. Rather than build all the tree diagrams in this book by hand, for example, I used an AST walker to generate DOT scripts. The templates I used are similar to those from the previous section. Because they aren't tied to the web link model, we can reuse them to build an AST visualizer in this section.

For simplicity, let's assume our trees follow Pattern 9, *Homogeneous AST*, on page 94. Given a tree like (VAR int x (+ 3 3)), we want to generate DOT that gives us a visualization like the tree on the top of the next page.

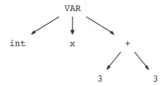

We need to generate DOT with the usual list of edges. But in this case, we have to define the nodes before we reference them in the edge list. DOT needs different tree nodes to have unique names. Since we have two 3 nodes in the tree, DOT wants us to give them different node names. The output looks like this:

```
...
node4 [label="+"];
node5 [label="3"];
node6 [label="3"];
...
node4 -> node5
node4 -> node6
...
```

We've already seen the templates, so we can focus on the differences. We need to add a line to the **file** template:

```
file(gname,nodes,edges) ::= <<
digraph <gname> {
    ...
    <nodes; separator="\n">     <! new !>
    <edges; separator="\n">
}
```

That extra expression spits out all the nodes separated by a newline, just as it does for edges. (Comments appear in between <!...!>.) The other thing we need is a **node** template:

trans/ast/DOT.stg

```
node(name,text) ::= <<
<name> [label="<text>"];
>>
```

Our visualizer object will inject a unique name for each node so we can associate it with the tree node text strings:

trans/ast/ASTViz.java

```
protected StringTemplate getNodeST(Tree t) {
    StringTemplate nodeST = templates.getInstanceOf("node");
    String uniqueName = "node"+counter++; // use counter for unique name
    nodeST.setAttribute("name", uniqueName);
    nodeST.setAttribute("text", t.payload);
    return nodeST;
}
```

Like we did in the previous section, we'll use a visualizer object whose toString() method creates a **file** template and renders it to text. The only problem is that our input model is a tree. We don't have a convenient list of Link objects. We have two choices. We can walk the tree and create a list of links as we did in the previous example. Or, we can walk the tree, creating **edge** template instances as we go. If we stuff them into the **file** template's edges attribute, ST automatically makes a list for us.

Here's the code to do a recursive depth-first walk:

`trans/ast/ASTViz.java`

```
/** Fill fileST with nodes and edges; return subtree root's ST */
protected StringTemplate walk(Tree tree, StringTemplate fileST) {
    StringTemplate parentST = getNodeST(tree);
    fileST.setAttribute("nodes", parentST); // define subtree root
    if ( tree.getChildCount()==0 ) return parentST;
    // for each child, create nodes/edges and inject into fileST
    for (Tree child : tree.children) {
        StringTemplate childST = walk(child, fileST);
        Object from = parentST.getAttribute("name");
        Object to   = childST.getAttribute("name");
        StringTemplate edgeST = getEdgeST(from, to);
        fileST.setAttribute("edges", edgeST);
    }
    return parentST;
}
```

It starts out by creating a **node** template for the current node and inserts it into the overall **file** template. Then, it recursively walks that node's children (if any). walk() returns the **node** template it creates for parameter tree.

To create **edge** templates from parent to child, we have to know the child's unique name. To get its name, we call getAttribute(). We can set and read template attributes all the way up until we render the templates to text. Once walk() creates the **edge** template, it embeds it within the **file** template by injecting it via setAttribute().

This example generates DOT visualizations for any AST, regardless of its structure. It can't generate something different depending on a subtree's structure or contents. For translation purposes, though, we need to distinguish between subtrees such as variable declarations and assignment statements. The next section demonstrates how to construct different templates for different subtrees and assemble them together into a template tree.

12.5 Using a Tree Grammar to Create Templates

A surprising number of translators spit out the same language that they read in. There are lots of useful things we can do such as refactoring, reformatting, instrumenting, or simplifying source code. In this section, we're going to build a translator that reads in some Cymbol code (the C++ subset from Pattern 19, *Symbol Table for Classes*, on page 167) and spits it back out in more or less the same shape. For example, here's a sample Cymbol file:

`trans/ast-st/s.cymbol`

```
void f(int a[], int x) {
        if ( x>0 ) return;
        else x = 10;
        a[3] = 2;
}
```

We want to read that in and send it back out using our translator program:

```
$ java Test s.cymbol
void f(int *a, int x) { // "int a[]" becomes "int *a"
    if ( (x > 0) ) return ;
    else x = 10;
    a[3] = 2;
}
$
```

The translator we're going to build epitomizes the most common architecture. It has three core components: a parser grammar (Cymbol.g) that builds the AST, a tree grammar (Gen.g) that constructs the template output model, and the actual templates themselves (Cymbol.stg).

Each rule in the tree grammar yields a template representing a single translated phrase. The tree traversal builds up the template hierarchy by embedding the templates returned from one rule in the template result of another. So, the input model traversal dictates the structure of the output model. The templates just say what the output looks like.

This approach makes it pretty easy to adapt a generator to another application. The tree grammar only cares about the name and attributes of the templates. It doesn't depend on what's inside the templates. To change the output language, then, all we have to do is swap out one group of templates for another. A lot of compilers use this approach to generate machine code for lots of different processors. (They use a tree grammar to map IR expression subtrees to assembly code patterns.)

For radically different output languages, though, sometimes we need a totally different hierarchy rather than just different text in the templates. In Section 12.7, *Building Retargetable Translators*, on page 337, we'll move control of the hierarchy into the templates.

Since we already know how to build ASTs, we're going to focus on the generator component in this section. That means exploring the tree grammar and the templates. So that we don't get overwhelmed right away by the full tree grammar, let's start with something simple.

Comparing Visitors and Tree Grammars

To make it easier to understand how tree grammar rules construct templates, let's compare them to visitor methods. Here's a tree grammar rule that matches an assignment subtree and returns an **assign** template:

```
assign : ^('=' ID e=expression) -> assign(a={$ID.text}, b={$e.st})
```

The template argument list is the interface between the grammar and the template. It injects attributes into the **assign** template: a={$ID.text} sets attribute a to the identifier's text, and b={$e.st} sets attribute b to the template returned from the call to rule **expression**. The template itself looks like this:

> trans/ast-st/Cymbol.stg

```
assign(a,b) ::= "<a> = <b>;"
```

If we were building this by hand, we'd make a visitor method that looks something like the following (assuming ANTLR's homogeneous CommonTree nodes):

```
StringTemplate genAssign(CommonTree n) { // match ^('=' ID expression)
    CommonTree idAST = (CommonTree)n.getChild(0);
    String id = idAST.getText();
    CommonTree exprAST = (CommonTree)n.getChild(1);
    StringTemplate exprST = gen( exprAST );
    StringTemplate st = templates.getInstanceOf("assign");
    st.setAttribute("a", id);
    st.setAttribute("b", exprST);
    return st;
}
```

As you can see, building the visitor manually is a lot more work and a lot more verbose. With this comparison in mind, let's go through the full Pattern 14, *Tree Grammar*, on page 119 now. It's our first big one.

Creating Templates with a Tree Grammar

Our tree grammar uses two important options. The tokenVocab options says which parser grammar created our trees, and the output option indicates that we want to build a template hierarchy:

```
trans/ast-st/Gen.g
tree grammar Gen;
options {
  tokenVocab = Cymbol;
  ASTLabelType = CommonTree;
  output = template;
}
```

As we move into the rules now, notice that there are no output literals in the tree grammar. Everything dealing with the output language is encapsulated in the templates. Conversely, there's no model logic in the templates. This model-view separation is the linchpin supporting retargetable code generators.

OK, let's start with the highest-level rule, **compilationUnit**, which matches all the various declarations:

```
trans/ast-st/Gen.g
compilationUnit
    :   ( d+=classDeclaration | d+=methodDeclaration | d+=varDeclaration )+
        -> file(defs={$d})
    ;
```

The rule collects a list of the templates returned by the declaration rules using the += list label operator. When using the output=template option, each rule returns an st property. The -> operator indicates which template to create for that rule. ANTLR looks for templates in the String-TemplateGroup that we pass into the generated tree walker via setTemplateLib().

The rule injects data into the template via the attribute assignments in the template argument list. In this case, it sets attribute defs to the list we collect while matching the trees for this rule.

Aside from matching multiple elements, it's common for grammars to match optional items. For example, to match a class definition, we might have to match a superclass.

`trans/ast-st/Gen.g`

```
classDeclaration
    :   ^('class' name=ID (^(':' sup=ID))? m+=classMember+)
        -> class(name={$name.text}, sup={$sup.text}, members={$m})
    ;
```

We can attach a label, sup, to the optional element and refer to it in the template argument list. Label reference $sup is null when the rule doesn't match a superclass. ANTLR automatically prevents null pointer exceptions when we reference known properties such as $sup.text.

Sometimes a rule does nothing but invoke another rule. Or, it needs to create a template from a single node. The **type** rule demonstrates both of these situations:

`trans/ast-st/Gen.g`

```
type:   primitiveType    -> {$primitiveType.st}
    |   ID               -> {%{$ID.text}}
    ;
```

The first alternative says to match rule **primitiveType** and return its template. The -> {...} syntax returns the template specified by the arbitrary expression in the curly braces. The second alternative matches an **ID** node and then creates a template again using the -> {...} arbitrary expression notation. In this case, it creates a template using a shorthand available to any ANTLR action. ANTLR translates %{x} to something like new StringTemplate(x). The overall expression, {%{$ID.text}}, then creates a template from the **ID** node's text.

That shorthand is also useful when you have a whole list of single node alternatives as we do in rule **primitiveType**:

`trans/ast-st/Gen.g`

```
primitiveType
@after {$st = %{$text};}
    :   'float'
    |   'int'
    |   'char'
    |   'boolean'
    |   'void'
    ;
```

The @after action sets the return template property st to the text matched for the rule. That way, we don't have to use a -> template action on each alternative.

There's one final complication we should look at before turning to the templates. The following **op** rule matches any of the binary operators including the < and <= relational operators:

trans/ast-st/Gen.g

```
op
// Text of operator is $start.getText(); $start is root token for op
@after {$st = %operator(o={$start.getText()});}
    :   bop | relop | eqop
    ;
```

As in **primitiveType**, we use the @after action to set the return template. But, in this case, we can't use %{$text} to create the return template from the single node it matches. There are two problems. First, we have an issue related to the < template expression delimiter characters. If we try to create template with new StringTemplate("<="), StringTemplate won't like it because < starts a template expression. We need to create a template with a single hole into which we can inject the operator string. That's why we need the **operator** template:

trans/ast-st/Cymbol.stg

```
operator(o) ::=  "<o>"
```

The second problem is that we need to create a template from the text of the operator node alone. In a tree grammar, $text evaluates to the input text from which the parser built the entire subtree. This is normally what you want. For example, if you're in a rule that matches a **while** statement, you want $text to mean the entire original **while** statement, not just the five characters while. Here, though, we don't want the original text for the expression since we might be translating it to something else. In other words, if we have input 3+4, the parser creates a tree that looks like ^(+ 3 4). If we asked for $text in **op**, we'd get 3+4, not +. That's why we create the template using $start.getText() instead of $text.

There's nothing else to point out in the tree grammar. The other rules don't introduce anything new, so let's move on to the templates now.

Defining Cymbol Templates

At the top level, our Cymbol output file looks like a list of definitions. We can emit them with a newline separator using template **file**:

trans/ast-st/Cymbol.stg

```
file(defs) ::= <<
<defs; separator="\n">
>>
```

The class definition template has to deal with optional superclasses:

trans/ast-st/Cymbol.stg

```
class(name, sup, members) ::= <<
class <name> <if(sup)>: <sup><endif> {
    <members>
};
>>
```

The ST expression <if(sup)>: <sup><endif> says to emit the superclass if it exists and prefix it with the ": " character sequence. In the method definition template, we use the familiar separator option on the argument list so that the arguments come out with a comma separator:

trans/ast-st/Cymbol.stg

```
method(name, retType, args, block) ::= <<
<retType> <name>(<args; separator=", ">) <block>
>>
```

The method body comes in as a **block** template (because tree grammar rule **methodDeclaration** calls rule **block**, which returns a **block** template):

trans/ast-st/Cymbol.stg

```
block(stats) ::= <<
{
    <stats; separator="\n">
}
>>
```

Since the parser strips the curly braces, we have to manually put them back in. This is sometimes overly cautious for the if statement, but it's necessary to ensure we group all statements associated with a block. As you can see in rule **if**, there aren't any curly braces around the stat1 and stat2 statement attributes:

trans/ast-st/Cymbol.stg

```
if(cond, stat1, stat2) ::= <<
if ( <cond> ) <stat1>
<if(stat2)>else <stat2><endif>
>>
```

The next template of interest is **call**. It doesn't use anything fancier than what we've seen so far, but we need to look at how its attribute list interacts with an invoking template:

trans/ast-st/Cymbol.stg

```
call(name, args) ::= <<
<name>(<args; separator=", ">)
>>
```

This template handles method calls inside expressions as well as method calls as statements. The only thing we need for a method call statement is a semicolon at the end:

`trans/ast-st/Cymbol.stg`

```
callstat(name, args) ::= "<call(...)>;" // call() inherits name,args
```

Having template **callstat** reuse **call** makes sense. The only strange thing is the ellipsis "..." in the argument list. That means we want **callstat**'s attributes to flow through automatically to **call** when we invoke it. In general, when template *x* calls template *y*, the formal arguments of *y* hide any *x* arguments of the same name because the formal parameters force you to define values. This prevents surprises and makes it easy to ensure any parameter value is empty unless you specifically set it for that template.

Here are a few more rules where it's easier to have parameters passed through rather than manually passing them down:

`trans/ast-st/Cymbol.stg`

```
decl(name, type, init, ptr) ::=
    "<type> <if(ptr)>*<endif><name><if(init)> = <init><endif>"
var(name, type, init, ptr) ::= "<decl(...)>;"
arg(name, type, init, ptr) ::= "<decl(...)>"
```

Templates **var** and **arg** embed **decl** and use the ellipsis to pass through the attributes of the same name.

The rest of the templates are reasonably straightforward or similar to those we've already seen.

Exercising the Translator

Let's put together a test rig now so that we can try our translator:

`trans/ast-st/Test.java`

```
// LOAD TEMPLATES (via classpath)
FileReader fr = new FileReader("Cymbol.stg");
StringTemplateGroup templates = new StringTemplateGroup(fr);
fr.close();
//  CREATE TREE NODE STREAM FOR TREE PARSERS
CommonTreeNodeStream nodes = new CommonTreeNodeStream(tree);
nodes.setTokenStream(tokens);          // where to find tokens
Gen gen = new Gen(nodes);
gen.setTemplateLib(templates);
Gen.compilationUnit_return ret = gen.compilationUnit();
System.out.println(ret.getTemplate());
```

As usual, we start by loading a group of templates, Cymbol.stg, using a StringTemplateGroup. Then, using the AST (variable tree) returned from the parser, we create the tree parser. In order for it to create templates, we have to tell it about the group we loaded via setTemplateLib(). The template we get back from **compilationUnit** is the root of the template tree, which we can print.

Here's how we build the software:

```
$ java org.antlr.Tool Cymbol.g Gen.g
«a warning you can ignore from ANTLR»
$ javac *.java
$ java Test s.cymbol
void f(int *a, int x) {
...
$
```

At this point, we've created templates by traversing some fairly simple input models. We started out walking a list of links and then moved on to ASTs. We didn't even have to worry about symbol table and type information in the ASTs. Further, although there were lots of templates to look at in this example, they weren't very big. To learn how to build more complicated translators, we need to look at some bigger and more complicated templates. In the next two examples, we'll get the chance. We're going to generate the SQL and Java code necessary to build an object-relational database mapping tool. We'll use Java's reflection API as an input model, which is essentially a symbol table that's available at run-time.

12.6 Applying Templates to Lists of Data

Building an object-relational database mapping is an excellent use of code generation. In this section, we're going to build one component of such a mapping by generating SQL schemas from Java class definitions. To keep things simple, we'll restrict ourselves to fields whose Java types maps easily to SQL types (such as integers, strings, floats, doubles, and Date objects).

To build this generator, we're going to use Java's reflection API as an input model and create a nested template hierarchy as we did in the previous section. This application is going to require some new skills, though. We have to get comfortable sifting and filtering the input model and then applying templates to that data. Since ST is a high-level DSL, it doesn't have a **foreach** or any other looping construct. We "apply" or "map" templates to multivalued attributes, as we saw in Section 12.1, *Getting Started with StringTemplate*, on page 314.

We'll attack this problem in three stages. First, we'll figure out how to represent Java objects using table rows and columns. Then, we'll filter the input model to get lists of array and nonarray fields. Finally, we'll use those lists in the templates to create the appropriate SQL table definitions.

Representing Objects in a Relational Database

The basic idea in an object-to-relational database mapping is to translate classes to tables and fields to columns in the corresponding table. Objects then map to rows in tables. For example, let's say we want to serialize objects of the following type:

trans/sql/Person.java

```java
public class Person {
    public String name;      // single-valued fields:
    public String SSN;
    public Date birthDay;
    public int age;
    public String[] roles;   // multi-valued fields:
    public Date[] vacation;
```

The single-valued fields become columns in a Person database table. The multivalued array fields, though, don't map directly to columns. That means we have to create a subordinate table for these fields. The rows in a subordinate table store the multiple values of an array field from the object. Each row has a *foreign key* that indicates the owner from the main table. In Figure 12.2, on the next page, we can see how subordinate tables for the roles and vacation fields point back into the main table for Person. The Person_ID fields are the foreign keys. Looking at the tables, we can piece together that Ter's Person object has two roles (mgr and coder) and no vacation. (There's no entry in table Person_vacation for column Person_ID==1.)

To create our schema, we need to generate some SQL. First, we need a table to hold the single-valued fields:

```sql
CREATE TABLE Person (
    ID INTEGER NOT NULL UNIQUE PRIMARY KEY,
    name TEXT,
    SSN TEXT,
    birthDay DATETIME,
    age INTEGER
);
```

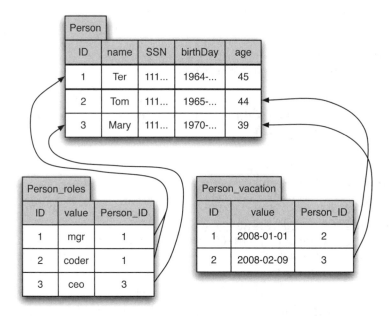

Figure 12.2: MAPPING PERSON OBJECTS TO DATABASE USING FOREIGN KEYS

Then, we need a new table for each multivalued field. For example, here is the subordinate table that handles array field roles:

```
CREATE TABLE Person_roles (
    ID INTEGER NOT NULL AUTO_INCREMENT UNIQUE PRIMARY KEY,
    roles TEXT,
    Person_ID INTEGER NOT NULL
);
```

Knowing the details of SQL is not really important here. We're focusing on how to generate this SQL. Let's get started with our generator by looking at how we extract data from the model and inject it into the templates.

Extracting Data from the Input Model

To trigger the schema generation, our test rig program creates an instance of GenSchema and then invokes genSchema() with Person's class definition object.

```
trans/sql/GenSchema.java
```
```
GenSchema gen = new GenSchema();
StringTemplate schemaST = gen.genSchema(Person.class);
System.out.println(schemaST.toString());
```

According to the schema from the last section, we need to deal with array and nonarray fields differently. This means that we need to extract data by walking the model:

```
trans/sql/GenSchema.java
```
```
protected void filterFields(Class c, List<Field> fields,
                            List<Field> arrayFields)
{
    for (Field f : c.getFields()) {
        if (f.getType().isArray()) arrayFields.add(f);
        else fields.add(f);
    }
}
```

Given a Class object, filterFields() fills two data structures according to the kinds of fields in the class definition object. Notice that we're following the input-driven approach here. We walk the input model once collecting data. The output-driven approach would force two complete walks of the input model, once to get the nonarray fields and then again to get the array fields.

Once we have the data we need, we can stuff it into the overall **objectTables** template via method genSchema():

```
trans/sql/GenSchema.java
```
```
public StringTemplate genSchema(Class c) {
    List<Field> fields = new ArrayList<Field>();
    List<Field> arrayFields = new ArrayList<Field>();
    filterFields(c, fields, arrayFields);
    StringTemplate classST = templates.getInstanceOf("objectTables");
    classST.setAttribute("class",       c);
    classST.setAttribute("fields",      fields);
    classST.setAttribute("arrayFields", arrayFields);
    return classST;
}
```

So, that's how all the attributes arrive at the templates. Now, let's see how those templates use the attributes.

Generating SQL with Templates

Once the main program injects the data into the overall **objectTables** template, its job is done. That root template directly or indirectly creates

> ## Java Objects Know Their Type
>
> Before we can generate SQL, we have to figure out how to get information about an object at run-time such as a Person. We could build a parser for Java and extract the list of fields from Person.java, but that's a lot of work. Instead, let's ask Java itself. Through the reflection API, Java gives us access to its symbol table at run-time. There are two key classes we need: Class and Field. Yep, there is a class called Class. Each Class instance contains information about a single class, including the list of fields. Field knows, among other things, its name and type (a Class instance). If that field is an array, getComponent-Type() returns the array element type. We can test whether a type is an array using isArray(). These reflection objects are similar to our ClassSymbol and VariableSymbol classes from Pattern 19, *Symbol Table for Classes*, on page 167.

every other template in our template hierarchy output model. It begins by creating the primary table that holds the single-valued fields and then includes a subordinate table for multivalue fields:

`trans/sql/SQL.stg`

```
objectTables(class, fields, arrayFields) ::= <<
CREATE TABLE <class.simpleName> (
    ID INTEGER NOT NULL UNIQUE PRIMARY KEY,
    <fields:columnForSingleValuedField(); separator=",\n">
);
<arrayFields:tableForMultiValuedField()>
>>
```

Template expression <class.simpleName> calls getSimpleName() on the incoming Class object. The simple name does not include any surrounding package name. For example, the fully qualified name of Date is java.util.Date, but the simple name is just Date.

To emit the columns, we apply the **columnForSingleValuedField** template to each Field object in the list of single-valued fields: <fields:columnForSingle-ValuedField()>. That expression creates and embeds a new template instance for each Field in fields. Finally, the **objectTables** template includes subordinate tables by walking over the arrayFields. This time, though, it applies template **tableForMultiValuedField** to each field. Before we get to that template, let's look at single-valued fields.

To emit a column, template **columnForSingleValuedField** includes template **column**:

trans/sql/SQL.stg

```
columnForSingleValuedField(f)::="<column(name=f.name, javaType=f.type)>"
```

If we didn't need to translate Java to SQL types, **column** would look something like this:

```
column(name,javaType) ::= "<name> <javaType>"
```

To generate correct SQL, we need to map **int** to **INTEGER** and **String** to **TEXT**, for example. To sequester all output literals in the templates instead of the input model and Java code, we can specify the mapping in ST:

trans/sql/SQL.stg

```
javaToSQLTypeMap ::= [
    "int":"INTEGER",     // "int" maps to "INTEGER"
    "String":"TEXT",
    "float":"DOUBLE",
    "double":"DOUBLE",
    "Date":"DATETIME",
    default : key        // If not found, yield key; don't map
]
```

We can access this map as if the key were a property of the map. For example, <javaToSQLTypeMap.int> evaluates to string INTEGER. The int is taken as the key to look up in the map. In our case, we need to look up a Java type's name, not a constant. Parentheses around an expression in ST evaluates the expression to a string. We can then ask ST to look up that string. $<m.(x)>$ means to evaluate x to a string and then use that as the key to look up in map m. So, the **column** template has the rather complicated-looking ST expression for the type:

trans/sql/SQL.stg

```
column(name,javaType)::="<name> <javaToSQLTypeMap.(javaType.simpleName)>"
```

OK, we have the main table; now we have to generate the subordinate tables that hold our multivalued fields. For each array field of the class, we need to apply template **tableForMultiValuedField**:

trans/sql/SQL.stg

```
tableForMultiValuedField(f) ::= <<
CREATE TABLE <class.simpleName>_<f.name> (
    ID INTEGER NOT NULL AUTO_INCREMENT UNIQUE PRIMARY KEY,
    <column(name=f.name, javaType=f.type.componentType)>,
    <class.simpleName>_ID INTEGER NOT NULL
);<\n>
>>
```

Each subordinate table has three columns: a unique identifier (ID), a column for the array field, and a foreign key. Since we have template **column** handy, we can reuse it by passing in the appropriate values.

To test it, we can run the main program in GenSchema to see what it generates:

```
$ java GenSchema
CREATE TABLE Person (
    ID INTEGER NOT NULL UNIQUE PRIMARY KEY,
    name TEXT,
    ...
);
...
$
```

Now that we can generate a schema, let's walk the reflection API again to generate Java code that reads and writes objects in the database.

12.7 Building Retargetable Translators

If we can easily make a translator generate different output, we say that it's *retargetable*. As we mentioned in Section 12.5, *Using a Tree Grammar to Create Templates*, on page 324, altering or swapping in new templates is one way to do this. The template hierarchy stays the same, just the contents of those templates change. This retargeting approach is really useful if you need to generate different SQL to suit different database vendors, for example. (Alas, we often do.)

In this section, we're going to learn another retargeting strategy that changes the output language by changing the template hierarchy. The interesting thing is that we assemble different hierarchies using the templates themselves, not using Java code. As before, all we have to do is switch template groups to switch targets. The difference here is that we don't have to change a tree grammar to create a different output model structure. With either strategy, retargetable code generators consist of a collection of templates and some code that traverses the input model to compute attributes.

To illustrate the approach, we're going to build a translator that can generate both the SQL from the previous section and some Java object serializer and deserializer methods. As we go along, we'll learn some advanced ST features such as dynamic scoping, lazy evaluation, and attribute renderers (that give ST special instructions about converting objects to text). If you can get through the majority of this example, you'll be ready to tackle most translation problems that come your way.

Let's start by looking at the code we need to generate.

Generating Java Code

We already know what SQL we need to generate, so let's work on the Java code output. (Warning: this section contains a lot of Java-specific code that talks to the database.) We want to generate PersonSerializer.java from the sample Person class from the previous section. For example, here's the method we need that saves the nonarray fields of the object into the primary table:

```
class PersonSerializer {
    ...
    public static void savePerson(Connection con, Person o)
        throws SQLException
    {
        PreparedStatement prep = con.prepareStatement(
            "INSERT into Person SET ID=?, "+
            "name=?, SSN=?, birthDay=?, age=?;");
        int Person_ID = ID++;
        prep.setInt(1, Person_ID);
        prep.setString(1+1, o.name);
        prep.setString(2+1, o.SSN);
        prep.setDate(3+1, new java.sql.Date(o.birthDay.getTime()));
        prep.setInt(4+1, o.age);
        save_Person_roles(con, o.roles, Person_ID);
        save_Person_vacation(con, o.vacation, Person_ID);
        if (prep.executeUpdate () != 1) {
            System.err.println("couldn't save "+o);
        }
    }
}
```

Given a database connection and a Person object to store, savePerson() writes the fields out to the main Person table. Then, we'll need some helper methods like the following to save the array fields in subordinate tables:

```
static void save_Person_roles(Connection con,
                              String[] roles,
                              int Person_ID)
    throws SQLException { ... }
```

You can take a look at the details in PersonSerializer.java. Since loading objects doesn't introduce any new generation concepts, we'll focus on saving objects.

Now that we have a goal in mind, let's extract data from the input model and inject it into the overall root template.

Injecting Data into the Root Template

To build a retargetable code generator, we need a common interface to the templates. Just like any library, we need to "publish" the templates and attributes available to our generator. In our case, we'll reference a common template called **output**, which then accesses the target-specific templates within. Here's what they look like in both the SQL and Java templates:

trans/sql/SQL2.stg

```
/** Common interface to templates for this target "*/
output(class, fields, arrayFields, nonPrimitiveTypes) ::=
  "<objectTables()>" // objectTables defines no args; no need for ... arg
```

trans/sql/persist.stg

```
output(class, fields, arrayFields, nonPrimitiveTypes) ::=
  "<serializerClass()>" // no need for ... "pass through" parameter
```

To make a common interface, the list of attributes has to be the same even if that target doesn't need every attribute. For example, the SQL target doesn't need the nonPrimitiveTypes attribute. (To generate Java code, we need a list of nonprimitive types so we can generate some **import** statements.) The easiest thing to do is to compute all possible attributes so we don't have to worry about which target we're generating on a particular run. Or, if the computations are expensive, we can limit ourselves to computing attributes needed by a particular target (passing in null instead).

Let's put our retargetable generator in DBGen.java. The main program decides which target to generate according to the command-line argument (-java or -sql):

trans/sql/DBGen.java

```
if ( args[0].equals("-sql") ) groupFile = "SQL2.stg";
else if ( args[0].equals("-java") ) groupFile = "persist.stg";
else {System.err.println("java DBGen [-sql|-java]"); return;}
```

To switch targets, we simply change template group files. Once we have the group file, we can load those templates into memory and then call a generic gen() method to build the template hierarchy from our sample Person class.

trans/sql/DBGen.java

```
// LOAD TEMPLATES
FileReader fr = new FileReader(groupFile);
StringTemplateGroup templates = new StringTemplateGroup(fr);
fr.close();
templates.registerRenderer(Class.class, new TypeRenderer());
// GEN OUTPUT
StringTemplate output = gen(templates, Person.class);
System.out.println(output.toString());
```

(We'll look at the registerRenderer() method in the next section.)

The gen() method computes the set of attributes with filterFields() and injects them into the **output** common root template:

trans/sql/DBGen.java

```
filterFields(c, fields, arrayFields, nonPrimitiveTypes);
StringTemplate classST = templates.getInstanceOf("output");
classST.setAttribute("class",             c);
classST.setAttribute("fields",            fields);
classST.setAttribute("arrayFields",       arrayFields);
classST.setAttribute("nonPrimitiveTypes", nonPrimitiveTypes);
```

Method filterFields() is the same as before except that it computes the extra nonPrimitiveTypes set of fields. So, all we need is this little bit of (shared) Java code to drive both targets.

Before we get to the templates, though, we need to look at how ST supports different renderings of the same data value.

Altering How ST Renders Attributes

ST (deliberately) has almost no built-in functionality to manipulate the attributes we inject. To maintain proper separation of concerns, we don't want the templates to become part of the program. And, if they're modifying data, they're part of the program. In practice, though, we sometimes do need to alter data to suit the display requirements of the output language. In this case, we need to capitalize some words.

The main program in DBGen calls registerRenderer() and passes in an instance of TypeRenderer. Our goal is to override ST's default behavior for rendering attributes to text. Without instructions to the contrary, ST calls toString() on objects to render them to text. But, before doing that, ST checks to see whether there's an *attribute renderer* registered for that type of object. A renderer has two versions of toString(), one to convert an object to text and one to convert an object to text with a specific format.

For example, from type int, we need to generate a call to setInt(), which means we need to capitalize type names. The second version lets us alter the conversion with a parameter specified in a template:

```
set<type; format="capitalized">(«args»);
```

The renderer gives us a way to hook in a snippet of formatting code for a particular type (in this case, Class) without forcing ST to support arbitrary code. Allowing arbitrary code allows model-view entanglement. ST passes the format option to the following method:

trans/sql/TypeRenderer.java

```java
public String toString(Object o, String formatName) {
    if ( formatName.equals("capitalized") ) {
        return capitalize(((Class)o).getSimpleName());
    }
    return toString(o);
}
```

While we're at it, we might as well make our lives a little bit easier. We're going to reference the simpleName property of Class objects a lot. So, instead of having to say <class.simpleName>, let's make it just <class>. Because of the renderer we've registered, ST renders that as the simple name for the class via the following method.

trans/sql/TypeRenderer.java

```java
public String toString(Object o) { return ((Class)o).getSimpleName(); }
```

OK, we've built everything except for the templates. Our Java code creates an overall template and injects all the data we need. Now it's time to figure out how to create the template hierarchy for the serializer and deserializer methods.

Constructing the Template Hierarchy

At this point, we've seen quite a few templates, some with fairly complicated attribute expressions. So, let's focus on the new and interesting bits in template group file persist.stg: dynamic scoping of attributes, implicit use of attribute renderers, and lazy evaluation.

First, let's see how dynamic scoping makes it easy to share attributes between templates. The main program, DBGen, creates a single instance of template **output**. That "interface" template then has to invoke all the other templates necessary to create the proper template hierarchy. For example, **output** immediately invokes **serializerClass** but without parameters. **serializerClass** can automatically see the attributes of any invoking template (a template higher up in the template hierarchy). So, **serializerClass** can see attributes class, fields, arrayFields, and nonPrimitiveTypes without us having to pass them down manually. (If **serializerClass** defined those attributes as formal parameters, though, we'd need to use the pass-through ellipsis, calling serializerClass(...) in **output**.)

For deeply nested templates, dynamic scoping is very convenient. Note that the attributes of **output** are not global variables. Only templates that **output** invokes can see its attributes. Here's the start of template **serializerClass**:

`trans/sql/persist.stg`

```
/** Inherit class, fields, arrayFields, nonPrimitiveTypes
 *   from output template that invokes me. */
serializerClass() ::= <<
// This file automatically generated by "java DBGen -java"
<imports()>
public class <class>Serializer { <! class inherited from above !>
```

Just so those comments are clear, the /**...*/ comment is an ST comment outside a template definition. The //... is literal text that goes in the output. The <!...!> comment is an ST comment inside the template that doesn't appear in the output.

Dynamic scoping works no matter how deep the template hierarchy. Notice that **serializerClass** invokes **imports**, which uses **output**'s nonPrimitiveTypes attribute to generate imports:

`trans/sql/persist.stg`

```
/** Inherit attribute 'class' from serializerClass */
imports() ::= <<
<nonPrimitiveTypes:{t | import <t.name>;<\n>}>
import java.util.ArrayList; <! used by support code !>
import java.util.List;
import java.sql.*;
>>
```

The templates in persist.stg make much more sense when you're familiar with ST's dynamic scoping.

Now, let's take a look at the **saveObjectMethod** template, which implicitly uses our TypeRenderer attribute renderer. ST renders attribute expression <class> using the renderer's toString(), not Class' toString(), for example. This template also uses the format option and so ST invokes the renderer's other toString() method.

`trans/sql/persist.stg`

```
saveObjectMethod() ::= <<
public static void save<class; format="capitalized">(Connection con,
                                                     Person o)
    throws SQLException
{
    PreparedStatement prep = con.prepareStatement(
        "INSERT into <class> SET ID=?, "+
        "<fields:{f | <f.name>=?}; separator=", ">;");
    int <class>_ID = ID++;
    prep.setInt(1, <class>_ID);
    <fields:saveField(); separator="\n">
    <arrayFields:saveArrayField(); separator="\n">
    if (prep.executeUpdate () != 1) {
        System.err.println("couldn't save "+o);
    }
}
>>
```

If there's one really complicated part of this example, it's the lazy evaluation. As with SQL generation, we have to worry about conversion between Java and SQL types. To save objects in the database, we have to generate code to set the elements of a PreparedStatement (which is like a built-in SQL template language that uses question marks as the "holes"). For injecting strings into the PreparedStatement, we can call setString() and pass in the appropriate string:

```
PreparedStatement prep = con.prepareStatement(
    "INSERT into Person SET ID=?, name=?, SSN=?, birthDay=?, age=?;");
prep.setString(3, o.SSN);
```

For Date objects, though, we need to convert them to SQL dates like this:

```
prep.setDate(4, new java.sql.Date(o.birthDay.getTime()));
```

We can encode this "switch on type" string mapping with an ST map:

`trans/sql/persist.stg`

```
javaToSQLValueMap ::= [
        "Date":"new java.sql.Date(<value>.getTime())",
        default : "<value>"
]
```

It has the same form as the int to INTEGER conversion we saw in the SQL example, but these map values are templates, not mindless strings. As you can see, they reference attribute value even though there's no obvious definition for it. Fortunately, that's no big deal because of lazy evaluation. Templates that look up values in this map will define attribute value. Once ST embeds the map result into the calling template, value will magically become visible. For example, here's a template that references the map:

```
fieldValue(type, value="o") ::= "<javaToSQLValueMap.(type.simpleName)>"
```

The assignment in the parameter list is a default parameter value assignment (like C++ default parameters). Attribute value is string o if nobody sets it explicitly.

This template hides all the complicated map lookup from the other templates. First, it evaluates type.simpleName to get a string like int or Date and then looks it up in the map. If it's a Date, the map returns the java.sql.Date instance creator template. If it's anything else, the map returns a template that evaluates to attribute value (the default case). So, template **fieldValue** returns either the value we pass in or that value wrapped in a **new** expression.

We can then use this template to save fields in both **saveObjectMethod** and **saveForeignObjectMethod** via **saveField**:

```
saveField(f) ::= <<
prep.set<f.type; format="capitalized">(<i>+1,
    <fieldValue(type=f.type, value={o.<f.name>})>);
>>
```

This template passes attribute value as an anonymous template {o.<f.name>}. Because of lazy evaluation, ST doesn't evaluate that template until template **fieldValue** references it. Because of dynamic scoping, **fieldValue** can see **saveField**'s f attribute because **saveField** calls that template. **fieldValue** doesn't explicitly reference f, but {o.<f.name>} does, and it's evaluated inside **fieldValue**.

The <i>+1 attribute expression computes the prepared statement "hole" to fill. Attribute i iterates from 1, but we need indexes starting at 2. (ID is index 1.) Since there's no way in ST to add values, we can use the generated Java code to compute the proper index.

OK, now that we have the templates to go with the code generator Java code, let's give the generator a try.

Testing Code Generation

First, let's have our generator spit out an SQL schema. Using command-line option -sql gets us the SQL for Person.

```
$ java DBGen -sql
CREATE TABLE Person (
    ID INTEGER NOT NULL UNIQUE PRIMARY KEY,
    name TEXT,
...
$
```

Using -java gets us the Java code:

```
$ java DBGen -java
// This file automatically generated by "java DBGen -java"
import java.util.Date;
import java.lang.String;

import java.util.ArrayList;
import java.util.List;
import java.sql.*;
public class PersonSerializer {
...
$
```

Ultimately, we need to shove that Java code into a file and compile:

```
$ java DBGen -java > PersonSerializer.java
$ javac PersonSerializer.java
$
```

If you're curious, you can continue on into the next section to see the generated code serialize and deserialize a Person with a MySQL database.

Testing Object Serialization

To verify that the code we generate is valid, we have to compile it, but we should also see whether it communicates properly with a database. Test.java in the source code directory creates a Person object, serializes it to a MySQL database, reads it back in, and prints it out. You don't need to go through this section if you're interested only in the translation mechanism. It's here just for completeness. The following code is the core of the test rig:

trans/sql/Test.java

```
// CREATE PERSON AND SERIALIZE
PersonSerializer.init(con);
GregorianCalendar cal = new GregorianCalendar(2000,10,5);
Person p = new Person("ter","555-11-2222",cal.getTime(), 9);
p.roles = new String[] {"ceo", "janitor"};
PersonSerializer.savePerson(con, p);         // SAVE Person TO DB
// READ PERSON BACK IN
String q="SELECT * FROM Person WHERE ID=1"; // GET FIRST Person
```

```
Statement stat = con.createStatement();
ResultSet rs = stat.executeQuery(q);
rs.next();
Person back = PersonSerializer.nextPerson(con, rs);
System.out.println("read back: "+back);
```

To get this to execute, we need to download the MySQL Connector/J 5.1[6] JDBC database driver and get the mysql-connector-java-5.1.8-bin.jar file from that distribution into our CLASSPATH environment variable.

Once we're set up, we can invoke the test rig using a particular server, user, password, and database (via command-line arguments):

```
$ java Test sql.cs.usfca.edu parrt parrt parrt
read back: Person{name='ter', SSN='555-11-2222', birthDay=2000-11-05,
 age=9, roles=[ceo, janitor], vacation=[]}
OK
$
```

The test rig connects to my (private) MySQL instance at sql.cs.usfca.edu. After the program executes, we find data in the main and subordinate tables:

```
mysql> select * from Person;
+----+------+-------------+---------------------+------+
| ID | name | SSN         | birthDay            | age  |
+----+------+-------------+---------------------+------+
|  1 | ter  | 555-11-2222 | 2000-11-05 00:00:00 |   9  |
+----+------+-------------+---------------------+------+
1 row in set (0.00 sec)
```

```
mysql> select * from Person_roles;
+----+---------+-----------+
| ID | roles   | Person_ID |
+----+---------+-----------+
| 19 | ceo     |         1 |
| 20 | janitor |         1 |
+----+---------+-----------+
2 rows in set (0.00 sec)
```

```
mysql> select * from Person_vacation;
Empty set (0.00 sec)
```

Since the Person object had no vacation elements, the corresponding subordinate table has no data.

---

6. http://dev.mysql.com/downloads/connector/j/5.1.html

Up Next

With the conclusion of this example, we have the skills necessary to build all sorts of generators. The primary lesson is that generators consist of a collection of templates and some code to traverse the model. The traversal code trawls for data, creates and combines templates, injects them with attributes, and builds up a template tree. Sometimes the input model traversal code is responsible for the entire template hierarchy, sometimes the templates do all the work, and sometimes they share this responsibility. In the end, we call toString() on the template tree root to generate text.

We're nearing the end of our adventure. We've learned a lot about language implementation by exploring and applying the common language design patterns. We know how to build readers, interpreters, generators, and translators. In the next chapter, we're going to lay out a number of sample projects to help you continue learning on your own.

## Chapter 13

Putting It All Together

We began this book by looking at the different kinds of language applications and then cracking a few of them open to see what their pipelines looked like. We then spent the majority of this book going through the common language design patterns and their implementations. In the previous chapter, we looked at a few larger examples (generating DSLs). In this final chapter, we're going to walk through some sample applications and outline the strategies and language pattern ingredients you'd need to implement them.

Now that you've gone through all the patterns in this book, you're ready to venture out on your own. My intention in this last chapter is to inspire you and to expose you to a variety of language applications. You'll have to build these "projects" yourself, but I'll give you a nudge in the right direction by pointing you to some appropriate patterns.

Let's start with a DSL from biology and then look at progressively more complicated applications.

13.1 Finding Patterns in Protein Structures

To get you thinking about nontraditional uses of languages, let's break out of our normal programming world. You might be surprised how many biologists (and other scientists) use parsers for pattern recognition and analysis. For example, there are DSLs for describing DNA/RNA sequences, chemical molecules, molecular formulas (such as H_2O), and so on. Just as with language examples from our world, scientists want to trigger actions upon recognizing various structures.

As an example, let's look at a DSL that molecular biologists use to describe RNA sequences. RNA sequences are chains of nucleotide units:

Adenine (A), Cytosine (C), Guanine (G), or Uracil (U). You can think of those letters as the language vocabulary or token set. We can break up the chains into tokens with Pattern 2, *LL(1) Recursive-Descent Lexer*, on page 33. Let's pick one linguistic structure within RNA sequences. In *The Language of Genes* [Sea02], Searls says that "...a folded RNA secondary structure entails pairing between nucleotide bases." For example, in sequence GAUC, G creates a dependency for a C down the line, and an A creates a dependency for a future U.

Say we wanted to look at a sequence of nucleotide bases and determine whether it was a "folded RNA secondary structure." It turns out that this notion of dependence between bases is exactly like matching parentheses and square brackets in a programming language. We built something similar in the implementation section of Pattern 3, *LL(1) Recursive-Descent Parser*, on page 38. Assuming only the G-C and A-U dependencies, we could use the following grammar to match RNA sequences:

```
rna : 'G' rna 'C'
    | 'A' rna 'U'
    |                      // allow an empty RNA sequence
    ;
```

If we needed to process sequences instead of just detecting them, we could either add actions to the grammar or build an AST (Chapter 4, *Building Intermediate Form Trees*, on page 73).

Directly processing pairs as we see them follows Pattern 29, *Syntax-Directed Translator*, on page 296. If we created an AST, we could walk it (Chapter 5, *Walking and Rewriting Trees*, on page 101) one or more times to extract information.

This parsing application is fairly simple, so let's move on to an application with a more complicated language.

13.2 Using a Script to Build 3D Scenes

Let's say we wanted to build an English-like scripting language to draw 3D scenes. The language might look something like this:

```
x = Cube
y = Sphere
y.radius = 20
draw x
draw y to the left of x and behind x
```

The fastest way to get this running is probably with Pattern 24, *Syntax-Directed Interpreter*, on page 225. Most likely we wouldn't care about speed. Issuing commands is a lot faster than rendering objects in 3D, so parsing and interpreting would not be the bottleneck. The interpreter would need Pattern 2, *LL(1) Recursive-Descent Lexer*, on page 33 and Pattern 3, *LL(1) Recursive-Descent Parser*, on page 38 or Pattern 4, *LL(k) Recursive-Descent Parser*, on page 43. To go beyond recognition, we'd need to add actions to the parser that respond to the different kinds of statements.

Further, our interpreter needs run-time support. In this case, we could use a hash table to represent global memory. For example, in response to assignment statement x=Cube, we'd create an internal representation of a cube and map x to that object in the hash table. Statement draw x would then look up x in the global memory to find which object to draw. Note the similarity with defining and resolving symbols from Pattern 16, *Symbol Table for Monolithic Scope*, on page 141.

Instead of building custom parsers for custom languages, some programmers lean heavily on XML as a universal format. We'll take a look at parsing and extracting information from XML in the next section.

13.3 Processing XML

The minute my students hear the term XML, they reach for a full XML parser. But, when we're facing a small lizard, there's no point in reaching for a dinosaur-crushing asteroid. XML parsers are big and slow, and if they build a tree in memory, they can't handle files bigger than the computer's memory or infinite streams from sockets. Remember that we can view even complicated files like English text in multiple ways: as sequences of characters, words, or sentences. If we can get away with inspecting tokens instead of sentences, we've got a much easier problem to solve.

Let's say we needed a list of all target tags from some XML file. grep makes short work of that without writing any code:

```
$ grep '<target' config.xml
<target name="init">
<target name="war" depends="clean, compile">
...
$
```

A tiny bit of code (or awk and sed) would clean that up into a simple list of target names. (We're assuming here that each target tag is on a line by itself.) This strategy follows Pattern 29, *Syntax-Directed Translator*, on page 296 where we recognize constructs and immediately process or emit output, which is how a full *Simple API for XML* (SAX) XML parser works. A SAX parser avoids creating a large tree in memory by triggering callbacks when it recognizes certain input nodes.

Sometimes solving the opposite of the problem at hand simplifies our task significantly. Take the problem of extracting all nontag text from an HTML file, which is useful if you're building a search engine or something similar. We could parse the HTML file into a tree and then print out all the leaf nodes. Building a Pattern 9, *Homogeneous AST*, on page 94 in memory follows the *Document Object Model* (DOM) XML strategy. There's an easier way, though.

Recognizing the text between tags is tough because it really has no syntax. On the other hand, recognizing tags is straightforward because we can just look for anything in between angle brackets (using Pattern 2, *LL(1) Recursive-Descent Lexer*, on page 33). Strip away the tags, and we're left with the text.

Once we're recognizing tags, we can extract lots of information without having to really parse the XML. Let's say we want to extract all rect tags from a file in the SVG graphics format. Since the rect has a number of attributes like x and y, it might spill over multiple lines. We need a real XML tag lexer, but we can scan the list of tags looking for rect with a simple loop, not a parser. This approach is analogous to Pattern 15, *Tree Pattern Matcher*, on page 123 because we focus on just the pattern of interest. ANTLR users will recognize this approach as filter mode for lexer grammars.

Let's take this one step further to verify that an XML document is well formed. We can solve this with a stack and a loop around "get next token" as we just did to extract rect tags. When we see an open tag, we push it onto the stack. When we see a close tag, we pop a tag from the top of the stack and check that it goes with the current close tag. </book> must match a previous <book>.

Many applications come with XML configuration files these days. In the next section, we'll look at a configuration DSL we can use instead.

13.4 Reading Generic Configuration Files

We use configuration files to set initial parameters and create initial data structures for applications. That means humans have to read and write those files. The problem is that XML is a generic data format, not a specialized DSL for initializing applications. Being good DSL-o-philes, we can do a lot better than XML for this niche.

What we want is a simple C-like notation that lets us build a list of objects with properties such as strings, ints, lists, and references to other configuration objects. Here's a simple example:

```
Site jguru {
        port = 80;
        answers = "www.jguru.com";
        aliases = ["jguru.com", "www.magelang.com"];
}
```

To begin, we need Pattern 2, *LL(1) Recursive-Descent Lexer*, on page 33 and Pattern 3, *LL(1) Recursive-Descent Parser*, on page 38 to recognize the various structures. Rather than build a tree or some other intermediate representation, we want to turn configuration files into object instances. For example, in this case, we want to create an object of type Site and set its three fields: port, answers, and aliases. We need to use Java reflection to do this just as we did in Chapter 12, *Generating DSLs with Templates*, on page 313. The difference is that we're going to convert text to objects using reflection rather than the other way around.

Beyond the syntax, we need to add actions into the grammar to build the list of configured objects. To keep the grammar clean, though, it's a good idea to move all the "new instance" and "set object property" functionality into a separate class. The actions then just trigger the appropriate method call in our support code. You can see an entire implementation on the ANTLR wiki.[1]

Instead of just converting input sentences into internal data structures, let's look at translating input to output with some slight modifications.

---

1. http://www.antlr.org/wiki/display/ANTLR3/Fig+-+Generic+configuration+language+interpreter

13.5 Tweaking Source Code

Let's say we want to tweak some source code, perhaps deleting the method bodies of all methods within a particular class file. We also don't want to mess up the formatting of the file.

First, let's see whether we can get away with using simple tools like awk or sed. Unfortunately, these tools aren't so good at matching patterns across lines and the starting { and ending } are most likely on different lines. Worse, it's hard to distinguish between the curlies of a method and the curlies of a class body or a statement block. We need context information because those curlies mean different things depending on the surrounding text. The minute we say "context," we know that purely lexical tools and Pattern 2, *LL(1) Recursive-Descent Lexer*, on page 33 aren't powerful enough. We just can't scan the input symbols for curly braces.

That means we need a parser for the input language. Depending on the language and depending on how we write the grammar or parser, we will need Pattern 3, *LL(1) Recursive-Descent Parser*, on page 38, Pattern 4, *LL(k) Recursive-Descent Parser*, on page 43, or Pattern 5, *Backtracking Parser*, on page 55. Naturally, we need Pattern 2, *LL(1) Recursive-Descent Lexer*, on page 33 to feed one of these parsers.

To actually modify the source code, we need to record the token or character index of the method body curly braces. Once we've got that, we've got two choices. One way is to strip that text region from the file. Or, we can print out all tokens (including whitespace tokens) as they come in unless they are in a method body region. ANTLR has a particularly handy and efficient class, TokenRewriteStream, for "editing" the token stream. (Pattern 21, *Automatic Type Promotion*, on page 193 has sample code that uses this class.) The grammar and associated editing action might look like this:

```
methodBody : a='{' statement+ b='}' {tokens.delete($a,$b);} ;
```

We might have a more difficult problem, though. If we want to strip the method body only if no one else calls it (dead code elimination), we need to examine all code in the project looking for references. We need to resolve every method call, f() and o.f(), to compute class-method pairs. Once we have the set of all invoked methods, we can invert that to get the list of "dead" methods. As we scan for method bodies, then, we can delete any method in that set. We'll need the symbol table management from Pattern 19, *Symbol Table for Classes*, on page 167 and the type inference algorithms from Chapter 8, *Enforcing Static Typing Rules*, on page 181 to resolve method calls.

Although deleting bits of text is a form of translation, it's more common to translate an input construct to an output construct instead of deleting it. In the next example, we'll look at reducing (translating) an augmented version of Java down to pure Java.

13.6 Adding a New Type to Java

Java doesn't have a built-in vector math type (java.util.Vector is not meant for mathematics and isn't a built-in type). Let's say we wanted to add type **vec** so that we can do things like this:

```
vec x = [1, 2, 3];
vec y = [2, 9, 10];
vec z = x * y;
```

First, we need a strategy to execute this code. The easiest thing to do is to translate this down to raw Java. That means we have to figure out a mapping from input to output. Most of the input is pure Java, so we can just leave that stuff alone. The best way to change a few things and leave everything else alone is to "edit" the token stream (TokenRewriteStream if you're using ANTLR). We know the start and stop tokens ([and]), so we can replace everything in between yielding something like this:

```
vec x = new vec (new int[] {1, 2, 3});
```

Replacing the vector multiplication is a little trickier. We need Pattern 19, *Symbol Table for Classes*, on page 167 and Pattern 20, *Computing Static Expression Types*, on page 184 to differentiate simple scalar multiplication from vector multiplication. To support all that machinery, we need to build an AST (Chapter 4, *Building Intermediate Form Trees*, on page 73). Once we've computed all the types, we need to walk the AST with Pattern 15, *Tree Pattern Matcher*, on page 123, looking for multiplication subtrees that result in a **vec**. To figure out the complete text for the multiplication expression, the parser needs to store token index information into the AST. The tree pattern matcher can then replace the appropriate token region with a method call. For example, x*y would become vec.mult(x,y).

To get started, grab an existing Java grammar, and add 'vec' to the **type** rule in the parser grammar. Also add [...] notation to **primaryExpression** or some other low-level expression rule. Don't forget to add a subclass of BuiltInTypeSymbol called vec for use with the symbol table and type computations.

In the next section, we're going to look at another translation task, one that's unusual because it changes the whitespace, not the input symbols.

13.7 Pretty Printing Source Code

Building a pretty printer even for a specific language is surprisingly difficult. It's even harder to build a general pretty printing engine. For an interesting research framework, take a look at the pretty printing language called BOX described by Merijn de Jonge in *Pretty-Printing for Software Reengineering* [Jon02]. General pretty printers require some serious voodoo, and language-specific pretty printers tend to be messy *ad hoc* code blobs. Let's see whether we can design a more formal language-specific pretty printer as a compromise.

We can make the problem dramatically easier if we relax it a little bit. Most pretty printers consider the right column a "do not exceed" hard limit. They must wrap everything before that edge. But, that's not what programmers do. We step over that right column occasionally to get a better-looking bit of code. Programmers have a few templates in their head for each language construct. For example, I personally use a few versions of varying width for the **if** statement. As I get closer and closer to the right edge, I use a narrower and narrower template to write out the code.

By mimicking what programmers do naturally, we can whip up a decent pretty printer. The basic idea is to create an AST from the input as usual and then walk the tree bottom-up to create a "pretty" output template for each node. In a template group file, we can create one or more templates for each kind of node using special template names: *name_i*. The larger the value of *i*, the narrower the template. So, for example, we could make two different templates, if_1 and if_2, to express a single-line and multiline version of an **if**.

The key to solving this pretty-printing problem lies in how we choose the templates. We're going to shuffle through the different template versions looking for one that plays nicely with the other templates we choose. To format a particular node, n, in the AST, we format n's children and then choose a template for n. If the template for n yields a line that blows past the right column, we reformat the entire subtree at and below n. To reformat a subtree, we look for a narrower and narrower template for n until either we find one that fits or we run out of templates for that construct. If the template for n is still too wide, we reformat n's children and use the narrowest template we have for n itself. It might still be too wide, but it's the best we can do. By accepting a few of these right column border violations, we end up with a much simpler pretty printer.

In the next section, we're going to step it up a notch and figure out how to build a compiler that translates source code down to machine code.

13.8 Compiling to Machine Code

Although few people build compilers for full programming languages, you might find yourself in a position where you need maximum runtime performance. For example, you might have a scripting or small programming language that executes on a small device like a phone. Because of battery life issues, phone processors run slowly compared to desktops. It might make sense to translate your language all the way down to the machine code to wrench the most speed from the slow CPU.

In Section 1.3, *C Compiler*, on page 14, we looked at the typical compiler application pipeline. There are many stages and a whole lot of tricky stuff going on. In a nutshell, we need patterns and techniques from Chapter 2, *Basic Parsing Patterns*, on page 21, Chapter 4, *Building Intermediate Form Trees*, on page 73, Chapter 3, *Enhanced Parsing Patterns*, on page 49, Chapter 7, *Managing Symbol Tables for Data Aggregates*, on page 155, Chapter 8, *Enforcing Static Typing Rules*, on page 181, and Chapter 11, *Translating Computer Languages*, on page 279. But, that's not all.

To make things more concrete, let's compile a C subset down to machine code. We've covered everything except optimization and machine code generation (the "back end") in this book. For example, we could use the following patterns to build the "front end:" Pattern 2, *LL(1) Recursive-Descent Lexer*, on page 33, Pattern 4, *LL(k) Recursive-Descent Parser*, on page 43, Pattern 9, *Homogeneous AST*, on page 94, Pattern 15, *Tree Pattern Matcher*, on page 123, Pattern 17, *Symbol Table for Nested Scopes*, on page 146, Pattern 22, *Enforcing Static Type Safety*, on page 201. That gets us to the point where we've verified the syntactic and semantic validity of the input. Unfortunately, optimizing and generating machine code from an AST (or any other intermediate representation) is really hard.

Low Level Virtual Machine[2] (LLVM) to the rescue. LLVM is a compiler infrastructure and, quite simply, one of the finest pieces of open source software available. Among other things, LLVM provides a virtual instruction set that's reminiscent of the instructions for Pattern 28, *Register-Based Bytecode Interpreter*, on page 267. From this intermediate representation, LLVM can generate highly optimized machine code for any of several processors (such as x86, ARM, MIPS, and SPARC). That is great news because we can generate that intermediate representation from an AST using Pattern 14, *Tree Grammar*, on page 119. So, to build a compiler, we combine the patterns mentioned earlier and then let LLVM do all of the heavy lifting. Please see my sample implementation[3] for more details. You can also think of this front end as a bytecode compiler suitable for use with the interpreters in Chapter 10, *Building Bytecode Interpreters*, on page 239.

Well, we've reached the end of a long road. You've just gotten a huge dose of language implementation technology. As you can see from the sample implementations in this book, being a language implementer means becoming familiar with lots of language tools. If you choose to use ANTLR and StringTemplate, I encourage you to join us on the friendly support lists.[4,5] There are a lot of nice people who can help you solve tricky language problems.

The patterns in this book and these sample applications will get you started building your own language applications. You're well on your way to being a solid language implementer. I encourage you to share ideas with other developers on this book's forum.[6] If you develop a nice grammar or application you'd like to share, please feel free to add it to the grammar list[7] or showcase[8] on http://antlr.org.

---

2. http://www.llvm.org
3. http://www.antlr.org/wiki/display/ANTLR3/LLVM
4. http://www.antlr.org/mailman/listinfo/antlr-interest
5. http://www.antlr.org/mailman/listinfo/stringtemplate-interest
6. http://forums.pragprog.com/forums/110
7. http://www.antlr.org/grammar/list
8. http://www.antlr.org/showcase/list

Appendix A

Bibliography

[ALSU06]   Alfred V. Aho, Monica S. Lam, Ravi Sethi, and Jeffrey D. Ull-
           man. *Compilers: Principles, Techniques, and Tools*. Addison-
           Wesley Longman Publishing Co., Inc., Boston, MA, USA,
           second edition, 2006.

[For02]   Bryan Ford. Packrat parsing: simple, powerful, lazy, linear
           time, functional pearl. In *ICFP '02: Proceedings of the Sev-
           enth ACM SIGPLAN International Conference on Functional
           Programming*, pages 36–47, New York, 2002. ACM Press.

[For04]   Bryan Ford. Parsing expression grammars: a recognition-
           based syntactic foundation. In *POPL '04: Proceedings of the
           31st ACM SIGPLAN-SIGACT Symposium on Principles of Pro-
           gramming Languages*, pages 111–122, New York, 2004. ACM
           Press.

[GHJV95]   Erich Gamma, Richard Helm, Ralph Johnson, and John
           Vlissides. *Design Patterns: Elements of Reusable Object-
           Oriented Software*. Addison-Wesley, Reading, MA, 1995.

[IdFC05]   R. Ierusalimschy, L.H. de Figueiredo, and W. Celes. The
           implementation of lua 5.0. *Journal of Universal Computer
           Science*, 11(7):1159–1176, 2005.

[Jon02]   Merijn De Jonge. Pretty-printing for software reengineering.
           In *International Conference on Software Maintenance (ICSM
           2002)*, pages 550–559. IEEE Computer Society Press, 2002.

[Par07]   Terence Parr. *The Definitive ANTLR Reference: Building Domain-Specific Languages*. The Pragmatic Programmers, LLC, Raleigh, NC, and Dallas, TX, 2007.

[Sea02]   David B. Searls.   The language of genes.   *Nature*, 420(6912):211–217, November 2002.

Index

C

I

J

L

N

O

P

The Pragmatic Bookshelf

Available in paperback and DRM-free PDF, our titles are here to help you stay on top of your game. The following are in print as of December 2009; be sure to check our website at pragprog.com for newer titles.

Title	Year	ISBN	Pages
Advanced Rails Recipes: 84 New Ways to Build Stunning Rails Apps	2008	9780978739225	464
Agile Coaching	2009	9781934356432	250
Agile Retrospectives: Making Good Teams Great	2006	9780977616640	200
Agile Web Development with Rails, Third Edition	2009	9781934356166	784
Augmented Reality: A Practical Guide	2008	9781934356036	328
Behind Closed Doors: Secrets of Great Management	2005	9780976694021	192
Best of Ruby Quiz	2006	9780976694076	304
Core Animation for Mac OS X and the iPhone: Creating Compelling Dynamic User Interfaces	2008	9781934356104	200
Core Data: Apple's API for Persisting Data on Mac OS X	2009	9781934356326	256
Data Crunching: Solve Everyday Problems using Java, Python, and More	2005	9780974514079	208
Debug It! Find, Repair, and Prevent Bugs in Your Code	2009	9781934356289	232
Deploying Rails Applications: A Step-by-Step Guide	2008	9780978739201	280
Design Accessible Web Sites: 36 Keys to Creating Content for All Audiences and Platforms	2007	9781934356029	336
Desktop GIS: Mapping the Planet with Open Source Tools	2008	9781934356067	368
Developing Facebook Platform Applications with Rails	2008	9781934356128	200
Enterprise Integration with Ruby	2006	9780976694069	360
Enterprise Recipes with Ruby and Rails	2008	9781934356234	416
Everyday Scripting with Ruby: for Teams, Testers, and You	2007	9780977616619	320
FXRuby: Create Lean and Mean GUIs with Ruby	2008	9781934356074	240
From Java To Ruby: Things Every Manager Should Know	2006	9780976694090	160
GIS for Web Developers: Adding Where to Your Web Applications	2007	9780974514093	275
Google Maps API, V2: Adding Where to Your Applications	2006	PDF-Only	83
Grails: A Quick-Start Guide	2009	9781934356463	200

Continued on next page

Title	Year	ISBN	Pages
Groovy Recipes: Greasing the Wheels of Java	2008	9780978739294	264
Hello, Android: Introducing Google's Mobile Development Platform	2009	9781934356494	272
Interface Oriented Design	2006	9780976694052	240
Land the Tech Job You Love	2009	9781934356265	280
Learn to Program, 2nd Edition	2009	9781934356364	230
Manage It! Your Guide to Modern Pragmatic Project Management	2007	9780978739249	360
Manage Your Project Portfolio: Increase Your Capacity and Finish More Projects	2009	9781934356296	200
Mastering Dojo: JavaScript and Ajax Tools for Great Web Experiences	2008	9781934356111	568
Modular Java: Creating Flexible Applications with OSGi and Spring	2009	9781934356401	260
No Fluff Just Stuff 2006 Anthology	2006	9780977616664	240
No Fluff Just Stuff 2007 Anthology	2007	9780978739287	320
Pomodoro Technique Illustrated: The Easy Way to Do More in Less Time	2009	9781934356500	144
Practical Programming: An Introduction to Computer Science Using Python	2009	9781934356272	350
Practices of an Agile Developer	2006	9780974514086	208
Pragmatic Project Automation: How to Build, Deploy, and Monitor Java Applications	2004	9780974514031	176
Pragmatic Thinking and Learning: Refactor Your Wetware	2008	9781934356050	288
Pragmatic Unit Testing in C# with NUnit	2007	9780977616671	176
Pragmatic Unit Testing in Java with JUnit	2003	9780974514017	160
Pragmatic Version Control Using Git	2008	9781934356159	200
Pragmatic Version Control using CVS	2003	9780974514000	176
Pragmatic Version Control using Subversion	2006	9780977616657	248
Programming Clojure	2009	9781934356333	304
Programming Cocoa with Ruby: Create Compelling Mac Apps Using RubyCocoa	2009	9781934356197	300
Programming Erlang: Software for a Concurrent World	2007	9781934356005	536
Programming Groovy: Dynamic Productivity for the Java Developer	2008	9781934356098	320
Programming Ruby: The Pragmatic Programmers' Guide, Second Edition	2004	9780974514055	864
Programming Ruby 1.9: The Pragmatic Programmers' Guide	2009	9781934356081	960
Programming Scala: Tackle Multi-Core Complexity on the Java Virtual Machine	2009	9781934356319	250

Continued on next page

Title	Year	ISBN	Pages
Prototype and script.aculo.us: You Never Knew JavaScript Could Do This!	2007	9781934356012	448
Rails Recipes	2006	9780977616602	350
Rails for .NET Developers	2008	9781934356203	300
Rails for Java Developers	2007	9780977616695	336
Rails for PHP Developers	2008	9781934356043	432
Rapid GUI Development with QtRuby	2005	PDF-Only	83
Release It! Design and Deploy Production-Ready Software	2007	9780978739218	368
Scripted GUI Testing with Ruby	2008	9781934356180	192
Ship it! A Practical Guide to Successful Software Projects	2005	9780974514048	224
Stripes ...and Java Web Development Is Fun Again	2008	9781934356210	375
TextMate: Power Editing for the Mac	2007	9780978739232	208
The Definitive ANTLR Reference: Building Domain-Specific Languages	2007	9780978739256	384
The Passionate Programmer: Creating a Remarkable Career in Software Development	2009	9781934356340	200
ThoughtWorks Anthology	2008	9781934356142	240
Ubuntu Kung Fu: Tips, Tricks, Hints, and Hacks	2008	9781934356227	400
iPhone SDK Development	2009	9781934356258	576

Fun with Java

Modular Java

This pragmatic guide introduces you to OSGi and Spring Dynamic Modules, two of the most compelling frameworks for Java modularization. Driven by real-world examples, this book will equip you with the know-how you need to develop Java applications that are composed of smaller, loosely coupled, highly cohesive modules.

Modular Java: Creating Flexible Applications with OSGi and Spring
Craig Walls
(260 pages) ISBN: 9781934356401. $34.95
http://pragprog.com/titles/cwosg

Programming Scala

Scala is an exciting, modern, multi-paradigm language for the JVM. You can use it to write traditional, imperative, object-oriented code. But you can also leverage its higher level of abstraction to take full advantage of modern, multicore systems. *Programming Scala* will show you how to use this powerful functional programming language to create highly scalable, highly concurrent applications on the Java Platform.

Programming Scala: Tackle Multi-Core Complexity on the Java Virtual Machine
Venkat Subramaniam
(250 pages) ISBN: 9781934356319. $34.95
http://pragprog.com/titles/vsscala